Weaving It Together

Connecting Reading and Writing

THIRD EDITION

4

Milada Broukal

HEINLE
CENGAGE Learning

Australia • Brazil • Japan • Korea • Mexico • Singapore • Spain • United Kingdom • United States

HEINLE
CENGAGE Learning

Weaving It Together 4: Connecting Reading and Writing, Third Edition
Milada Broukal

Publisher: Sherrise Roehr

Acquisitions Editor: Tom Jefferies

Development Editor: Catherine Black

Director of Global Marketing: Ian Martin

Director of US Marketing: Jim McDonough

Senior Product Marketing Manager: Katie Kelley

Marketing Manager: Caitlin Driscoll

Marketing Assistant: Anders Bylund

Director of Content and Media Production: Michael Burggren

Content Project Manager: Mark Rzeszutek

Print Buyer: Susan Spencer

Cover Design: Page2 LLC

Compositor: Glyph International

For product information and technology assistance, contact us at **Cengage Learning Customer & Sales Support, 1-800-354-9706**

For permission to use material from this text or product, submit all requests online at **cengage.com/permissions**
Further permissions questions can be emailed to **permissionrequest@cengage.com**

Library of Congress Control Number: 2009936066

ISBN-13: 978-1-4240-5739-9

ISBN-10: 1-4240-5739-6

Heinle
20 Channel Center Street
Boston, MA 02210
USA

Cengage Learning is a leading provider of customized learning solutions with office locations around the globe, including Singapore, the United Kingdom, Australia, Mexico, Brazil, and Japan. Locate your local office at: **international.cengage.com/region**

Visit Heinle online at elt.heinle.com

Visit our corporate website at **www.cengage.com**

Text Credits: p. 14: Excerpt from *Frank Gehry* by Caroline Evensen Lazo. Published by Twenty-First Century Books © 2006. p. 45: From *Great Expressions* by Marvin Vanoni. Text © 1989 by Marvin Vanoni. Reprinted by permission of HarperCollins Publishers. p. 72: From *Symbiosis* by Nicolette Perry. Reprinted by permission of Continuum. © 1983. p. 101: Courtesy of the JFK Presidential Library. p. 126: From BURGER. *Personality* (with Infotrac®), 6E. © 2004 Wadsworth, a part of Cengage Learning, Inc. Reproduced by permission. www.cengage.com/permissions. p. 155: Excerpt from *Sociology* by Craig Calhoun, Donald Light, and Suzanne Keller. Published by The McGraw-Hill Companies, Inc. p. 185: "BST and Milk Yield (For debate)" by Nigel Collins. Published in *Catalyst: GCSE Science Review,* volume 12, issue 3. February 1, 2002. Reproduced with permission of Philip Allan Updates. p. 213: "Clone Farm" by Andrea Graves. Reproduced with permission of *New Scientist.* © 2001 Reed Business Information. p. 232: Excerpt from "Winterblossom Garden" by David Low. Reprinted by permission of David Low. p. 239: Excerpt from THE INTERPRETER OF MALADIES by Jhumpa Lahiri. © 1989 by Jhumpa Lahiri. Reprinted by permission of Houghton Mifflin Harcourt Publishing Company. All rights reserved.

Printed in the United States of America
1 2 3 4 5 6 7 11 10 09

Brief Contents

Contents

A Message from the Author

Approach

Weaving It Together, **Book 4**, is the fourth in a four-book series that integrates reading and writing skills for students of English as a second or foreign language. The complete program includes the following books: Book 1–Beginning Level; Book 2–High Beginning Level; Book 3–Intermediate Level; and Book 4–High Intermediate Level.

The central premise of *Weaving It Together* is that reading and writing are interwoven and inextricable skills. Good readers write well; good writers read well. With this premise in mind, *Weaving It Together* has been developed to meet these objectives:

1. To combine reading and writing through a comprehensive, systematic, and engaging process designed to integrate the two effectively.
2. To provide academically bound students with serious and engaging multicultural content.
3. To promote individualized and cooperative learning within moderate- to large-sized classes.

Through its systematic approach to integrating reading and writing, *Weaving It Together* teaches ESL and EFL students to understand the kinds of interconnections that they need to make between reading and writing in order to achieve academic success.

Organization of the Text

Weaving It Together, **Book 4** contains eight thematically organized units, each consisting of two interrelated chapters. The units begin with a set of questions to engage the student in the theme of the unit. Each chapter begins with a reading, moves on to a set of activities designed to develop critical reading skills, and culminates with a series of interactive writing exercises.

Each chapter contains the same sequence of activities:

1. **Pre-Reading and Predicting Activities:** Each chapter opens with a picture, a set of pre-reading discussion questions, and a predicting exercise. The pre-reading activity prepares students for the reading by activating their background knowledge and encouraging them to call on and share their experiences. The predicting activity prepares students for the ideas and vocabulary in the reading.
2. **Reading:** Each reading is a high-interest passage related to the theme of the unit. Selected topics include colors, healing pets, and secret languages. The final unit includes readings from literature.

3. **Vocabulary:** Three types of vocabulary exercises practice the vocabulary contained in the reading. "Vocabulary in Context" uses the new words in the context in which they were used in the reading. "Vocabulary Building" and "Vocabulary in New Context" help students extend their vocabulary skills to new contexts by, for example, learning to recognize collocations, synonyms, or antonyms. Additionally, once per chapter a "Word Partnership" box provides a complete collocation of a vocabulary word taught in that chapter. These were included to expand students' knowledge of how words go together to improve reading fluency.

4. **Reading Comprehension:** Three types of exercises to check students' reading comprehension: "Looking for Main Ideas" focuses on a general understanding of the reading: "Looking for Details" concentrates on developing skimming and scanning skills: "Making Inferences and Drawing Conclusions" activates students' critical thinking skills.

5. **Discussion Questions:** Students work in small or large groups to discuss questions that arise from the reading. The discussion questions ask students to relate their experiences to what they have learned from the reading.

6. **Critical Thinking Questions:** These questions are much more challenging than the discussion questions. When students think critically about a given topic, they have to consider their own relationship to it, and thus, the interaction with the topic is greater. Students interact in small or large groups to discuss or debate these questions, giving the classroom a more meaningful environment.

7. **Writing Skills/Organizing:** In connection with each of the 16 readings, a different aspect of essay writing is developed. These aspects include essay organization, structure, transitions, and rhetorical devices the students may use to develop their own essays. Exercises following the instructional text reinforce the organizational techniques introduced.

8. **Student Model Essay:** Each unit, with the exception of Unit 1, contains an essay written by an international student whose writing skills are slightly more advanced than those of the writers who will use **Book 4** of *Weaving It Together*. The essay follows the general rhetorical form of North American academic prose and provides natural preparation for the discrete points taught in the organizing section.

9. **Writing Practice:** Students are presented with a choice of topics and then guided through the writing process step by step. First, they pre-write using a brainstorming technique to activate their background knowledge. Three techniques are presented on pages 254–256. Then they create an outline. The next step is to write a rough draft of the essay. *Weaving It Together* encourages students to write several drafts, since writing is an ongoing process. Then either working alone or with a

partner, students check their essays and make any necessary alterations. Next, students work with a partner or their teacher to correct spelling, punctuation, vocabulary, and grammar. Finally, students prepare the final version of the essay.

Weaving It Together: Optional Expansion and Review Activities

The final page of each unit, entitled "Weaving It Together," offers three types of expansion and review activities:

1. **Timed Writing:** To prepare them for exam writing, students are given a 50-minute timeframe to write on a topic or skill similar to the one they have worked on in the unit. Teachers may change the 50-minute timeframe to one that suits their requirements.
2. **Connecting to the Internet:** These activities give students the opportunity to develop their Internet research skills. This activity may be done in a classroom setting under the teacher's guidance, or—if students have Internet access—as a homework task leading to a classroom presentation or discussion.
3. **What Do You Think Now?:** Students are asked to review their answers from the "What Do You Think?" questions at the start of each unit. The questions review the information they learned while completing the unit.

Journal Writing

In addition to having students do the projects and exercises in the book, I strongly recommend that students be instructed to keep a journal in which they correspond with you. It gives them an opportunity to tell you what they like, what they dislike, what they understand, and what they don't understand. By having students explain what they have learned in the class, you can discover whether they understand the concepts taught and identify language concerns and trouble spots that need further review. In its finest form, journal writing becomes an active dialogue between teacher and student that permits you to learn more about your students' lives and to individualize their language instruction.

Note for the New Edition

In this new edition of **Weaving It Together**, **Book 4**, I have added a quiz at the beginning of each unit to engage students in the theme of the unit. The quiz is repeated at the end of the unit, so that students can check how much information they have learned from the unit. In addition to the discussion questions, critical thinking discussion questions have been added to give students the opportunity to develop their thinking skills. For those who need to write under constrictions of time, a timed writing activity has been included at the end of each unit. I have also expanded the Internet activities. I hope that you will enjoy using these new features and that **Weaving It Together** will continue to help you toward success.

1 Artists

What Do You Think?

Answer the questions with your best guess. Circle **Yes** or **No**.

Do you think . . .

1. Frida Kahlo was an artist from Spain?	**Yes**	**No**
2. Frida Kahlo was famous in her lifetime?	**Yes**	**No**
3. Frida Kahlo was the wife of Frank Gehry?	**Yes**	**No**
4. Frank Gehry is a famous American painter?	**Yes**	**No**
5. the Guggenheim Museum in New York was the work of Frank Gehry?	**Yes**	**No**

Pre-Reading

1. Discuss the answers to these questions with your classmates.

    1. Most of Frida Kahlo's works are portraits of herself. What do you think this tells us about her?

    2. Which other famous artists painted self-portraits? What do the portraits say about their lives and feelings?

    3. Describe the life of an artist you know. Do you think it is difficult to be an artist?

    4. Do artists have to face hardships that other working people don't?

2. Match the name of each artist with the facts about his or her life. Then say which artist is your favorite and why.

Salvador Dali   Claude Monet   I.M. Pei
Paul Gauguin   Georgia O'Keefe   Vincent van Gogh

    1. This artist studied art in Chicago and New York and then became a teacher. He/she went back to being a painter in 1918. In 1924, this artist married a photographer. He/she loved the New Mexico desert so much that he/she went to live there in 1929. This artist painted dramatic abstract landscapes, flowers, and other objects of nature. He/she was known for his/her independent lifestyle.

2. This artist was born in Paris and studied art there. While in Paris, he/she met other future impressionists like himself/herself. After a period of poverty in the 1870s, he/she became more financially secure. He/she then moved to a town in France called Giverny and painted works in series, such as *Rouen Cathedral* and *Water Lilies*.

3. This artist is considered a tragic painter because he/she never achieved recognition in his/her lifetime. In 1888, he/she moved from Paris to Arles in the south of France. Gauguin visited him/her there, and the two had violent disagreements, which may have led to his/her first mental seizure. He/she started to express his/her emotional state in his/her work. In 1890, this artist moved north to Auvers-sur-Oise, where he/she committed suicide.

4. This artist is one of the most famous surrealist artists. This artist was only six when he/she sold his/her first painting. By the time this artist reached the age of 75, he/she was so famous that a letter would reach him/her addressed only with the word *España* (Spain, which was his/her native country) and the sketch of a moustache. His/her works are highly realistic in style and have a strange, dreamlike imagery.

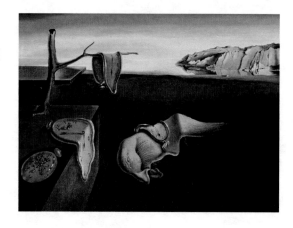

5. In 1883, this artist gave up his/her job as a stockbroker and became a full-time painter. He/she left his/her spouse and children and emigrated from Paris to

Tahiti. He/she was attracted to Polynesia because he/she believed primitive art and life were superior to so-called civilization. He/she painted the life of the people of the islands. Although this artist became less happy with life in Tahiti, he/she remained there until his/her death.

6. This architect is known all over the world for his/her buildings, which include the Bank of China Tower in Hong Kong, the Museum of Islamic Art in Qatar,

and—most of all—the glass pyramid in the courtyard of the Louvre Museum in Paris. When the pyramid was first built in 1989, people were either amazed or shocked by it. This architect was born in China and became a U.S. citizen in 1954.

Reading 1

Frida Kahlo: Triumph Over Tragedy

CD 1,
Track 1

1   Independence, rebelliousness, self-assurance—these are traits shared
by many famous people. They are found particularly among artists, and
certainly in Frida Kahlo, who belonged to the first generation of famous North
American women artists.

5   Even as a child, Mexico's best-known woman painter exhibited an
independent, rebellious spirit and lack of restraint that often got her into
trouble. She preferred to run, jump, and skip instead of walk, and she found
it difficult to control herself even in church, where she giggled and teased her
younger sister.

10   At the age of six, however, Frida's life changed dramatically. She got
polio and was confined to her bed for nine months. The disease left Frida's
right leg shorter and thinner than her left, and when she had recovered
enough to return to school, she walked with a limp. She was often teased
by her playmates, and although that was emotionally painful for her, she
15   compensated by being outgoing and gained a reputation as a "character."
Her father encouraged her to play sports to strengthen her leg, and eventually
she was able to walk quite well. Frida's father, Guillermo, a professional
photographer and amateur painter, was a great influence in her life.

    In 1922, at the age of 15, Frida was enrolled at the National Preparatory
20   School in Mexico City, which was near her hometown of Coyoacán. This was
the beginning of the postrevolutionary period in Mexico, and the country was
experiencing a time of cultural rebirth as well as reform. There was a strong
spirit of nationalism and pride in Mexico's heritage. Frida identified with the
revolution intellectually, emotionally, and spiritually.

25   After a few months at the school, Frida adopted a radical[1] new look. Although
her father, whom she adored, was European, Frida rejected her European clothes
in favor of overalls.[2] She cut her thick, black hair short like a boy's and rode

---

[1]**radical:** completely different
[2]**overalls:** loose pants fastened over the shoulders, usually worn by workers over other
clothes

around Coyoacán on a bicycle—shocking everyone. She even changed her birth
date from 1907 to 1910 to show her sympathy with the Mexican Revolution and
to identify herself with the beginnings of modern Mexico.

Frida thrived on[3] intellectual, social, and cultural stimulation at school.
She made friends easily and quickly became part of the notorious Cachuchas,
a group of seven boys and two girls—intelligent yet rebellious students who
named themselves after the caps worn at the school. Their keen[4] minds were
matched only by their contempt for authority and capacity for trouble. Frida's
natural independence and mischievous[5] nature fit right in. She cut classes
and joined in their escapades.[6]

One day, the Cachuchas let a donkey loose in a classroom. Another time,
one of the Cachuchas set off fireworks next to a dog, who ran wildly through
the school creating chaos. Frida was even expelled from school once, but
managed to regain entrance by boldly appealing to the minister of education.

Meanwhile, Frida was developing a strong sense of self-assurance and
belief in herself. She showed an aptitude for science and intended to go
on to medical school and become a doctor. Although she didn't become a
physician, her studies in biology and physiology later influenced her work. In
many of her paintings, hearts, glands, and other organs are displayed, both
inside and outside the body.

A turning point[7] occurred in Frida's life in September 1925, when she was
involved in a near-fatal accident. The bus in which she was riding home after
school collided with a trolley car. The impact caused a metal rail to break
loose, piercing Frida's entire body with the steel rod. The Red Cross doctors
who arrived and examined the victims separated the injured from the dying,
giving the injured first priority. They took one look at Frida and put her with
the hopeless cases.

The doctors eventually treated Frida, and miraculously she survived. She
suffered a broken spine, collarbone, and pelvis and two broken ribs. Her right
leg was broken in 11 places, and her right foot was crushed. Her left shoulder
was dislocated. From that point on, Frida Kahlo would never live a day
without pain.

---

[3]**thrived on:** grew vigorously or developed successfully with
[4]**keen:** sharp, quick at understanding
[5]**mischievous:** likely to cause trouble
[6]**escapades:** wild or exciting acts, usually causing trouble
[7]**turning point:** a time of important change

Although Frida recovered enough to lead a fairly normal life, the accident had severe psychological and physical consequences. She had to abandon her plans to become a doctor, and she had to recognize that she would be a near-invalid for the rest of her life. Her slowly healing body kept her in bed for months, and it was during this time that Frida began to paint. She read every book on art she could get her hands on. Exactly one year after her accident, she produced her first painting, a self-portrait dedicated to[8] her school boyfriend, the leader of the Cachuchas.

Some artists look to nature or society for their inspiration, but Frida Kahlo looked inward. After her crippling accident, Frida depicted her pain in haunting,[9] dreamlike self-portraits. Most of her 200 paintings explore her vision of herself. In *The Broken Column* (1944), her body is open to reveal a cracked column in place of her spine. In *The Wounded Deer* (1946), a small deer with Frida's head and a body pierced with arrows runs through the woods.

In 1929, Frida married the celebrated Mexican artist Diego Rivera. It would be an emotionally turbulent marriage, however, with a divorce in 1939 and remarriage in 1940. Diego made no secret of his infidelities and caused Frida much pain, although his devotion and admiration for her as an artist never diminished. Diego's betrayal of Frida's devotion inflicted great injury on her, as is revealed in a series of paintings depicting their relationship. "I have suffered two accidents in my life," she wrote, "one in which a streetcar ran over me. The other is Diego."

Frida's condition required many operations to try to straighten her spine and repair her foot. But with each one, her condition seemed to worsen. Often she painted in bed with an easel[10] her mother had designed for her. Her health seriously declined when she was in her forties, but Frida always kept her lively spirit. By then she was internationally known. When a Mexican gallery wanted to have a major exhibition of her work, she arranged to have her elaborately decorated, four-poster bed[11] carried into the gallery so that she could receive people.

---

[8]**dedicated to:** made as a tribute to
[9]**haunting:** not easily forgotten, remaining in the mind
[10]**easel:** a wooden frame that holds a canvas while it is being painted
[11]**four-poster bed:** a bed with four corner posts designed to support curtains

Frida died in July 1954, in the same room of the bright blue house in which she had been born. She left her work as her legacy,[12] to be sure. But equally inspirational is her life story—and the fact that, by transforming pain into brilliant art, Frida Kahlo triumphed[13] over misfortune.

---

[12]**legacy:** something received by others after a person's death
[13]**triumphed:** was victorious or succeeded

Vocabulary

A. Vocabulary in Context

Select the letter of the answer that is closest in meaning to the **bold** word or phrase.

1. Independence, rebelliousness, **self-assurance**—these are traits shared by many famous people.
   a. optimism
   b. confidence
   c. strength
   d. moodiness

2. Kahlo showed a lack of **restraint** that often got her into trouble.
   a. stress
   b. force
   c. self-control
   d. laziness

3. In church, she giggled and **teased** her sister.
   a. made fun of
   b. encouraged
   c. punched
   d. punished

4. Although she was often teased by her playmates, and this was emotionally painful for her, Frida **compensated** by being outgoing.
   a. rewarded herself
   b. made up for it
   c. forgave them
   d. attacked them

5. Kahlo became part of the **notorious** Cachuchas, a group of seven boys and two girls—intelligent yet rebellious students who named themselves after the caps worn at the school.
   a. unpopular
   b. fearless
   c. disreputable
   d. unequaled

6. The Cachuchas' keen minds were matched only by their **contempt for** authority and capacity for trouble.
   a. doubt of
   b. devotion to
   c. envy of
   d. hatred of

7. In September 1925, Kahlo was involved in a **near-fatal** accident.
   a. dangerous
   b. alarming
   c. unavoidable
   d. deadly

8. The **impact** of the bus colliding with the trolley car caused a metal rail to break loose.
   a. crash
   b. disaster
   c. conflict
   d. noise

9. After her accident, Kahlo **depicted** her pain in self-portraits.
   a. advertised
   b. taught
   c. portrayed
   d. determined

10. Kahlo's marriage to Diego Rivera was emotionally **turbulent**.
   a. stormy
   b. romantic
   c. strong
   d. delicate

Word Partnership	Use **impact** with:
adj.	**historical** impact, **important** impact
v.	**have an** impact, **make an** impact, **die on** impact
prep.	**on** impact

B. Vocabulary Building

Match the adjectives with the nouns as they were used in the context of the reading. Look back at the reading to check your answers. Add two more nouns that may be used with each adjective.

   a. accident   c. decoration   e. look
   b. artist   d. group   f. turbulence

1. _e_ radical   ___look___   _____   _____

2. ____ notorious   _____   _____   _____

3. ____ fatal   _____   _____   _____

4. ____ celebrated   _____   _____   _____

5. ____ emotional _____ _____ _____

6. ____ elaborate _____ _____ _____

C. Vocabulary in New Context

Make questions about Frida Kahlo's life, using each of the word combinations from Part B. With a partner, take turns asking and answering your questions.

Example:

In what way did Frida have a *radical* look?

Reading Comprehension

A. Looking for the Main Ideas

Answer the questions with complete sentences.

1. What is the main idea of paragraph 3?
2. What is paragraph 9 mostly about?
3. Which line states the main idea of paragraph 11?
4. Which sentences contain the main idea of paragraph 12?

B. Skimming and Scanning for Details

Scan the reading quickly to find the answers to these questions. Circle the letter of the best answer.

1. As a young girl, Frida Kahlo was _____.
   a. sweet-natured   c. lazy
   b. studious   d. rebellious

2. Polio left Kahlo with a limp, and as a result she became _____.
   a. shy and withdrawn   c. polite and graceful
   b. outgoing and unconventional d. unfriendly and mean

3. Kahlo's father was a _____.
   a. photographer   c. psychologist
   b. politician   d. professor

4. At school, Kahlo joined _____.

a. the revolution

b. the debating team

c. a group of rebellious students

d. an art club

5. When Kahlo was in school, her goal was to become _____.

a. an artist

b. a scientist

c. a doctor

d. a revolutionary soldier

6. Which area of study eventually influenced Kahlo's painting?

a. math

b. physiology

c. history

d. literature

7. Kahlo began to paint _____.

a. when she was still a child

b. after an accident left her bedridden

c. during the Mexican Revolution

d. while she was a member of the Cachuchas

8. Which of the following does not describe Kahlo's artwork?

a. She painted many beautiful landscapes.

b. She often used herself as a subject for her work.

c. She painted pictures showing pain and suffering.

d. She painted even when she was very ill.

9. Kahlo considered her marriage to Diego Rivera _____.

a. one of the best things that ever happened to her

b. a convenient arrangement

c. essential to the advancement of her career

d. a painful aspect of her life

10. At the time of her death, Kahlo was _____.

a. still an unknown artist

b. not accepted as an accomplished artist

c. sorry she had ever taken up art

d. a famous North American woman artist

C. Making Inferences and Drawing Conclusions

Some of the following statements can be inferred from the reading, and others cannot. Circle the number of each statement that can be inferred.

1. Shy, withdrawn people are not likely to achieve fame as bold, confident people.
2. Sometimes tragic incidents can turn out to be positive influences in our lives.
3. Frida Kahlo was influenced by events that occurred both to her and in the outside world.
4. Kahlo was easily intimidated by those in positions of authority.
5. Several events in Kahlo's life prove that she had a weak character.
6. If Kahlo had not been involved in the bus accident, she probably would never have become a famous artist.
7. Kahlo used her art as a way to express her personal feelings.
8. Kahlo's painting can be described as cheerful and optimistic.
9. Kahlo's marriage to Diego Rivera influenced her art.
10. Kahlo's physical disabilities would eventually have led her to withdraw from society.

Discussion Questions

Discuss the answers to these questions with your classmates.

1. How do you think painting helped Frida Kahlo with her problems?
2. Many of Kahlo's paintings express pain and tragedy. Do you like to see this in a work of art? If so, why? If not, what would you like to see?
3. What is your opinion of the mischievous acts carried out by the Cachuchas? Why did they do these things? Was their behavior acceptable? Why or why not?
4. Is it important to know about an artist's life in order to understand his or her work?

Critical Thinking Questions

Discuss the answers to these questions with your classmates.

1. Many people judge a work of art by how realistic it is and by the technical skill of the artist. They may look at a piece of modern art and say, "Anyone can do that." Is evidence of an original mind also important? Discuss.
2. Lots of famous people were difficult and rebellious in their youth, and people who knew them often thought they wouldn't amount to anything. Discuss how certain traits can cause problems in childhood but can lead to greatness in adulthood.
3. If not for Frida's accident, she would have become a doctor. If you had a choice of living an ordinary life or a life of greatness that includes great suffering, which would you choose, and why?

How a Building Changed a City

Frank Gehry is a world-renowned architect. The Guggenheim Museum in Bilbao, Spain, the Walt Disney Concert Hall in Los Angeles, California, and the Millennium Park in Chicago, Illinois, are some of his well-known projects. The following excerpt is taken from a biography called Frank Gehry *by Caroline Evensen Lazo (copyright 2006, Twenty-First Century Books, pages 56–61). It describes the effect that Gehry's architecture of the Guggenheim had on the city of Bilbao.*

1   The city of Bilbao had been in deep financial trouble during the 1980s. Though it was the largest city in Northern Spain, it was on the verge of becoming a slum. Shipyards and steel plants had shut down due to rising competition from other areas. The unemployment rate soared, making life
5   almost unbearable in Bilbao. Could the city ever regain its past reputation as one of Spain's richest industrial centers? What could the city do to restore its glorious past? Was it even possible to do so? Those were some of the basic questions that faced the city leaders.

They answered those questions by building a new railway station,
shopping center, a new airport, and other necessary features that help make
a city work. Yet the town needed something dramatic to put it in the spotlight,
to attract visitors and businesses alike. Government leaders turned to the
Solomon R. Guggenheim Foundation. It operates the legendary Guggenheim
Museum in New York City. The foundation also operates an empire of art
collections around the world. Thomas Krens, head of the Guggenheim
Museum in New York, invited three architects—from Austria, Japan, and the
United States—to submit plans. Gehry presented a remarkable plan for a site
along the Nervion River, which runs through Bilbao. He created his model out
of wood, foam core, and paper. Gehry's plan clearly surpassed the other two.
But could it actually be built?

Soon after Gehry had been selected as the architect of the new museum,
local Bilbao residents began to ask, *Quien es Frank Gehry?* (Who is Frank Gehry?)
They soon found out. In 1991 Gehry and his team geared up for the Bilbao
project and the awesome task of injecting new life into a disintegrating city.

Gehry had used the computer software program CATIA on earlier projects,
but he used it to the fullest in constructing the new Guggenheim Museum in
Bilbao. CATIA did not serve as a tool in the design process, but it checked the
design and helped to keep costs down. It also made construction plans easier.

Gehry used titanium (a silvery gray metallic element) on the exterior of
the Guggenheim Museum. "Thin titanium planes project from the ground
and float like strange jellyfish against the sky," architecture critic Steen Estvad
Petersen wrote. Located on the Nervion River, the building reflects the river's
wavy motion, and depending on the sun and time of day, the titanium
changes from gray to gold to red—much like the Weisman Museum on the
Mississippi River.[1]

Like Gehry's early family life, marked by boom and bust, chaos and order,
his design for the Guggenheim in Bilbao is full of contrasts. Rectangular
spaces lead to circular galleries with curving walls. The galleries differ in
design according to the art on exhibit. That is the art of architecture. And
Gehry proved to be the master of it.

---

[1]The Weisman Art Museum on the Mississippi River was designed by Frank Gehry.

In his essay "Jumbo Architecture," in *Frank O. Gehry: The Architect's Studio*, Steen Petersen summarized the general impact of Gehry's Guggenheim Museum:

45
50

> The enormous atrium [skylighted court] towers up though the building like a Gothic cathedral and is spanned by concrete, steel, titanium, elevator shafts, walkways, and skylights in wild confusion. . . . Gehry's museum is a total rhythmic composition . . . which, depending on temperament [mood] and taste, can be experienced as a miracle or a nightmare. . . . Frank O. Gehry is a decided loner and perhaps the only living architect who has been fully able to eliminate the boundaries between art and architecture.

The Guggenheim in Bilbao not only restored the city's reputation, but announced it around the world. And the incredible economic and cultural boom that resulted became known as the "the Bilbao effect." No one in Bilbao asks, *Quien es Frank Gehry?* anymore!

Vocabulary

A. Vocabulary in Context

Look at the reading to help you choose the best answer to each of the following questions.

1. Which phrase in paragraph 1 means "is going to happen very soon"?

2. Which of these words is similar in meaning to **soared** as it is used in paragraph 1?
a. went up and down
b. dropped down
c. flew out
d. went up a lot and fast

3. Which word in paragraph 3 means "was much better than"?

4. What phrase in paragraph 4 has the same meaning as **prepared to do** something?

5. Which definition of **disintegrating**, as it is used in the reading, is correct?
a. deteriorating
b. rotting
c. dead
d. imaginary

6. The best substitute for the word **boom** in paragraph 7 is _____.

    a. crash   c. success

    b. increase   d. shock

7. Which word in paragraph 7 means "failure"?

8. The best substitute for the word **impact** in paragraph 8 is _____.

    a. shock   c. impression

    b. experience   d. forecast

9. In his essay "Jumbo Architecture," which word does Steen Petersen use to describe Frank O. Gehry as a person who is alone in doing something?

10. Another way of expressing **eliminate** as it is used in paragraph 9 would be _____.

    a. reduce   c. create

    b. remove   d. disconnect

B. Vocabulary Building

1. Match the adjectives with the nouns as they were used in the context of the reading. Look back at the reading to check your answers. Add two more nouns that may be used with each adjective.

    a. trouble   c. motion   e. spaces

    b. boom   d. process   f. program

1. _b_ cultural   _boom_   _____   _____

2. ____ financial   _____   _____   _____

3. ____ design   _____   _____   _____

4. ____ rectangular   _____   _____   _____

5. ____ wavy   _____   _____   _____

6. ____ software   _____   _____   _____

2. Use the nouns and adjectives in Exercise 1 to complete these sentences about architecture.

  1. The Guggenheim Museum in Bilbao gave the city not only an economic but also a _____ _____.

  2. Many architects use a _____ _____ to help design their buildings.

  3. The building project came to a stop because the owners were in _____ _____.

  4. In the old days, there were no computers to help in the _____ _____ of a building. Everything was drawn and calculated by hand.

  5. The museum has different kinds of spaces from _____ _____ to circular galleries.

  6. The forms Gehry uses in the building create a _____ _____ to harmonize with the river it overlooks.

C. Vocabulary in New Context

Now make new sentences using the adjective and noun combinations you chose in Part B, Exercise 1.

Reading Comprehension

A. Looking for the Main Ideas

Some of the following statements from the reading are main ideas, and some are supporting statements. Find the statements in the reading. Write **M** in the blank in front of each main idea. Write **S** in front of each supporting statement.

_____ **1.** The city of Bilbao had been in deep financial trouble during the 1980s.

_____ **2.** Shipyards and steel plants had shut down due to rising competition from other areas.

_____ **3.** The foundation also operates an empire of art collections around the world.

_____ **4.** He created his model out of wood, foam core, and paper.

_____ **5.** Gehry had used the computer software program CATIA on earlier projects, but he used it to the fullest in constructing the new Guggenheim Museum in Bilbao.

_____ **6.** It also made construction plans easier.

_____ **7.** Like Gehry's early family life, marked by boom and bust, chaos and order, his design for the Guggenheim in Bilbao is full of contrasts.

_____ **8.** Rectangular spaces lead to circular galleries with curving walls.

B. Skimming and Scanning for Details

Scan the reading quickly to complete the following sentences. Fill in the blanks.

1. Two of Frank Gehry's most well-known projects are the _____ in Los Angeles and the _____ in Chicago.

2. Bilbao is the largest city in _____.

3. Bilbao needed something dramatic to attract _____ and _____.

4. The head of the Guggenheim Museum in New York invited architects from _____, _____, and the _____ to submit plans.

5. The computer software CATIA helped to _____ on the project.

6. On the exterior of the museum, Gehry used titanium, which is _____.

7. The building reflects the river's _____.

8. The galleries have designs that differ according to the _____.

9. Steen Petersen describes the enormous atrium as towering up through the building like a _____.

10. The economic and cultural growth the resulted from the museum became known as _____.

C. Making Inferences and Drawing Conclusions

Some of the following statements are facts from the reading. Other statements can be inferred from the reading. Write **F** in the blank in front of each factual statement. Write **I** in front of each inference.

_____ **1.** Before the Gehry-designed museum was built, Bilbao was on the verge of becoming a slum.

_____ **2.** Bilbao's city leaders showed great vision in their attempts to restore the city to its old glory.

_____ **3.** The Guggenheim Foundation holds a powerful position in the art world.

_____ **4.** Gehry's plans were chosen over those of two other architects.

_____ **5.** Bilbao residents questioned who Frank Gehry was.

_____ **6.** The museum design has many contrasts, just like Gehry's own life.

_____ **7.** There will most likely be people who don't like the Gehry design for the museum.

_____ **8.** Frank Gehry's designs for buildings are not strictly practical and useful.

Discussion Questions

Discuss the answers to these questions with your classmates.

1. What are some of the most famous buildings and cities in your country? Why are they admired?

2. What are some of the great architectural wonders around the world? What makes them great?

3. Which cities would you like to visit and why?

Critical Thinking Questions

Discuss the answers to these questions with your classmates.

1. What is your favorite type of architecture and why? Do you prefer ancient or modern architecture? Do you like Gehry's design for the Bilbao museum? Why or why not?

2. Do you think buildings should be designed to be practical or as pieces of art? What are do you think of the blending of art and architecture?

3. What does Steen Petersen mean when he says, "Gehry's museum . . ., depending on temperament [mood] and taste, can be experienced as a miracle or a nightmare"? Do you agree with this opinion?

Writing

Writing Skills

A. Organizing: *The Essay*

An essay consists of several paragraphs that develop one topic. An essay has three parts:

1. *The Introduction.* The introduction is generally one paragraph that introduces the topic and tells the reader what is to come in the following body paragraphs. The introduction contains the thesis statement, which is the central idea of the essay. The thesis statement usually comes at the end of the introduction.
2. *The Body Paragraph.* The number of body paragraphs depends on the number of main points you want to discuss. The body paragraphs support the thesis statement in the introduction.
3. *The Conclusion.* The concluding paragraph ends the essay. It sums up the main points or restates the thesis statement. It also leaves the reader with a final thought or comment on the topic.

The number of paragraphs an essay should have depends on the depth of the writer's examination of the topic. For this level, essays written in class should contain from 2 to 4 paragraphs, as well as an introduction and a conclusion.

Essay Form

Introduction	General statements
	Thesis statement
Body Paragraphs	Each body paragraph supports the thesis.
	Body Paragraph A develops a single point related to the thesis.
	Body Paragraph B develops a second point related to the thesis.
	Body Paragraph C develops another point related to the thesis.
Conclusion	The conclusion restates the thesis or summarizes the main points and gives a final comment.

The Introduction

The function of an *introduction* in an essay is to introduce the topic and present the thesis. An introduction should be interesting enough to make the reader want to continue on to find out what you have to say.

Several strategies can help make your introduction more interesting to the reader. Here are some suggestions:

1. *Start with a strong opinion.* Starting with a strong opinion can catch the reader's attention because the reader may not have thought of this point of view before.

> There are no creatures on earth less practical than humans. And nothing shows our frivolity better than fashion. From women's hoop skirts to men's high hats, fashion victims through the ages have endured the ridiculous, the uncomfortable, and the absolutely dangerous in their desire to be fashionable. Even our feet, which are normally planted firmly on the ground, have suffered the pains of keeping up with the latest craze.

2. *Start with a question.* Starting with a question is a way of breaking into a subject. You can then use the rest of the essay, including the thesis statement, to answer the question.

> Cleanliness is considered a virtue, but just what does it mean to be clean? As most of us have had the unpleasant occasion to discover, one person's definition can be quite different from another's. From Istanbul to Indianapolis, people have their own ways of keeping clean and their own reasons for doing so.

3. *Start with a quotation.* Starting with a quotation can make your introduction lively. The quotation should be directly linked to the main idea of the essay. It might be a well-known saying, a remark from a well-known person, or a line from a song or poem.

> "Let me have men about me that are fat," says Shakespeare's Julius Caesar to Marcus Antonius. In Julius Caesar's opinion, fat people are more trustworthy than thin ones—that is, those with a "lean and hungry look," who "are dangerous."

4. *Start with an anecdote.* Starting with an anecdote or story makes an abstract idea more real to the reader. The anecdote should be related to the thesis.

> Imagine walking on the surface of Mars. You follow the channels where water is believed to have once flowed, hike across the flat plains covered with rocks of all sizes, and jump the basin called Hellas, measuring more than 930 miles across. After you

explore the polar caps, you climb the huge volcano Olympus Mons, which is twice as high as Earth's highest peak. Seem impossible? It may be in the real world, but not in virtual reality.

An introduction has two parts:

1. General statements
2. Thesis statement

General Statements

The first sentence in an introductory paragraph should be a very *general statement* about the topic. Its purpose is to get the reader's attention (see the above introductions) and to give background information on the topic. Each statement that follows the general statement should be more specific than the one before it, usually ending with the thesis statement. Your introduction, therefore, will have a funnel shape, as shown in the diagram below.

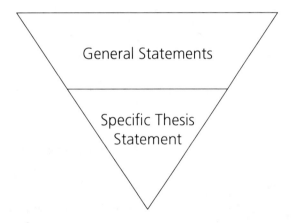

Thesis Statement

The *thesis statement* is usually the last sentence in the introduction. It is also the most important sentence in the introduction. A thesis statement gives the specific topic and central idea of the whole essay. It states the writer's approach to (method of organization) or attitude toward the central idea and may list the subtopics that will be discussed in the body paragraphs. Each of the topic sentences in the body paragraphs should relate to the thesis statement.

Remember these points about a thesis statement:

1. It states the main topic.
2. It may list subdivisions of the topic.
3. It may indicate the method of organization.
4. It should be expressed in a complete sentence.
5. It should express an opinion, an idea, or a belief. (It should not be a plain fact.)
6. It should express only one idea about a topic. (If it expresses more than one idea, the essay will lack unity.)
7. It should not just announce a topic.

Examples:

Not a thesis statement: Diet colas contain artificial sweeteners.

Thesis statement: Artificial sweeteners in diet colas may be dangerous to one's health.

Not a thesis statement: Advertising on American television is becoming more sophisticated, and there are some interesting movies.

Thesis statement: Advertising on American television is becoming more sophisticated.

Not a thesis statement: I am going to write about traffic problems in Thailand.

Thesis statement: Traffic problems in Thailand disrupt people's lives.

The Body Paragraphs

The number of paragraphs in the body of an essay written for this class may range from 2 to 4. The function of the *body paragraphs* is to explain or prove the thesis statement.

Remember the following points about body paragraphs:

1. *The main idea of the body paragraph should support the thesis statement.* If the thesis statement is about the advantages of exercise— "Regular exercise is beneficial to health."—then the topic sentence of each body paragraph should be about how regular exercise is beneficial to health.
2. *Each body paragraph should discuss one aspect of the thesis.* If you are writing about the benefits of exercise, then each body paragraph might discuss one benefit of exercise for health.
3. *The body paragraphs should follow a logical order.* The order of the paragraphs is determined by the type of organization you are using. Each body paragraph should follow the other smoothly through the use of transitions.

Once you have written a thesis statement, you can develop the topics for the body paragraphs in several ways, depending on your thesis statement. You can focus each body paragraph on one of the reasons, steps in a process, advantages and disadvantages, causes, effects, examples, or points of comparison and contrast.

A simple way of developing body paragraphs is to look at the central idea of the thesis statement and turn it into a question. The answers to the question will help you decide on the body paragraphs.

Example:

Thesis statement: Regular exercise is beneficial to health.

Question: In what way is regular exercise beneficial to health?

Answers:

Exercise is good for blood circulation.
It burns up extra calories.
It keeps the body and muscles flexible.

The central idea of the thesis statement is "beneficial to health." Asking the question "in what way?" provides the answers above. Each body paragraph could focus on a different benefit of exercise.

In the following example, the body paragraphs could deal with points of similarity.

Example:

Thesis statement: Hawaii and Alaska have some similarities.

Question: What similarities?

Answers:

Both are not connected to the 48 contiguous states.
Both have a large population of native peoples.
Both are expensive states in which to live.

The Conclusion

The final paragraph, or *conclusion*, should make the reader feel that you have completed what you set out to do in your thesis statement. The conclusion is often introduced or signaled by a transition, such as "in conclusion," "to sum up," or "thus."

A conclusion consists of:

- a restatement of the thesis in different words.

or

- a restatement of the main points of the essay and a final comment on the subject, based on what you have written.

What you say in the conclusion depends on what ideas you developed in your essay. Do not, however, bring up a new topic in the conclusion.

Read the following introduction and sample concluding paragraph.

1   There is a difference between being an onlooker and being a true observer of art. Onlookers just walk by a work of art, letting their eyes record it while their minds are elsewhere. They have no true appreciation of art. Observers, on the other hand, are informed and appreciative. They have spent the time
5   and energy to educate themselves so that art will be meaningful. They don't just exist side by side with art; they live with it and are aware of its existence in even the smallest part of their daily lives.

In conclusion, onlookers are unaware and unappreciative of the art surrounding them in their daily lives. Observers, having educated themselves,
10   are able to admire, enjoy, and appreciate art at any level, from a bold and imaginative magazine advertisement to an architecturally classic public building to an Impressionist painting in an art museum. Rather than allow the rich visual world to slip by them, observers pause to let their eyes and minds absorb artistic images of all kinds. Their deep appreciation of artistic
15   expression stretches their intellectual and emotional experiences, thus opening up new areas of enjoyment.

B. Exercises

1. Read the following sentences. Some are thesis statements, and some are not. Put a check mark in the box next to each thesis statement.

☐   Art has played a vital role in society since the earliest cave dwellers painted scenes on cave walls.

☐   Art today is more varied than at any other time in history, and art is one way to help people with emotional problems.

☐   Art is a form of human expression and thus a means of fulfilling an important human need.

☐   I am going to write about the function of art during the Renaissance.

- ☐ We can enrich our lives by developing a more active appreciation of the art we live with.
- ☐ For children, painting and drawing are play activities.
- ☐ Folk art is a term applied to works made by individuals with no academic training in art.
- ☐ Folk art is a spontaneous, personal, and appealing form of art.
- ☐ Modern artists enjoy much greater freedom than artists of even a few generations ago, and photography is now considered an art form of its own.
- ☐ The social role of artists has changed over time.
- ☐ A patron is a person who buys or orders works of art.
- ☐ Without patrons, artists could not prosper.

2. Read the following introductory paragraphs and answer the questions that follow.

1.   There is a difference between being an onlooker and being a true observer of art. Onlookers just walk by a work of art, letting their eyes record it while their minds are elsewhere. They have no true appreciation of art. Observers, on the other hand, are informed and appreciative. They have spent the time and energy to educate themselves so that art will be meaningful. They don't just exist side by side with art; they live with it and are aware of its existence in even the smallest part of their daily lives.
a. What is the topic?
b. What is the thesis statement?
c. What device is used to catch the reader's interest?

2.   What is art? People in the past always thought they knew what art was. Today, however, art is harder to define. Art in this century is far more complex, for several different reasons. People are exposed to the art of many times and cultures. Much of modern art is difficult to classify. And to further complicate things, we now have works of art created in media undreamed of a few decades ago, including electronic images that may disappear within moments of their creation. It's no wonder that people are asking what exactly art is and isn't, and how we can tell the difference.
a. What is the topic?
b. What is the thesis statement?
c. What device is used to catch the reader's interest?

3. "The only difference between me and a madman is that I am not mad," said Salvador Dali, probably the most famous Surrealist artist. Like many other modern artists, such as Vincent van Gogh, Edvard Munch, and Jean Dubuffet, Dali was interested in the relationship between madness and creativity. Certainly the works of these artists, with their swirling lines, strange scenes, and fantastic dreamlike quality, appear to be the products of unstable minds. Van Gogh produced a whole body of work while in an asylum, so the question of whether madness contributed to his work, and might even have been the force behind it, is a valid one. Where does creativity end and madness begin? Is the line that separates them so thin as to be unrecognizable? These are questions that must be explored in any study of the relationship between madness and creativity in the world of art.

    a. What is the topic?

    b. What is the thesis statement?

    c. What device is used to catch the reader's interest?

3. Following each thesis statement are two supporting topic sentences that relate to the question being asked. Write a third topic sentence.

  1. Thesis: There are advantages to having a small family.
    Topic sentences:
      I. Parents can afford more things.
      II. Making family decisions is easier.
      III. _____.

  2. Thesis: Watching television has harmful effects on society.
    Topic sentences:
      I. Family members no longer talk to each other.
      II. People lose interest in their communities.
      III. _____.

  3. Thesis: New York and Los Angeles differ in many ways.
    Topic sentences:
      I. There are climatic differences.
      II. There are differences in cultural life.
      III. _____.

4. Thesis: Computers have benefited society in several ways.
Topic sentences:
   I. Operations can be done faster.
   II. Fewer workers are needed, saving money for employees.
   III. _____.

5. Thesis: There are advantages to stopping smoking.
Topic sentences:
   I. You can have a better social life.
   II. You can get back your self-esteem.
   III. _____.

4. Read the following introductions, and write your own concluding paragraphs.

1.   What is art? People in the past always thought they knew what art was. Today, however, art is harder to define. Art in this century is far more complex for several different reasons. People are exposed to the art of many times and cultures. Much of modern art is difficult to classify. And to further complicate things, we now have works of art created in media undreamed of a few decades ago, including electronic images that may disappear within moments of their creation. It's no wonder that people are asking what exactly art is and isn't, and how we can tell the difference.

2.   "The only difference between me and a madman is that I am not mad," said Salvador Dali, probably the most famous Surrealist artist. Like many other modern artists, such as Vincent van Gogh, Edvard Munch, and Jean Dubuffet, Dali was interested in the relationship between madness and creativity. Certainly the works of these artists, with their swirling lines, strange scenes, and fantastic dreamlike quality, appear to be the products of unstable minds. Van Gogh produced a whole body of work while in an asylum, so the question of whether madness contributed to his work, and might even have been the force behind it, is a valid one. Where does creativity end and madness begin? Is the line that separates them so thin as to be unrecognizable? These are questions that must be explored in any study of the relationship between madness and creativity in the world of art.

A. Summarize

Write a one-paragraph summary of Reading 1. Check your summary with the Summary Checklist on page 269.

B. Paraphrase

Paraphrase paragraph 1 (which begins "The city of . . .") of Reading 2. Look at pages 264–267 to find out about paraphrasing. Begin paraphrasing with "According to Lazo, . . ." or "Based on Lazo's book, ..."

Weaving It Together

⏱ Timed Writing

Write an introduction with a thesis statement, 2 or 3 topic sentences, and a full conclusion about art or an artist you like. You have 50 minutes to write it.

Connecting to the Internet

A. Use the Internet to research the life of the following artists: Jackson Pollock, Takashi Murakami, Maya Lin, Anish Kapoor, and Bridget Riley. Make a list with the name of each artist and the type of art for which he or she is most famous. Then write a short article about the life and work of one of these artists or of another artist that you admire.

B. Use the Internet to look up the lives of the following architects: Alvar Aalto, Frank Lloyd Wright, Fumihiko Maki, Ludwig Mies van der Rohe, and Renzo Piano. Make a list with the name of each architect and the work for which he or she is most famous. Then write a short article about the life and work of one of these architects or of another architect that you admire.

What Do You Think Now?

Refer to page 1 at the beginning of this chapter. Do you know the answers now? Complete the sentence or circle the best answer.

1. Frida Kahlo was an artist from _____.
2. Frida Kahlo was/was not famous in her lifetime.
3. Frida Kahlo was the wife of _____.
4. Frank Gehry is a famous American _____.
5. The Guggenheim Museum in New York was/was not the work of Frank Gehry.

Chapter 2

Language

Heere bigynneth the Knyghtes Tale.

Whilom, as olde stories tellen us,
Ther was a duc that highte Theseus;
Of Atthenes he was lord and governour;
And in his tyme swich a conquerour
That gretter was ther noon under the sonne.

Here begins the Knight's Tale.

Once, as old stories tell, there was a prince
Named Theseus that in Athens ruled long since,
A conqueror in his time; for rich lands won
There was no greater underneath the sun.

What Do You Think?

Answer the questions with your best guess. Circle **Yes** or **No**.

Do you think . . .

1. English was a mix of five languages at one time?	**Yes**	**No**
2. the first English dictionary came out in 1855?	**Yes**	**No**
3. Shakespeare spelled his name in different ways all the time?	**Yes**	**No**
4. the word *window* originally meant "wind eye"?	**Yes**	**No**
5. The English dish called pie came from the word *circle*?	**Yes**	**No**

Pre-Reading

1. Discuss the answers to these questions with your classmates.

    1. Look at the manuscript written in Old English and the modern translation on page 33. Which words are spelled differently today?

    2. There were no spelling rules when Old English was spoken. What problems do you think this situation caused for people?

    3. Do you think spelling rules are important? Why or why not?

    4. What spelling rules do you know in English?

2. Six words in the list below are spelled wrong. Find the misspelled words and correct them. Use a dictionary to check your answers.

    a. pronunciation (the way you say a word)

    b. batchelor (unmarried male)

    c. superintendant (manager)

    d. exerpt (selected passage from a book or film)

    e. absorption (process of being absorbed)

    f. tarrif (import fee)

    g. occurence (happening)

    h. newstand (place where you buy newspapers and magazines)

    i. separate (to move apart)

    j. nighttime (at night)

3. Do you know the American and British spellings of these words?

American	British
color	**5.**
1.	centre
2.	behaviour
theater	**6.**
jail	**7.**
3.	judgement
program	**8.**
4.	skilful
check	**9.**
draft	**10.**

Reading 1

Spell It in English

CD 1,
Track 3

The British Isles

1   English spelling is confusing and chaotic, as any student of English knows all too well. "How can the letters *ough* spell so many different sounding words," they ask,

5   "like *dough*, *bough*, *rough*, and *through*?" And what about a word like *colonel*, which clearly contains no *r* yet pretends it does, and *ache*, with its *k* sound instead of the *chuh* sound of *arch*? And why does *four* have

10   a *u* while *forty* doesn't? There are no simple rules for English spelling, but there is an explanation behind its complexity. We have only to look back in history.

      Over the centuries, the English language

15   has been like a magnet, attracting words from numerous other languages. It all started with the Britons, an ancient people living in a part of Western Europe that eventually became the British Isles.[1] The Britons spoke a language called Celtic, which was a combination of the early forms of Irish,[2] Scottish,[3]

20   and Welsh.[4] When the Britons were conquered by the Romans and later the Germanic tribes, their language was also invaded. The merging of the languages gave birth to Old English (an early form of the Modern English we know), and a Latin alphabet replaced, with a few exceptions, the ancient Germanic alphabet. In the ninth century, the conquering Norsemen from

---

[1]**the British Isles:** Great Britain (England, Scotland, Wales) and Ireland
[2]**Irish:** the language of Ireland
[3]**Scottish:** the language of Scotland
[4]**Welsh:** the language of Wales

25 Scandinavia added their pinch of language spice,[5] as did the French in the 11th century.

By the 14th century, English, with its mix of at least five languages, had evolved into what is called Middle English and had become Britain's official language. At that time, however, its spellings were far from consistent or
30 rational. Many dialects had developed over the centuries, and sometimes people adopted the spelling used in one part of the country and the pronunciation used in another. For instance, today we use the western English spellings for *busy* and *bury*, but we give the first the London pronunciation *bizzy* and the second the Kentish[6] pronunciation *berry*. Of course, this all
35 happened when English was primarily a spoken language, and only scholars knew how to read and write. Even they appear to have been quite indifferent to matters of consistency in spelling and were known to spell the same word several different ways in a single sentence.

Even after William Caxton set up England's first printing press in the late
40 15th century and the written word became available to everyone, standard spelling wasn't considered very important. As a matter of fact, the typesetters in the 1500s made things even worse by being very careless about spelling. If a blank space needed to be filled in or a line was too long, they simply changed the spellings of words to make them fit. Moreover, many of the
45 early printers in England were from Germany or Holland and didn't know English very well. If they didn't know the spelling of a word, they made up one! Different printers each had their favorite spellings, so one word might be spelled five or six different ways, depending on who printed the passage.

Throughout this period, names and words appear in many different forms.
50 For instance, *where* can be found as *wher, whair, wair, wheare, were,* and so on. People were even very liberal about their names. More than 80 spellings of Shakespeare's name have been found, among them *Shagsspeare, Shakspeare,* and even *Shakestaffe.* Shakespeare himself didn't spell his name the same way in any two of his six known signatures—he even spelled his name two
55 different ways in his will.

By the late 16th century and early 17th century, some progress had been made in standardizing spelling due to the work of various scholars. By then, however, English spelling was far from a simple phonetic system. For one

---

[5]**pinch of language spice:** a little bit of variety in the language
[6]**Kentish:** of Kent, a county in southeast England

thing, word pronunciations had changed too rapidly for a truly phonetic
60 spelling to keep up. Also, English had borrowed from many languages and
ended up having far too many sounds (more than 40) for the 26 letters in
its Roman alphabet. By the time printing houses finally began to agree on
standard spellings, many of these written forms were only a shadow of their
spoken selves. In other words, spelling and pronunciation sometimes had
65 little in common.

Finally, in 1755, Samuel Johnson gave English its first great dictionary. His
choice of spellings may not have always been the best or the easiest, but the
book helped to make the spellings of most English words uniform. Eventually,
people became aware of the need for "correct" spelling. Meanwhile, on the
70 other side of the Atlantic, Noah Webster was standardizing American English
in his *American Dictionary of the English Language* and *American Spelling Book*.
Although the British had been complaining about the messiness of English
spelling for some time, it was the Americans, with their fanaticism for
efficiency, who screamed the loudest. Webster not only favored a simplified,
75 more phonetic spelling system, but also tried to persuade Congress to pass a
law making the use of nonstandard spelling a punishable offense.

Mark Twain[7] was of the same mind—but laziness figured into his
opinion. He wasn't concerned so much with the difficulty of spelling words
as with the trouble in writing them. He became a fan of the "phonographic
80 alphabet," created by Isaac Pitman, the inventor of shorthand—a system
in which symbols represent words, phrases, and letters. "To write the word
'laugh,'" Twain wrote in *A Simplified Alphabet*, "the pen has to make fourteen
strokes—no labor is saved to penman." But to write the same word in the
phonographic alphabet, Twain continued, the pen had to make just three
85 strokes. As much as Twain would have loved it, Pitman's phonographic
alphabet never caught on.

Interest in reforming English spelling continued to gain momentum on
both sides of the Atlantic. For a while, it seemed as if every famous writer and
scholar had jumped on the spelling bandwagon.[8] Spelling reform associations
90 began to pop up everywhere. In 1876, the American Philological Association
called for the "urgent" adoption of 11 new spellings: *liv, tho, thru, wisht,
catalog, definit, gard, giv, hv, infinit,* and *ar.* In the same year, the Spelling
Reform Association was formed, followed 3 years later by a British version.

[7]**Mark Twain:** an American author (1835–1910) who wrote many books, including
The Adventures of Tom Sawyer and *The Adventures of Huckleberry Finn*
[8]**jump on the bandwagon:** join a popular movement

In 1906, the philanthropist Andrew Carnegie gave $250,000 to help establish the Simplified Spelling Board. The board quickly issued a list of 300 words that were commonly spelled two ways, such as *ax* and *axe*, and called for using the simpler of the two. The board helped to gain acceptance for quite a few American spellings, including *catalog, demagog,* and *program.*

Eventually the Simplified Spelling Board got carried away with its work, calling for such spellings as *tuff, def, troble,* and *yu.* The call for simplified spelling quickly went out of fashion, particularly with the onset of World War I and the death of Andrew Carnegie. The movement never died out completely, however. Spelling reform continued to be an ongoing, if less dramatic, process, as it had been for centuries. Without the benefit of large donations or outside agencies, many words have shed useless letters. *Deposite* has lost its *e,* as have *fossile* and *secretariate. Musick* and *physick* have dropped their needless *k's,* and *catalogue* and *dialogue* have shed their last two vowels.

As long as the world goes around, language will continue to change. New words will be added to English; spellings will be altered. But because people are most comfortable with the familiar, it's not likely that we'll ever see a major change in the way most words are spelled. Anyway, what would we do without the challenge of English spelling?

Vocabulary

A. Vocabulary in Context

Select the letter of the answer that is closest in meaning to the **bold** word or phrase.

1. The **merging** of the different languages gave birth to Old English.
a. crossing
b. confusion
c. blending
d. complication

2. By the 14th century, English, with its mix of languages, had **evolved** into what is called Middle English.
a. improved
b. appeared
c. spread
d. developed

3. Even scholars were quite **indifferent** to matters of consistency in spelling and were known to spell the same word several different ways in a single sentence.

a. uncaring about

b. superior about

c. unsocial about

d. confused about

4. People were even **liberal** about the spelling of their names, using different spellings on the same page.

a. receptive

b. interested

c. understanding

d. free

5. Americans, with their **fanaticism** for efficiency, complained the most about the messiness of English spelling.

a. spirit

b. obsession

c. excitement

d. fascination

6. Interest in reforming English spelling continued to **gain momentum** on both sides of the Atlantic.

a. be temporary

b. become stable

c. grow stronger

d. get weak

7. The **philanthropist** Andrew Carnegie gave $250,000 to help establish the Simplified Spelling Board.

a. person who is an expert in language

b. person who actively helps others

c. person famous for his or her written work

d. person known for his or her wealth

8. The Spelling Board outlived its usefulness when it **got carried away** with its work.

a. became overenthusiastic about

b. was removed from

c. got to continue

d. became successful in

Word Partnership	Use **momentum** with:
v.	**build** momentum, **gain** momentum, **gather** momentum, **have** momentum, **lose** momentum, **maintain** momentum

9. The call for simplified spelling went out of fashion with the **onset** of World War I.

a. outcome
c. end
b. tragedy
d. start

10. Many words **shed** useless letters.

a. changed
c. dropped
b. kept
d. added

B. Vocabulary Building

1. Match the adjectives with the nouns as they were used in the context of the reading. Look back at the reading to check your answers. Add two more nouns that may be used with each adjective.

a. change
c. offense
e. spelling
b. language
d. process
f. system

1. _b_ official   language   _____   _____

2. ____ standard   _____   _____   _____

3. ____ punishable   _____   _____   _____

4. ____ phonetic   _____   _____   _____

5. ____ ongoing   _____   _____   _____

6. ____ major   _____   _____   _____

2. Use the nouns and adjectives you listed in Exercise 1 to complete these sentences about English spelling.

1. Spelling reform continues to be an _____ _____.

2. _____ _____ was introduced with the first dictionaries.

3. It is unlikely that there will be any _____ _____ in English spelling now.

4. Spelling did not represent the _____ _____ of English.

5. Middle English became the _____ _____ of Britain
      by the 14th century.

   6. Webster wanted to make the use of nonstandard spelling a
      _____ _____.

C. Vocabulary in New Context

Now make new sentences using the adjective and noun combinations you chose
in Part B, Exercise 1.

Reading Comprehension

A. Looking for the Main Ideas

Circle the letter of the best answer.

   1. What is the main idea of paragraph 3?
      a. By the time English had become a written language, the influence of
         several languages and dialects had made spelling and pronunciation very
         inconsistent.
      b. Scholars didn't help the problem of spelling inconsistency, because they
         often spelled words several different ways.
      c. In Britain, English words had different spellings and pronunciations in
         different parts of the country.
      d. By the 14th century, English had evolved into Middle English and was
         Britain's official language.

   2. Paragraph 6 is mostly about _____.
      a. how progress had been made in standardizing spelling by the 17th century
      b. why English spelling and pronunciation were often very different
      c. how English had many more sounds than it had letters in its alphabet
      d. why printing houses played a role in standardizing spelling

   3. Paragraph 12 is mainly concerned with _____.
      a. the work of the Simplified Spelling Board
      b. why the call for simplified spelling went out of fashion
      c. the many words that have been shortened by dropping useless letters
      d. the ongoing changes in the English language

B. Skimming and Scanning for Details

Scan the reading quickly to find the answers to the following questions. Write complete sentences.

1. According to the reading, what combination of languages formed the Celtic language?

2. Name four conquering peoples whose languages affected the development of the English language.

3. Before the invention of the printing press, English was mostly what kind of language?

4. Why were the typesetters of the 1500s not very helpful when it came to making spelling standard?

5. Who was responsible for giving English its first great dictionary?

6. What kind of spelling system did Noah Webster favor?

7. What is shorthand, and who invented it?

8. What purpose did spelling reform associations serve?

9. In the last sentence of paragraph 11, to what does the last *their* refer?

10. Why are we not likely to see major changes in the way most words are spelled?

C. Making Inferences and Drawing Conclusions

The answers to these questions are not directly stated in the reading. Circle the letter of the best answer.

1. The reading implies that _____.
   a. conquering tribes forced the Britons to speak their languages
   b. English was a "pure" language before the 14th century
   c. the influence of other languages made English a rich but complicated language
   d. when Britain made English its official language, it stopped foreign words from entering the language and making it even more complicated

2. From the reading, it can be concluded that _____.

    a. scholars weren't much more educated than the masses

    b. until the first dictionaries were written, even educated people weren't overly concerned with the spelling of words

    c. the invention of the printing press didn't have a significant influence on the English language

    d. there was no real need for an English dictionary before Johnson wrote his in 1755

3. It can be inferred from the reading that _____.

    a. if it weren't for Mark Twain, many English words would now be spelled differently

    b. Andrew Carnegie never played a significant role in the area of American spelling

    c. spelling reform associations had less influence on English spelling changes than the natural course of language changes today

    d. thanks to many concerned people, spelling is simpler now than it was 200 years ago

4. The author's tone is _____.

    a. informal

    b. sentimental

    c. insincere

    d. argumentative

Discussion Questions

Discuss the answers to these questions with your classmates.

1. How would you simplify English spelling?

2. If a spelling system based on pronunciation were devised in English, on whose pronunciation would you base it?

3. Do you know any special strategies for remembering difficult spellings in English?

4. Do you know of any new spellings of words used on the Internet?

Critical Thinking Questions

Discuss the answers to these questions with your classmates.

1. Why do you think proposals to reform English spelling have not won support?
2. What does language tell us about the country and people who speak it?
3. Why are you learning English? Do you think people should know more than one language? Why or why not?
4. In some countries, the people of that country speak several different languages. What problems can this cause? Are there any advantages? Do you think the world should have a universal language? Why or why not?

Reading 2

May I Borrow a Word?

The following extracts are taken from pages 154–155 of the book Great Expressions, *by Marvin Vanoni (William Morrow & Co., New York, 1989). They illustrate the historical development of the words* window, pie, *and* bangs.

Window

1   **E**arly Norse[1] carpenters had few tools and no building materials other than wood, stone, and straw. Consequently, they were forced to
5   build houses as simply as possible. There were no iron hinges;[2] doors usually hung on leather thongs.[3]

Since doors had to be closed in cold weather, some form of ventilation had to be provided. This was usually done by leaving a hole, or "eye," in the roof. Through it smoke and foul air could escape. Because the wind frequently whistled through it, the air hole was called *vindr auga* (wind eye).

English builders borrowed the Norse term, modified it to window, and developed new techniques by which the eye that once admitted the wind now holds it out.

---

[1]**Norse:** people who lived in Scandinavia in ancient times
[2]**hinges:** pieces of metal used to join a door to its frame
[3]**thongs:** a long, thin strip of leather

Pie

Until the late eighteenth century, the bird now called magpie was termed simply "pie." Then, as now, such a bird was likely to be a habitual collector. It was not unusual to find a pie's nest filled with pebbles, bits of broken glass, string, chicken feathers, and so on.

At some unrecorded time, an inspired housewife thought

of placing a crust around a small pot of stew. She used whatever ingredients at hand—meat, fowl, or fish, plus a few vegetables and perhaps an egg or two. Her menfolk[4] liked the odd conglomeration and, casting about for a name, compared it with a pie's nest, which was filled with a variety of odds and ends. So they called the new dish *pie*.

First used in writing around 1303, the word came to include many varieties of pie. No other language has a word that is even distantly related to the name of the most popular of English dishes.

Bangs

The term we now use to describe a particular hairstyle once referred to the way a horse's tail looked!

Money problems in the middle of the nineteenth century hurt many of the rich sportsmen. Some sold

---

[4]**menfolk:** men in a family or society

55

60

65

their stables[5] and horses. Others merely reduced their staff and kept only their best animals. The shorthanded stable crews couldn't groom horses as carefully as before. It had been customary to spend hours trimming a horse's tail; in the new age of austerity, grooms[6] just cut the tail off square, or "banged it off."

Soon bangtail animals were winning horse races everywhere. Designers took note, and it wasn't long before fashionable women were displaying their hair in bangs.

---

[5]**stables:** buildings in which horses are kept
[6]**grooms:** people whose job is to look after horses in a stable and keep them clean

Vocabulary

A. Vocabulary in Context

Select the letter of the answer that is closest in meaning to the **bold** word or phrase.

1. Since doors had to be closed in cold weather, some form of **ventilation** had to be provided.
   a. a way to let light in
   b. an opening to get in and out
   c. a system to allow air in and out
   d. a way to see outside

2. Through it smoke and **foul** air could escape.
   a. clean and fresh
   b. thick or dark
   c. light and fragrant
   d. dirty or impure

3. An **inspired** housewife thought of placing a crust around a small pot of stew.
   a. having a good idea
   b. being desperate
   c. feeling concerned
   d. having a great need for

4. She used whatever ingredients at hand—meat, **fowl**, or fish.
   a. cow
   b. bird
   c. sea creature
   d. lamb

5. Her menfolk liked the odd **conglomeration**.
   a. mess
   b. confusion
   c. combination
   d. sample

6. They compared it with a pie's nest, which was filled with a variety of **odds and ends**.
   a. a blend of ingredients
   b. several different locks of hair
   c. an assortment of small pieces
   d. a number of things that belong together

7. The **shorthanded** stable crews couldn't groom horses carefully as before.
   a. having many faults or defects
   b. having less people than needed
   c. being able to do something quickly
   d. being rudely impatient

8. The shorthanded stable crews couldn't **groom** horses carefully as before.
   a. provide training to
   b. give medical attention to
   c. give food and water to
   d. care for by cleaning and brushing

9. It had been customary to spend hours **trimming** a horse's tail.
   a. cutting in a neat and tidy way
   b. cutting in a rough or ragged way
   c. cutting extremely short
   d. cutting straight or square

10. In the new age of **austerity**, grooms just cut the tail off square, or "banged it off."
   a. living with great style
   b. living by society's rules
   c. living in a different or radical way
   d. living with less luxury and comfort

B. Vocabulary Building

1. Read the list of verbs below. Find verbs in the readings that have the same meaning.

   1. alter (window)   _____modify_____

   2. let in (window)   _____

   3. make a loud, high sound when moving (window)   _____

   4. call or name (pie)   _____

   5. show/show off (bangs)   _____

   6. pay attention (bangs)   _____

C. Vocabulary in New Context

Use the verbs you listed in Part B to complete these sentences.

1. _____ of what I say, you will see that it will be so.

2. He always _____ the same tune in the shower.

3. The expensive restaurant doesn't _____ people dressed in casual clothes.

4. Many movie stars _____ their designer clothes at the Academy Awards.

5. The Old English word *nekename* was later _____ to *nickname,* an added name.

6. When all the roads are so full with vehicles that none of them can move, it is _____ as *gridlock.*

Reading Comprehension

A. Looking for the Main Ideas

Some of the following statements from the reading are main ideas, and some are supporting statements. Write **M** in the blank in front of each main idea. Write **S** in front of each supporting statement.

_____ **1.** Early Norse carpenters had few tools and no building materials other than wood, stone, and straw.

_____ **2.** Since doors had to be closed in cold weather, some form of ventilation had to be provided.

_____ **3.** Through it smoke and foul air could escape.

_____ **4.** Then, as now, such a bird was likely to be a habitual collector.

_____ **5.** It was not unusual to find a pie's nest filled with pebbles, bits of broken glass, string, chicken feathers, and so on.

_____ **6.** At some unrecorded time, an inspired housewife thought of placing a crust around a small pot of stew.

_____ **7.** She used whatever ingredients at hand—meat, fowl, or fish, plus a few vegetables and perhaps an egg or two.

_____ **8.** Money problems in the middle of the nineteenth century hurt many of the rich sportsmen.

_____ **9.** Some sold their stables and horses.

_____ **10.** Others merely reduced their staff and kept only their best animals.

B. Skimming and Scanning for Details

Scan the reading quickly to complete the following sentences.

1. In Norse homes, there were no iron hinges; doors usually hung on

_____.

2. In Norse homes, ventilation was provided by _____.

3. The air hole in Norse homes was called _vindr auga,_ or wind eye, because

_____.

4. Until the _____ century, the bird now called magpie was termed simply "pie."

5. The men compared the housewife's new dish with a _____.

6. The word _pie_ was first used in writing around the year _____.

7. The term we now use to describe a particular hairstyle once referred to

_____.

8. In the middle of the nineteenth century, many of the rich sportsmen had _____ problems.

9. To save time, the stable crews cut the horse's tail in a _____ shape.

10. _____ noticed the new tails on the horses and soon fashionable women were displaying their hair in bangs.

C. Making Inferences and Drawing Conclusions

Some of the following statements are facts taken from the reading. Other statements can be inferred from the reading. Write **F** in the blank in front of each factual statement. Write **I** in front of each inference.

_____ **1.** The Norsemen were not technologically advanced.
_____ **2.** The Norsemen used whatever was locally available for building.
_____ **3.** The Norse houses were very simple.
_____ **4.** A hole in the roof was made for ventilation.
_____ **5.** English builders developed new techniques to make windows.

_____ **6.** The magpie lines its nest with items it collects.

_____ **7.** Using a crust to contain food was a uniquely English idea.

_____ **8.** Problems can sometimes lead to interesting changes in society.

_____ **9.** Stable crews didn't have the time to spend on grooming the horses that they had once had.

_____ **10.** Cutting off the horses' tails had a positive effect on their performance.

Discussion Questions

Discuss the answers to these questions with your classmates.

1. Certain English words are formed by combining parts of two other words, usually the first part of one and the last part of another. An example is _smog,_ which is a combination of _smoke_ and _fog._ Other examples include _brunch_ and _motel._ Words formed with this technique are called _portmanteau_ words. Create five new portmanteau words.

2. Describe the process you would use in learning a new language.

3. Imagine that four of you are together in a deserted part of the world. None of you speak the same language. Describe the process of creating a language to communicate with one another.

Critical Thinking Questions

Discuss the answers to these questions with your classmates.

1. Every day, new words are being added to our language. What changes in the past 100 years have had the greatest impact on the creation of new words? How are these new words created? Name at least 10 words that have come into our languages in the past 25 years alone. What new changes do you think will occur to add even more new words in the next century?

2. What can we tell about a person from the language that he or she speaks? In other words, what does language say about us? How do you think humans first learned language?

3. Historically, diplomats have been compared to poets, actors, and orators. What is the "language of diplomacy," and how do you think it developed? How is language used by diplomats to overcome the differences between nations and cultures?

Writing

Writing Skills

A. Organizing: *The Process Essay*

In Reading 1, we saw how English spelling developed over time into what it is today. In Reading 2, we saw how the words *window, pie,* and *bangs* originated and how they came to mean what they mean today. Both of these readings use a chronological (time) order.

One type of process essay describes events in the order they occurred over a period of time, such as a morning, a day, a childhood, or the duration of a war. A history or a biography usually describes events over a period of time.

Another type of process essay describes a technical process, such as how a computer works or how hair is transplanted or how chocolate is made. (This type of essay contains many verbs in the passive form.)

Yet another type of process essay is the "how to" essay, in which you tell someone how to do or make something. This type is used to discuss topics such as how to prepare a special dish or how to get a driver's license.

The essential component in all process essays is time order. Use time experiences and transition signals to indicate the time sequences clearly.

Thesis Statement for the Process Essay

The thesis statement for a process that is historical should name the process and indicate chronological order through words like *developed* or *evolved*.

Example:

Chinese is one of the world's oldest languages, and its written form, like that of most languages, developed from the pictograph.

The thesis statement for a technical process should name the process and indicate that it involves a series of steps.

Example:

Hair transplantation is a fairly simple process.

It may also name the main steps in the process.

Example:

The main steps in the process of hair transplantation are removal of the desired number of hair transplants, removal of small plugs in the bald area, and insertion of the hair transplants.

The thesis statement for a "how-to" essay is the same as the one for a technical process. It should name the process or item and indicate that it involves a number of steps.

Examples:

Baking your own bread can be quite easy if you follow these steps.

Rescue breathing for a person who is unconscious involves a sequence of steps that must be followed carefully.

Organizing the Process Essay

Deciding how to divide a process essay into paragraphs can be tricky. If you are writing a historical or narrative piece about a chronological process, divide your paragraphs by major time periods, as in the student essay on pages 56 and 57. However, if you are writing about how to do something, the following guidelines will help you:

Introduction:

Introduce the topic and explain why the process is performed, by whom it is performed, and in what situation it is performed. You may list the main steps of the process in the order they are performed.

Body Paragraphs:

Start to describe the process, introducing the first step in a topic sentence. You may at this point state the equipment and supplies needed for the process. Divide the process into three or four major steps. Each major step should be described in a body paragraph. For example, if you were describing a wedding ceremony in your country, the first major step would be the preparations, the next would be the ceremony, and the last would be the reception or banquet.

Conclusion:

Summarize by restating the main steps and describing the result. The type of conclusion will depend on the type of process you are describing (see the student essay on pages 56 and 57).

Time Expressions

Time may be indicated by a preposition with a date or historical period: *in 1920, by the 16th century, over the next 10 years,* or other time expressions. We will look at some prepositions commonly used with time.

During indicates the duration of the activity from beginning to end, usually without stating the length of time.

Example:

During her first year at college, she performed remarkably.

For indicates the length of time or an appointed time.

Examples:

I waited *for* an hour.

My appointment was *for* three o'clock.

Since indicates a period of time from its beginning to the present.

Example:

He has been living there *since* 1920. (He is still there.)

Other prepositions of time indicate when or how long: *as, in, on, to, till, up to, upon, as early as, as soon as, from/to,* and *as late as.*

Examples:

The process should be completed *in* three hours.
The class will have a test *on* Friday.
He worked *till* ten o'clock.
She spends *up to* three hours every day rehearsing.
Leave to thaw for an hour *upon* taking it out of the freezer.
She woke up *as soon as* it was daylight.
Cook the beans *from* 25 *to* 35 minutes.

Dependent clauses can be introduced by prepositions used as adverbs (*after, before, until*) or by adverbs (*when, while*).

Examples:

After (or *when*) you have made a rough draft, start revising your work.

Before starting on the second draft, make sure that your details support your topic sentences.

Don't forget to look up the spelling of words you are unsure of *when* you are editing.

Do not be distracted *while* you are editing each sentence.

Other useful words that indicate a sequence in a process are ordinal numbers (*first, second, third*) and interrupters (*next, then, later, simultaneously, eventually*). The expressions *previous to, prior to,* and *just before* place an action before another action.

Examples:

Prior to writing your research, make sure you have all the information at hand.

Next, revise your draft.

B. Exercises

1. Look back at Reading 1 and underline all the words that indicate time or sequence.

2. Fill in the blanks using the following time words. Each choice can be used only once.

1561	in 1499	still
after	in 1542	then
during	in 1637	until
for	later	when
		while

The first European to discover the Amazon River was Spanish explorer Vicente Pinzon **1.**_____. He had been on Columbus's first voyage seven years earlier and was **2.**_____ determined to find a route to the Orient.

3._____ he sailed into the mouth of the Amazon and looked at the mighty river ahead of him, he thought he had gone around the world and hit the Ganges River in India. He stopped at some islands in the mouth of the river and **4.**_____ sailed on.

Forty-three years **5.**_____, **6.**_____, Francisco de Orellana became the first European to travel the entire river, although that was not what he set out to do at all. **7.**_____ a Spanish expedition became stranded in the jungles of Eastern Peru, Orellana was sent down the Napo River to find food. But starvation, sickness, and Indian attacks took place, and Orellana couldn't get back upriver. Instead, he followed tributaries to the Amazon, and **8.**_____ 16 months of incredible hardships, he and what was left of his party made it all the way to the sea.

In **9.**_____, the notorious Lope de Aguirre traveled the Amazon **10.**_____ on the run from Spanish troops. He left a trail of death and destruction throughout the Amazon, all the way to the sea.

No one traveled the entire river **11.**_____ another 76 years, **12.**_____ a Portuguese captain, Pedro Teixeira, became the first to complete an upriver "ascent" **13.**_____.

Writing Model: The Process Essay

Read the following process essay written by a student.

The Chinese Art of Writing

1   Chinese is one of the most remarkable pieces of art in language that humankind has ever made. In elementary school, Chinese teachers ask their students to write not only correctly but beautifully by printing a picture for each character. Chinese is different from Western languages such as German,
5   French, or English because it has no alphabet. Instead, it contains 50,000 characters. If a person knows 5,000 of the most commonly used characters, he or she can read a newspaper. How many characters a person knows indicates how intellectual that person is. Chinese is one of the world's oldest languages, and its written form, like that of most languages, developed from
10   the pictograph.

Thi Chi is credited with the invention of the written Chinese language 5,000 years ago. He created the first Chinese characters by imitating the shapes of living things in the world. The sign for *sun* was a circle with a wavy line through it to show heat (⊝). The sign for *mountain* had three peaks (Ⱄ). The sign for a *child* was a child reaching for mother (⧸). The sign for *man* looked like a man (⧸). These signs or pictographs could be easily understood because they looked like real things.

Then, after a few centuries, the Chinese made these pictographs easier to draw. The signs were called characters and are used to this day. These are some of the examples of the changes: the character for *sun* became 日; the character for *mountain* became 山; and the character for *child* became 子. Two lines at 120 degrees (人) now represent *man*.

Later, it became necessary to express more ideas, so strokes were added to the characters or characters were combined. With extra strokes, a character had a new meaning. For example, a man with arms outstretched at 180 degrees (大) represents *big*, and two short lines on each side of a man (小) means *small*. Characters were combined to make new words, as in the example of the character for *to bark* (口犬), which is made up of the combination of *mouth* (口) and *dog* (犬). Another example of this kind is the character for *good* (好), which is made up of a woman and child because in China, as well as everywhere, a mother with her child is a good thing. Sometimes a character is repeated to make a different word, as in the character for *forest* (林), which is the repetition of *tree* (木).

From the first character that Thi Chi created, Chinese words have expanded to more than 10,000. The Chinese language also had an influence on other Asian languages such as Japanese and Korean, which somehow contain some Chinese characteristics. Chinese is not only a tool for people to communicate with but also an important subject for Chinese artists to study. Chinese fine handwriting, or calligraphy, was considered a branch of painting, and calligraphy was often combined with painting in a work of art. Chinese can be considered as one of the most beautiful languages in the world without question.

Chun Che
Taiwan

Student Essay Follow-Up

1. What is the writer trying to do in this essay?
2. Underline the thesis statement.
3. Are time signals used through each phase of the process?
4. Underline the topic sentence in each of the body paragraphs. Are the topic sentences supported?
5. Is the process of development clear?

Writing Practice

A. Write a Process Essay

Write a process essay, using chronological order or steps, on one of the following topics. In your essay, try to include **3** or more vocabulary words from the readings in this chapter.

1. Write a process essay on how you recovered from an illness or accident.
2. Write a process essay on learning a foreign language.
3. Write a process essay on a ceremony in your country (for example, a wedding). Indicate the sequence of steps clearly.

B. Pre-Write

Work alone, with a partner, or in a group.

1. Brainstorm the topic. Look at pages 254–256 to find out about brainstorming. Choose the pre-writing technique you prefer.
2. Brainstorm how to divide your process essay into 3 or 4 parts.
3. Work on a thesis statement.

C. Outline

1. Organize your ideas.
   Step 1: Write your thesis statement.
   Step 2: Divide your steps into 3 or 4 paragraphs.
   Step 3: Provide details of each step in the paragraphs.

2. Make a more detailed outline. The essay form on page 21 will help you.

D. Write a Rough Draft

Look at page 257 to find out about writing a rough draft.

E. Revise Your Rough Draft

Use the Revision Checklist on page 258.

F. Edit Your Essay

Use the Editing Checklist on page 259. Check your work for errors in subject and verb agreement. For example, the words *everybody* and *nobody* take a singular verb.

Example:

Error: Everybody find English spelling difficult to understand.

Correct: Everybody finds English spelling difficult to understand.

*pro
agree*

When you find a mistake of this type, you can write the symbol "pro agree" (pronoun agreement). Look at page 260 for other symbols to use when editing your work.

G. Write Your Final Copy

When your rough draft has been edited, you can write the final copy of your essay.

Additional Writing Practice

A. Summarize

Write a one-paragraph summary of Reading 1. Check your summary with the Summary Checklist on page 269.

B. Paraphrase

Paraphrase paragraph 1 of "Window" in Reading 2. Look at pages 264–267 to find out about paraphrasing. Begin paraphrasing with "According to Vanoni, . . ." or "Based on Vanoni's work, ..."

C. Research

Choose a process, procedure, or event leading to a change over a period of time. Consult appropriate sources in the library and/or use your own experience or that of friends to gather information.

The following are suggested topics:

- How the education system works (in the United States or your country)
- How the digestive system works
- How a holiday is celebrated (in the United States or your country)
- How babies learn to talk
- How to learn to use a computer
- How you get a divorce
- How a volcano explodes

You may use your research later to write a process essay.

Weaving It Together

⏱ Timed Writing

Choose one of the following topics that you have not already written about in "Writing Practice," or choose the topic that you have researched. You have 50 minutes to write an essay.

1. Write a process essay on how you recovered from an illness or accident.
2. Write a process essay on learning a foreign language.
3. Write a process essay on a ceremony in your country (for example, a wedding). Indicate the sequence of steps clearly.
4. Write a process essay, using chronological order or steps, about the topic you researched.

Connecting to the Internet

A. Use the Internet to look up the movement for "spelling reform" in English. Who started it? Does it still exist?

B. There are over 6,900 known languages. Use the Internet to research "world languages." Make a list of **10** languages that interest you. Beside each language, state the country or people who speak the language, and provide some information about the origin of the language.

C. There are many theories about the origins of language in humans. Use the Internet to look up the origins of language. Based on one of these theories, write a short essay about the process by which humans learned language.

What Do You Think Now?

Refer to page 33 at the beginning of this chapter. Do you know the answers now? Complete the sentence or circle the best answer.

1. English was/wasn't a mix of five languages at one time.
2. The first English dictionary came out in _____.
3. Shakespeare spelled/didn't spell his name in different ways all the time.
4. The word *window* originally meant/didn't mean "wind eye."
5. The English dish called pie came from _____.

3 Hygiene

What Do You Think?

Answer the questions with your best guess. Circle **Yes** or **No**.

Do you think . . .

1. people in Europe did not bathe for about 1,000 years?	**Yes**	**No**
2. the ancient Romans started public baths?	**Yes**	**No**
3. the average American today showers or bathes 5 times a week?	**Yes**	**No**
4. there are 5 species of fish that clean other fish?	**Yes**	**No**
5. large fish don't eat small fish that go into their mouths to clean them?	**Yes**	**No**

Pre-Reading

1. Discuss the answers to these questions with your classmates.
    1. Look at the picture on page 62. Describe what is happening.
    2. What reasons are there for taking a bath, in addition to getting clean?
    3. What is your opinion of public baths? Why do you think they are important in some cultures?

2. Read the following questions. Circle **T** for true and **F** for false. Then compare your answers with those of your classmates.
    1. The ancient Romans did not place much emphasis on personal cleanliness. **T** **F**
    2. Up until the 1870s in Europe and America, doctors washed their hands only after surgery—not before. **T** **F**
    3. Shrimps clean other fish in the sea. **T** **F**
    4. In colonial Pennsylvania and Virginia, there were laws that forced people to bathe at least once a month. **T** **F**
    5. During the Middle Ages in Europe, people bathed when they were baptized and seldom after that. **T** **F**
    6. For thousands of years, people have been aware that germs cause disease. **T** **F**

How Clean Is Clean?

**CD 1,
Track 5**

1   **C**leanliness is considered a virtue, but just what does it mean to be
clean? As most of us have had the unpleasant occasion to discover, one
person's definition can be quite different from another's. From Istanbul to
Indianapolis, people have their own ways of keeping clean and their own
5   reasons for doing so.

Cleanliness has had a long and varied history with mixed reviews.
Sometimes it's popular; sometimes it's not. Throughout the ages, personal
cleanliness has been greatly influenced by religion, culture, and technology.
Moreover, bathing has served many functions in addition to hygiene. Baths
10   are also places for social gathering, mental and physical relaxation, and
medicinal treatment. Archaeological evidence suggests that bathing is as
old as the first civilizations. Soaplike material has been found in clay jars of
Babylonian origin, dating back to about 2800 B.C.E.[1] One of the first known
bathtubs came from Minoan Crete, and a pretty sophisticated plumbing
15   system of clay pipes is known to have existed in the great palace of King
Minos, built in 1700 B.C.E. The ancient Egyptians didn't have such plumbing
expertise, but are known to have had a positive attitude toward hygiene. They
washed with soapy material made of animal and vegetable oils and salts and
sat in a shallow kind of bath while attendants poured water over them.

20   The Greeks prized cleanliness, although they didn't use soap. Instead, they
rubbed oil and ashes on their bodies, scrubbed with blocks of rocks or sand,
and scraped themselves clean with a curved metal instrument. A dip in the
water and anointment with olive oil followed. They were no doubt clean, but
how would they smell if we followed them down the street today?

25   There were public Grecian baths as well as private ones, but they didn't
serve the social purpose of the Roman baths. It seems that no one in history
has indulged in bathing the way the Romans did. Nearly a dozen large and
magnificent public bathhouses dotted the city, and many hundreds of private

---

[1]**B.C.E.:** Before Christian Era

baths were found in homes. Emperor Caracalla's bath could accommodate
1,600 bathers at a time. Emperor Diocletian entertained crowds of more than
3,000 in the marble splendor of his bath, finished in 305 C.E.[2] Apparently the
Romans had lots of time on their hands, because bathing was not just an
exercise; it was an event. First, a bather entered a warm room to sweat and
to engage in lengthy conversations. Fine oils and sand were used to cleanse
the body. Next came a hot room where the bather would be treated to even
more sweating, splashing with water, more oils and scraping, and yet more
talk. Finally, the Romans concluded the process by plunging into a cool and
refreshing pool. In the early years of the baths, men and women had separate
areas, but eventually the sexes mixed and the baths lost their virtuous
purpose.

So corrupt were Roman society and its baths that the fathers of the
early Christian church discouraged bathing. The hygienic practices of the
Greeks and Romans were repressed to such an extent that Europe during
the Middle Ages has been said to have gone a thousand years without a
bath. Queen Isabella of Castille boasted that she had bathed only twice in
her life—at birth and before her marriage. Religion wasn't the only reason
why Europeans didn't bathe. Although the royal and wealthy sometimes
indulged, commoners found bathing virtually[3] impossible. With no running
water, polluted rivers, and soap taxed as a luxury item, the ordinary citizen
had little opportunity to bathe. As a result, people lived in filth,[4] clothing was
infested with vermin,[5] and disease was rampant.

Early Americans, being of European origin, brought their dirty habits with
them. By the 1800s, however, both Europeans and Americans were reforming
their ways. As it became known that filth led to disease, governments began
to improve sanitation standards. Wash houses were built, and bathing
became a good thing again. In the United States, tubs, water heaters, and
good indoor plumbing put bathing within the reach of ordinary citizens. They
like it so much that today the average American claims to shower or bathe
more than seven times a week.

In America, clean means not only free of dirt, but free of odor as well—
or, rather, human odors, because millions of dollars are spent each year on

---

[2]**C.E.:** Christian Era
[3]**virtually:** almost
[4]**filth:** very dirty conditions
[5]**vermin:** insects that live on the body of humans or animals

powders and perfumes that cover up any natural smells that might slip by. As any deodorant ad will tell you, to have body odor (B.O.) is a grave social offense.

In many Middle Eastern countries, cleanliness has religious overtones that link spiritual and physical purification. The Jewish people have many religious laws relating to hygiene, both personal and in the preparation of food. Muslims, too, live by some very strict rules related to cleanliness. For example, they are required to wash certain parts of their bodies, such as their feet and hands, before they pray. Since the time of Mohammed, sweat baths, or *hammams*, have been recommended. They serve not only as places for cleansing but also as retreats and opportunities for socializing. As a matter of fact, the Crusaders,[6] who enjoyed hammams, brought the idea of the public bath back to Europe with them and introduced the use of thermal baths as therapy for a variety of ills.

For many Middle Easterners, baths are a sort of ritual, a major affair that takes longer than an hour. Bathing begins with a steam, followed by rubbing the body with a hard towel, then soaping and rinsing. People usually want to lie down after a bath. Since it takes so long and is so exhausting, they indulge in these baths once a week.

Asian cultures are very strict and ritualistic about their cleanliness. The Japanese in particular are known for their personal hygiene, which extends from removing their shoes and putting on special slippers before entering any house or building to extensive washing before meals.

It is logical to conclude that cleanliness has many different meanings and is judged by a variety of standards. *Clean* means pure, in a religious sense, as well as clean of body. For some, it means being "squeaky clean"[7] and smelling like roses. For others, a more "natural" state is acceptable. Whether it means washing one's hands and face or a head-to-toe scrubbing, cleanliness is a cultural practice, with enough stories and emotions behind it to make a real soap opera.

---

[6]**the Crusaders:** men who went on military expeditions undertaken by Christian powers in the 11th, 12th, and 13th centuries to win the Holy Land from the Muslims
[7]**squeaky clean:** extremely clean

Vocabulary

A. Vocabulary in Context

Select the letter of the answer that is closest in meaning to the **bold** word or phrase.

1. A dip in the water and **anointment with** olive oil followed.
   a. a rub with
   b. application of
   c. a soak in
   d. a wash with

2. No one in history **indulged in** bathing the way the Romans did.
   a. pleased themselves by
   b. made rules against
   c. talked and wrote about
   d. had the patience for

3. The baths lost their **virtuous** purpose.
   a. practical
   b. natural
   c. small
   d. good

4. The hygienic practices of the Greeks and Romans were **repressed**.
   a. encouraged
   b. defined
   c. held back
   d. debated

5. Queen Isabella **boasted** that she had bathed only twice in her life.
   a. said proudly
   b. argued often
   c. expressed quickly
   d. denied strongly

6. The clothing of commoners was often **infested with** vermin.
   a. free of
   b. decorated with
   c. made by
   d. full of

7. Disease was **rampant**.
   a. not commonly found
   b. easily controlled
   c. avoided at all cost
   d. spread everywhere

8. In America, body odor is a **grave** social offense.
   a. serious
   b. harmful
   c. rare
   d. frequent

Word Partnership	Use **indulge** with:
adj.	**freely** indulge
prep.	indulge **in something**
n.	indulge **children**

9. In many Middle Eastern countries, cleanliness has religious **overtones**.
   a. rituals
   b. meaning
   c. controls
   d. results

10. Sweat baths also served as **retreats**.
   a. locations for parties
   b. opportunities to get work accomplished
   c. places to get away and rest
   d. areas in which to exercise

B. Vocabulary Building

1. Match the adjectives with the nouns as they were used in the context of the reading. Look back at the reading to check your answers. Add two more nouns that may be used with each adjective.

a. treatment   c. overtones   e. relaxation
b. offense   d. hygiene   f. evidence

1. _e_ mental   _relaxation_   _____   _____

2. _____ medicinal   _____   _____   _____

3. _____ archaeological   _____   _____   _____

4. _____ social   _____   _____   _____

5. _____ religious   _____   _____   _____

6. _____ personal   _____   _____   _____

2. Use the nouns and adjectives you listed from Exercise 1 to complete these sentences about cleanliness.

1. Ruins of many ancient civilizations show _____ _____ of baths.

2. Bathing is a form of _____ _____.

3. If you are sick, bathing can be a form of _____ _____.

4. In some cultures, bathing is not only for cleanliness; it also has _____ _____.

5. If your body smells, it can be a _____ _____.

6. _____ _____ is more important in some cultures than in others.

B. Vocabulary in New Context

Do you agree with the sentences in Exercise 2? Are they true or false? Give some examples.

Reading Comprehension

A. Looking for the Main Ideas

Circle the letter of the best answer.

1. What is the main idea of paragraph 2?
   a. Bathing has many different functions in society besides that of cleansing the body.
   b. Indoor plumbing was achieved by the Minoans in Crete almost 4,000 years ago, although their technology didn't immediately spread to other parts of the world.
   c. The Egyptians made up for their lack of sophisticated plumbing by having servants pour water over them while they bathed.
   d. Cleansing of the body has been done for thousands of years in many different ways and for many different reasons.

2. Paragraph 4 is mostly about _____.
   a. the size of the Roman public bathhouses and the emperors who built them
   b. the social purposes of the Roman baths and their eventually corrupting influence
   c. the extent, purpose, and rituals of the Roman baths
   d. the differences between Roman baths and Greek baths

3. Paragraph 8 is mainly concerned with _____.
   a. Crusaders bringing the idea of public baths to Europe
   b. religious laws connected with cleanliness in the Middle East
   c. the importance of sweat baths in some countries
   d. the use of baths as a treatment for illness

B. Skimming and Scanning for Details

Scan the reading quickly to find the answers to these questions. Write complete sentences.

1. According to the reading, what three things have influenced the bathing habits of people over the centuries?
2. According to the reading, how were the Greeks different from the Egyptians in their bathing habits?
3. In the last sentence of paragraph 3, to what does the word *them* refer?
4. What bathing rituals were a part of the three stages of bathing in the Roman baths?
5. Why did the leaders of the early Christian church discourage bathing?
6. What three problems prevented commoners in Europe from taking baths?
7. What finally prompted Europeans and Americans to change their cleanliness habits?
8. What Muslim tradition influenced the introduction of therapeutic thermal baths in Europe?
9. To what does the word *people* in paragraph 9, sentence 3, refer?
10. What are two hygienic habits of the Japanese?

C. Making Inferences and Drawing Conclusions

The answers to these questions are not directly stated in the reading. Circle the letter of the best answer.

1. The reading implies that _____.
   a. only the most advanced societies recognized the importance of cleanliness
   b. cleanliness can mean only one thing: a body free from dirt and odors
   c. soap and bathtubs have not always been necessary for cleanliness
   d. little evidence exists regarding the cleanliness habits of early civilizations

2. From the reading, it can be concluded that _____.
   a. religion has always had a detrimental effect on society's personal cleanliness
   b. over the ages, some societies have valued personal cleanliness more than others
   c. during the Middle Ages, Europeans had no need to be concerned with personal cleanliness
   d. technology has had little effect on Americans' bathing habits

3. It can be inferred from the reading that _____.

    a. Middle Eastern traditions have had no influence on Western habits of cleanliness

    b. overwashing can be hazardous to a person's health

    c. the Grecian baths served a social purpose

    d. bathing is a ritualistic and meaningful activity that can be viewed in a cultural context

4. The author's purpose is to _____.

    a. amuse

    b. inform

    c. convince

    d. dispute

Discussion Questions

Discuss the answers to these questions with your classmates.

1. What is the most usual way of washing or taking a bath in your country?

2. How important are grooming activities such as brushing your teeth or combing your hair?

3. How is body odor regarded in your country and in other countries?

4. What is your definition of cleanliness?

Critical Thinking Questions

Discuss the answers to these questions with your classmates.

1. How do you think hygiene and cleanliness became intertwined with religion? What purposes did it serve? Has it been a benefit to humanity?

2. Why do you think cleansing rituals are important to people? What purposes do they serve?

3. How is modern life changing our knowledge and habits related to cleansing?

Reading 2

**CD 1,
Track 6**

Eat My Bugs, Please

The following passage is from the book Symbiosis *by Nicolette Perry (Blandford Press, Dorset, Poole, England, 1983). It describes the cleaning habits of fish.*

Figure 1[2]

1 $\quad$ **C**leaning symbioses[1] are found in the sea, in freshwater, on land and in the air, but the greatest
5 $\quad$ number of examples concern marine species. It is essential for all creatures to have some method of keeping themselves clean
10 $\quad$ and free from parasites. If they do not, they will probably fall ill from infected wounds or the effects of disease and blood loss from parasites. For those species that are unable to clean themselves it is obviously vital to find some other animal to perform this cleaning function.
15 $\quad$ This chapter is concerned with describing some typical examples of cleaning symbioses as well as the more extraordinary ones.

$\quad$ The vast majority of cleaners are fish; at least 45 species are known cleaners and there may well be more. Fish that are habitually cleaned often have to modify their usual behavior to allow the cleaners to do their work.
20 $\quad$ It is not normal for aggressive species like shark, barracuda, and moray eels to allow small fish to swim safely near them. With known cleaner species, however, these and other fish change their attitude completely and allow the

---

[1]**symbiosis:** the living or working together of two different organisms in a mutually beneficial relationship

[2]**Figure 1:** There are at least 45 species of fish that are known cleaners (engage in cleaning symbiosis with other fish). One example is the goby (pictured), which clean the Nassau Grouper. The Black Surgeonfish goes from black to blue while being cleaned by the *Labroides dimidiatus*.

cleaners all over their bodies without displaying any ferocity[3] towards them. The clients will slow down or stop completely (unusual behavior for most fish, as they usually move all the time), open and close their mouths and gill[4] covers and assume awkward-looking postures to help the cleaners. It is quite possible that some species have become extinct because of an inability to establish a cleaning symbiosis. So many individuals could have fallen foul of ectoparasites,[5] fungi and bacteria that the population was made inviable.

Some fishes change color while being cleaned. Black Surgeonfish go from black to blue when they are being cleaned by *Labroides dimidiatus*. The Goatfish changes from pale brown to pink while the same cleaner picks it over for parasites.

Fishes being groomed guard their cleaners against danger by warning them of the approach of predators. The Nassau Grouper when cleaned by gobies[6] warns its cleaner by suddenly closing its mouth, leaving only a small gap to allow the goby to escape. Even if the grouper is in imminent danger itself it takes time to warn the goby. This shows the regard that the client feels for its cleaner and the service that it performs.

Several species of cleaner set up cleaning stations in one particular place. The local fish soon realize where the cleaner is located and will visit it whenever they require cleaning. Quite astonishing numbers of fish are cleaned in this way: not only territorial species that would normally be found in the area but also migratory ones which have gone out of their way to visit these stations. Client fish will patiently wait their turn to be cleaned, and even form orderly queues.

Quite a considerable amount of observational and experimental work has been done on these cleaning stations. Limbaugh, for example, discovered that over three hundred fish can be cleaned by a single Senorita Fish in a six-hour period. These fish go back to the same cleaner every few days for another session and this enables them to remain in peak condition.

Limbaugh also did some experiments in waters off the Bahamas. He removed all the cleaner fish from one locality and observed the effects on the species normally found there. Within two days the numbers of fish were severely reduced and within two weeks almost all the territorial fish had

---

[3]**ferocity:** fierceness, violence
[4]**gill:** the organ through which a fish breathes
[5]**ectoparasites:** parasites that live on the exterior of the host
[6]**gobies:** a kind of cleaner fish

disappeared. Those that remained had developed the fuzzy marks that are an indication of fungal infection. It had been shown in previous experiments that the introduction of cleaners into an aquarium infected by fungi can restore its inhabitants to health.

From the above the value of cleaning symbiosis in the marine habitat can easily be seen. Without the work of all the cleaners of the ocean, the effects of parasites, fungi, and injury would kill many more species than they do already. The Senorita Fish is an example of a typical cleaner. It is of the wrasse family and lives off the coast of California. It is an active, small, cigar-shaped fish that the local people call the Senorita because of its cleaning habits. Its client fishes include the Topsmelt, Black Sea Bass, Opaleye, Blacksmith Fish, and many more. These fish are almost all much larger than the cleaner and would normally prey on wrasses of the Senorita's size. They do not attack the Senorita, however, but wait patiently until it is their turn to be cleaned, hold themselves still and often in the most peculiar postures while being attended to. The fish in the area of the coast that the Senorita Fish inhabits are especially troubled by fungal infection, and removal of the white growths caused by the fungi is the cleaner's most important function. The cleaning phenomenon has been observed for many years to the extent that one species is popularly called the Cleaner Fish or Wrasse. It is a small, slim fish with cyan-colored[7] body, striped with darker blue or black. The cleaner fish goes one stage further than the Senorita in that it actively attracts clients by "dancing." It swims in a vertical position, head downwards, and undulates its body from side to side. This is a most unusual posture for fish, as they usually swim horizontally to the sea bed. This "dancing" makes the cleaner noticeable to even the most myopic fish, and it has become the cleaner's trade mark.

Clients line up, as with the Senorita, until it is their turn to be cleaned, and also allow the little fish to enter their mouths and gill cavities unharmed. The contents of various species' stomachs have been examined to assess the quantity of cleaner fish that are eaten, both by fish that are known clients and others. It has been found that very few cleaners are consumed by any species, although fish of similar size make up the bulk of the diet. So few cleaner fish are eaten that it seems probable that the small number that are are taken accidentally by absent-minded clients rather than actively predated upon.

[7]**cyan-colored:** greenish-blue

Vocabulary

A. Vocabulary in Context

Circle the letter of the best answer.

1. Which of the following phrases could be substituted for **fallen foul of** in paragraph 2?
   - a. been the cause of
   - b. been eliminated by
   - c. eaten enough of
   - d. been harmed by

2. Which of the following is closest in meaning to the word **inviable** as used in paragraph 2?
   - a. unable to communicate
   - b. unable to survive
   - c. unable to move
   - d. unable to be eaten

3. Which word in paragraph 4 means "attended to or cared for"?

4. In paragraph 4, what does **imminent** mean?
   - a. immediate
   - b. constant
   - c. great
   - d. frequent

5. Which of these words is closest in meaning to **peak** as it is used in paragraph 6?
   - a. top
   - b. average
   - c. inferior
   - d. artificial

6. Something **fuzzy**:
   - a. is hard and clear.
   - b. is covered with fluffy particles.
   - c. changes shape.
   - d. changes color.

7. In paragraph 8, what does **undulates** mean?
   - a. looks right to left as it passes
   - b. advances in stops and starts
   - c. moves back and forth in a wavy form
   - d. swims quickly in a straight line

8. What is the meaning of **myopic** in paragraph 8?
   - a. unable to see faraway objects clearly
   - b. able to see in the dark
   - c. having sharp eyes and good hearing
   - d. unable to distinguish large objects

9. Which of these words is closest in meaning to **assess** as used in paragraph 9?

   a. judge

   b. compare

   c. confirm

   d. view

10. Which phrase in paragraph 9 means "the greater part of"?

B. Vocabulary Building

Match the verbs with the nouns as they were used in the context of the reading. Look back at the reading to check your answers. Add two more nouns that may be used with each verb.

a. station

b. smaller fish

c. ferocity

d. behavior

e. effects

f. service

1. __d__ modify   _behavior_   _____   _____

2. ____ display   _____   _____   _____

3. ____ perform   _____   _____   _____

4. ____ set up   _____   _____   _____

5. ____ observe   _____   _____   _____

6. ____ prey on   _____   _____   _____

C. Vocabulary in New Context

Make questions about cleaner fish, using each of the word combinations in Exercise 1. For example, How do larger fish _modify_ their _behavior_? With a partner, take turns asking and answering your questions.

Reading Comprehension

A. Looking for the Main Ideas

Some of the following statements from the reading are main ideas, and some are supporting statements. Write **M** in the blank in front of each main idea. Write **S** in front of each supporting statement.

_____ **1.** If they do not, they will probably fall ill from infected wounds or the effects of disease and blood loss from parasites.

_____ **2.** Fish that are habitually cleaned often have to modify their usual behavior to allow the cleaners to do their work.

_____ **3.** With known cleaner species, however, these and other fish change their attitude completely and allow the cleaners all over their bodies without displaying any ferocity towards them.

_____ **4.** The clients will slow down or stop completely (unusual behavior for most fish, as they usually move all the time), open and close their mouths and gill covers and assume awkward-looking postures to help the cleaners.

_____ **5.** Some fishes change color while being cleaned.

_____ **6.** Fishes being groomed guard their cleaners against danger by warning them of the approach of predators.

_____ **7.** Even if the grouper is in imminent danger itself it takes time to warn the goby.

_____ **8.** Several species of cleaner set up cleaning stations in one particular place.

_____ **9.** These fish go back to the same cleaner every few days for another session and this enables them to remain in peak condition.

_____ **10.** Within two days the numbers of fish were severely reduced and within two weeks almost all the territorial fish had disappeared.

B. Skimming and Scanning for Details

Scan the reading quickly to complete the following sentences.

1. Even normally aggressive species like _____, _____, and _____ allow small cleaner fish to swim near them.

2. Some species may have become extinct because of an inability to _____.

3. The Goatfish will change from _____ to _____ while being cleaned by a cleaner fish.

4. The Nassau Grouper warns its cleaner fish that predators are in the area by _____.

5. Many larger fish will not wait for the cleaner fish to come to them. Instead, they _____.

6. In a _____-hour period, a single _____ fish can clean over 300 fish.

7. If cleaner fish are taken out of an area they usually inhabit, the client fish that remain after the others have left the area will _____.

8. If cleaner fish are put in an aquarium with fish infected by _____, the cleaner fish can _____.

9. The cleaner fish, or Wrasse, attracts clients by doing a dance that involves

_____.

10. In appearance, the Senorita Fish is _____ and _____-shaped.

C. Making Inferences and Drawing Conclusions

Some of the following statements are facts taken from the reading. Other statements can be inferred from the reading. Write **F** in the blank in front of each factual statement. Write **I** in front of each inference.

_____ **1.** Parasites are dangerous to the health of all creatures.
_____ **2.** If a living creature can't clean itself, then some other animal has to do the job.
_____ **3.** In a symbiotic relationship, both creatures benefit.
_____ **4.** Even the simplest animals can adapt to situations when their lives depend on it.
_____ **5.** Most of the animals whose job it is to clean others are fish.
_____ **6.** Some fish actually change color while they are being cleaned.
_____ **7.** A client fish will even go so far as to protect its cleaner fish, even when the client fish is put in danger.
_____ **8.** Without cleaner fish, all fish would probably become extinct.
_____ **9.** Even normally aggressive client fish will wait patiently for their turn with a cleaner fish.
_____ **10.** A fish's survival instinct is stronger than its desire to eat the smaller cleaner fish.

Discussion Questions

Discuss the answers to these questions with your classmates.

1. Discuss the cleanliness habits of other animals.
2. Discuss the relationship between cleanliness and health in humans and animals.
3. Discuss five ways in which our environment could be cleaned up.
4. What is your definition of cleanliness?

Critical Thinking Questions

Discuss the answers to these questions with your classmates.

1. What are the greatest dangers posed to fish populations today? What are some ways in which these problems are being confronted? What more can be done?
2. Why does the behavior of the host and cleaner fish amaze us so much? What parallels does it have to human behavior? What can it teach us?
3. Water is a symbol of cleansing and purity. What are some ceremonies, rites, or rituals that use water in this way? Have you participated in any of these? If so, which one(s) and what did it mean to you?

Writing

Writing Skills

A. Organizing: *Literal* and *Extended Definitions*

Sometimes a definition appears in an essay to clarify a word. The definition may be expressed in a sentence or a paragraph, or it may even be the entire essay. The reason for this is that there are two kinds of definitions.

The first kind of definition gives the literal, or dictionary, meaning.

Example:

Cleanliness is the state of being free from dirt.

A literal definition is usually expressed in one sentence.

When you want to give a personal interpretation of a word, you use an extended definition. The extended definition may differ from the literal meaning because the word is defined in a particular or personal way. The meaning of an abstract word or concept such as *cleanliness* is often given in an extended definition, because such a word can be interpreted in different ways.

Example:

In America, clean means not only free of dirt but free of odor as well.

The extended definition involves various kinds of supporting ideas. Reading 1 tells how the word *cleanliness* was defined by the Romans and the Greeks and in the Middle Ages. We are then given examples of similarities and differences in ideas of cleanliness among different cultures today.

In Reading 2, cleanliness is seen through the world of fish. We are given examples of how various species of cleaner fish and their clients go about the process of cleaning, and we are told of the importance of cleanliness to fish, without which many species would die.

Introduction to the Definition Essay

In the introduction to a definition essay, state the term you are going to define. Then either define it yourself or use a dictionary definition, naming the dictionary and quoting from it. In your thesis statement, restate the term you are going to define and tell how you are going to define it, giving the three or four aspects from which you will illustrate your definition. Look back at the thesis statement of the student essay to see the three aspects of daily life the student used.

Using Etymologies

In your introduction, you may want to summarize the word's origin, or etymology. Look at pages 267–270 to find out about summarizing. Sometimes the original meaning of the word is quite different from its present meaning, and you may want to show this. The *Oxford English Dictionary* and many other unabridged dictionaries give detailed histories of the origin and development of words. For example, in *Webster's New Collegiate Dictionary*, we see that the word *boycott* comes from Charles Boycott, a land agent in Ireland who was ostracized for refusing to reduce rents; the word *prejudice* comes from the Latin *praejudicium*, which is made up of *prae*, meaning "before," and *judicium*, which means "judgment."

Using a Clear Definition

Many times, a form of the word or the word itself is used as part of the dictionary definition. This approach does not make the meaning clear. For example, avoid defining *cleanliness* as "the state of being clean." Your definition will be clearer if you say, "Cleanliness is the state of being free from dirt."

Points to Remember in Organizing a Definition Essay

- Each body paragraph in your essay should illustrate an aspect of the definition that you stated in your thesis.
- Support each aspect with clear examples.
- The conclusion should summarize your personal definition and give a final comment on the term.

B. Exercises

1. It is important to make your literal definitions accurate. Look at the definitions below. Which are accurate? Which are not? Rewrite the definitions that are not accurate.

1. Art is a mirror of the human soul.
2. Thermostats are devices that regulate heaters and cooling machines, turning them on and off so that they maintain the required temperature.
3. Wind means destruction from devastating storms or benefits from harnessing energy with windmills.
4. Powered flight is the realization of man's fondest dream over thousands of years.
5. A keynote address is an opening address that outlines the issues to be considered.
6. A mammal is a vertebrate animal with self-regulating body temperature and the capability for milk production by the female.
7. Mountain sickness is a sickness people get when they are in the mountains.
8. Separation anxiety is a negative emotional state that occurs in small children when they are parted from their parents.
9. Good sense is something everyone should hope to have.
10. Education is the key to prosperity.

2. Work with a partner, a group, or alone. Look up the following words in a dictionary and write down their literal meanings. Then write 3 or 4 ways that the definitions might be extended to include personal, social, or cultural meanings.

Example:

Touch

Literal Meaning: to bring a bodily part in contact with something
Extended Meaning: Different functions in society:
  a. professional/functional
  b. social/polite
  c. to express friendship and warmth
  d. to express love and intimacy

or

Different forms in different cultures:

a. North America

b. Latin America

c. Asia

or

Necessity for growth and development of certain animals:

a. monkeys

b. cats

c. dogs

1. Space
   Literal Meaning: _____
   Extended Meaning: _____

2. Time
   Literal Meaning: _____
   Extended Meaning: _____

3. Smell
   Literal Meaning: _____
   Extended Meaning: _____

4. Aggressiveness
   Literal Meaning: _____
   Extended Meaning: _____

5. Modesty
   Literal Meaning: _____
   Extended Meaning: _____

6. Respect
   Literal Meaning: _____
   Extended Meaning: _____

3. The following terms have been defined using a form of the term itself. Rewrite each definition without repeating the term being defined. Make sure the meaning of the word is clear.

1. fanaticism: fanatic outlook or behavior

2. loyalty: the quality or state of being loyal

3. education: the action or process of being educated

4. happiness: the state of being happy

5. creativity: the quality of being creative
6. friendship: the state of being friends
7. independence: the quality or state of being independent
8. leadership: the quality of a leader

Writing Model: The Definition Essay

Read the following definition essay written by a student.

Cleanliness

1   According to Webster's dictionary, the word *cleanliness* means "habitually kept clean." In fact, the quality, state, or condition of cleanliness is often determined by people's own culture, religion, occupation, or lifestyle. To comprehend the sense of cleanliness, each individual or culture has to be
5   considered. In my country, Japan, our basic sense of cleanliness may be more clearly defined by looking at basic aspects of our lives such as our buildings, our food, and hygiene.

Traditionally, it is the custom in Japan to keep our homes clean, since a clean house is a reflection of one's self. One way in which we keep our homes
10   clean from outside dirt and germs is by taking off our shoes when entering our homes or even public places such as schools, local hospitals, and some restaurants. Upon entering a home, shoes are taken off and slippers are worn. Since shoes are taken off when entering someone's home, it is crucial that our socks be clean and have no holes in them. In the home, certain areas or rooms
15   such as the bathroom or the yard require changing into different slippers which are used for that area. Also, our bathrooms are separated from our toilets, since the latter is considered to be a dirty place and therefore must be separate from the clean tub area. Needless to say, our floors are immaculately clean and must be scrubbed at least once a week.
20   When eating, there are other aspects of cleanliness that we consider. In a restaurant, clean chopsticks are provided just as clean silverware is provided in Western restaurants. However, it is difficult for a wooden chopstick to be kept really clean, so the Japanese discovered the disposable chopstick. Like most people, we wash our hands before eating, but in addition to this most

25 restaurants provide diners with hot, steamed towels to clean their hands with before a meal. In the home, members of a family each have their individual chopsticks, rice bowl, and tea cup. Being clean and hygienic is important to the Japanese. Westerners visiting Japan may see people wearing white gauze masks, like the ones used by surgeons, when they walk or bike through the city. People

30 wear these because they may have hay fever or they may have a cold and do not wish to spread their germs to others or they may be afraid of air pollution. Also, when we have a cold we use paper tissues, which we throw away after use. We do not use a handkerchief to blow our noses with. Handkerchiefs are used for drying hands after washing or for wiping our mouths. It is considered good manners to

35 always carry paper tissues with us wherever we go. Another custom we have when we come home from outside is to wash our hands with soap and water and rinse our mouths with water.

In conclusion, although the quality, state, or condition of cleanliness is determined by each individual, culture also plays a significant role. In Japan, there

40 are general cultural norms with regard to cleanliness that most people follow in their daily lives. The main objective in every culture with regard to cleanliness is to keep people healthy.

Noriko
Japan

Student Essay Follow-Up

1. Underline the thesis statement.
2. Which three aspects of life in Japan does the writer focus on to define cleanliness?
3. Are all three aspects developed in the body paragraphs?
4. Examine paragraph 2. Do all the ideas support and illustrate the topic sentence?
5. Do you like the writer's definition of cleanliness? Explain your answer.

Writing Practice

A. Write a Definition Essay

Write an essay on one of the following topics. In your essay, try to include **3** or more vocabulary words from the readings in this chapter.

1. Write a definition essay, using 3 or 4 examples, on honesty.
2. Write a definition essay on the concept of friendship. Illustrate your definition in 3 or 4 ways.
3. Write a definition essay on alcoholism.
4. Write a definition essay on respect, providing illustrations.

B. Pre-Write

Work alone, with a partner, or in a group.

1. Brainstorm the topic. Look at pages 254–256 to find out about brainstorming.
2. Write down any mental associations you make with the word to be defined. Brainstorm for examples that can illustrate the word.
3. Work on a thesis statement.

C. Outline

1. Organize your ideas.

   Step 1: Write your thesis statement.

   Step 2: Select at least three examples that illustrate the term.

   Step 3: Read your examples over again to make sure they all define the term.

2. Make a more detailed outline. The essay form on page 21 will help you.

D. Write a Rough Draft

Look at page 257 to find out about writing a rough draft.

E. Revise Your Rough Draft

Use the Revision Checklist on page 258.

F. Edit Your Essay

Use the Editing Checklist on page 259. Check your work for faulty shifts in point of view using inconsistent pronouns. If you start writing in the first person, you should not shift to second or third person within the same sentence.

Example:

Error: A person who exercises to avoid <u>his or her</u> problems is not necessarily reducing stress, especially if <u>you</u> have to go back to the same old problem the next day.

Correct: A person who exercises to avoid his or her problems is not necessarily reducing stress, especially if he or she [*or the person*] has to go back to the same old problem the next day.

p.o.v.

When you find a mistake of this type, you can write the symbol "p.o.v." (point of view). Look at page 260 for other symbols to use when editing your work.

G. Write Your Final Copy

When your rough draft has been edited, you can write the final copy of your essay.

Additional Writing Practice

A. Summarize

Write a one-paragraph summary of Reading 1. Check your summary against the Summary Checklist on page 269.

B. Paraphrase

Paraphrase paragraph 2 in Reading 2. Look at pages 264–267 to find out about paraphrasing. Begin with either "According to Perry, . . . " or "Based on Perry's article, ..."

C. Research

Choose a particular concept (an abstract word) and define it in 2 or 3 ways in an extended definition such as the one in Reading 1. To gather information, you should consult a dictionary, look at related sources in the library, and/or draw on your own experience or that of your friends.

The following are suggested concepts:

- beauty
- democracy
- education
- fanaticism
- freedom
- intelligence
- love
- natural
- patriotism
- peace
- prejudice
- trust

You may use your research later to write a definition essay. The extended definition is discussed on page 80.

Weaving It Together

⏱ Timed Writing

Choose one of the following topics that you have not already written about in "Writing Practice," or choose the topic that you have researched. You have 50 minutes to write an essay.

1. Write a definition essay, using 3 or 4 examples, on honesty.
2. Write a definition essay on the concept of friendship.
3. Write a definition essay on alcoholism.
4. Write a definition essay on respect.
5. Write a definition essay on the topic you researched.

Connecting to the Internet

A. The ritual of space cleansing (or space clearing) is found in many cultures including China, Tibet, Bali, Japan, and others. Use the Internet to find out about space cleansing. Based on your research, write a definition of space cleansing (or clearing), explain what it means to various cultures, and describe some of the methods used in this ritual.

B. There are many types of bathing and cleansing places/rituals around the world, including the Russian *banya*, Finnish *sauna*, Turkish *hammam*, Native American sweat lodge, and Japanese *ofuro*. Use the Internet to look up these places. Based on your research, write a brief description of each of these bathing/cleansing places. Then choose one and write about what it means to the people of that culture. Indicate which Web site(s) provided the information for your research.

What Do You Think Now?

Refer to page 62 at the beginning of this chapter. Do you know the answers now? Complete the sentence or circle the best answer.

1. People in Europe bathed/did not bathe for about 1,000 years.
2. The ancient _____ started public baths.
3. The average American today showers or bathes _____ times a week.
4. There are _____ species of fish that clean other fish.
5. Large fish eat/don't eat small fish that go into their mouths to clean them.

 4 Groups, Organizations, and Societies

What Do You Think?

Answer the questions with your best guess. Circle **Yes** or **No**.

Do you think . . .

1. Doctors Without Borders started in France?	**Yes**	**No**
2. Doctors Without Borders is completely funded by governments?	**Yes**	**No**
3. Doctors Without Borders has operations in 15 countries?	**Yes**	**No**
4. Peace Corps volunteers serve for a one-year period?	**Yes**	**No**
5. Peace Corps volunteers do not receive a monthly salary even for basic food and board?	**Yes**	**No**

Pre-Reading

1. Discuss the answers to these questions with your classmates.

   1. What groups or organizations can you name? Do you belong to any of these groups or organizations?
   2. What are some organizations that are dedicated to doing good in the world?
   3. Can you name some organizations that are harmful to society?

2. Read the following descriptions of some groups, organizations, and societies. Then find their names among those listed below.

The Amish	Mormons	Scientology
Big Brothers Big Sisters	Quakers	Scouts
Greenpeace	Red Cross	
Masons	Salvation Army	

   1. This organization teaches young people to be good citizens and trains them to become leaders. Members are taught to do their duty to God, to their country, and to other people. Their mottos are "Be prepared" and "Learn by doing." The organization was started in Great Britain in 1907 by Robert Baden-Powell. Today, over 5 million Americans belong to this organization.

   2. This group originated in Switzerland but is now centered in the United States and Canada. The largest communities are found in Ohio, Pennsylvania, Indiana, Iowa, and Illinois. This group believes in separation from the world. Members are forbidden to go to war, to swear oaths, or to hold public office. Their doctrine requires them to farm and to lead a simple life. The use of electricity and telephones is forbidden. Education is limited to the eighth grade.

   3. This international organization calls attention to the environmental dangers of such actions as oil drilling, nuclear bomb testing, and dumping of radioactive wastes. The group also opposes whaling, the spread of nuclear weapons, and the inhumane killing of animals. Members use direct action and nonviolent methods of protest. They go where an activity that they consider harmful is occurring. Without using force, they try to stop the activity. The organization was founded in 1969 by a group of Canadians.

4. The men and women who belong to this organization devote their lives to helping people in need and spreading the Christian faith. The organization is supported by gifts of money from people who admire its work. This group is organized like an army. Its projects include providing medical care for the poor, inexpensive lodging for the homeless, and employment agencies to help people find jobs.

5. This is one of the oldest and largest fraternal organizations in the world. It is dedicated to the ideals of charity, equality, morality, and service to God. Members of this organization donate millions of dollars each year to charitable projects. The organization has millions of members worldwide, including 3 million in the United States. Membership in this organization is for males only. Recently, a similar organization was started for women. This is a secret organization; therefore, members will not say publicly that they belong to it.

Reading 1

Crisis, Disaster, and Doctors Without Borders

CD 1, Track 7

1   **E**ven in wealthy countries with technologically advanced health-care systems, obtaining medical care can sometimes be difficult. Imagine being in a developing country where there is a war going on. There are no hospitals. There are no doctors. There is no medicine. You are injured and very sick. How

5 can you get medical help?

    In 1971, a group of doctors got together in France and created an organization called *Médecins Sans Frontières*, or MSF, which translates to "Doctors Without Borders." These doctors believed that all people have the right to medical care, whatever their race, religion, or political affiliation—

10 and that meeting their needs is more important than respecting national borders. The doctors wanted to give emergency aid to victims of war, epidemics, and disasters, whether natural or human in origin. To do this, they organized volunteer teams of health-care workers to go to often dangerous and remote areas.

15   At first, Doctors Without Borders was a very small organization. It consisted of volunteers who lived on money they earned from other jobs. Other international organizations considered the volunteers from Doctors Without Borders to be "amateurs" or "tourists." The organization did not grow very much, because the volunteers did not ask for charity from the public for their

20 service.

    After 1978, because of world conflicts and the growth of refugee camps everywhere, the organization's activities spread like the roots of a tree. Doctors Without Borders began to take a more professional approach. It realized it needed funds and started to use the kinds of fund-raising techniques used

25 in American political campaigns. This seemed to work well, and with the money it raised, Doctors Without Borders organized itself better and got better technology for dealing with emergencies. First, it began to pay an

administrator and to give a small amount of money to doctors who were sent out for 6 months. Expanding from its origins in France, it developed sections in other countries—first in Belgium, Switzerland, the Netherlands, and Spain and later in other countries such as Australia and Canada. To encourage people to join the organization and give stability to its volunteers, it began to pay the doctors who worked in the headquarters, to give travel allowances, and to give a stipend of $700 a month to doctors who worked on long-term missions in the field. Since the 1980s, the number of doctors and nurses joining the organization has increased. In 1987, a U.S. branch of Doctors Without Borders was established in New York to allow American doctors to become involved. Having trained and worked in an organized and advanced medical system, American doctors wanted to see how big an impact their skills could have in a less developed country.

Doctors Without Borders is very efficient and quick to come to the aid of people in a crisis. However, before Doctors Without Borders decides it is needed in an area where there is a humanitarian crisis, it sends out an experienced team. The job of the team is to evaluate the medical and nutritional needs of the people in that area. The team looks at the transport and security facilities as well as the political environment. The team then sends its information to one of the operational offices. The Operations Department makes the final decision to intervene and starts the mission. People in this department decide who is going to be sent, the materials needed, and the medical priorities. Each mission is coordinated by one of the organization's sections. Then, within 24 hours, Doctors Without Borders sends emergency kits, which include generators and operating rooms that are the size of a conference table. These kits were developed by Doctors Without Borders and are used as models by emergency relief organizations worldwide. The kits are so complete that they can be used to provide medical assistance to thousands of people for several months. In 1991, within 10 days of the departure of hundreds of thousands of Kurdish refugees from Iraq, Doctors Without Borders sent 75 airplanes loaded with 2,500 tons of equipment and supplies. After the kits are sent, teams of volunteers go to the crisis area and start their work.

Another of the missions of the organization is to bear witness and speak out. Doctors Without Borders is neutral and impartial as an organization and demands complete freedom in performing its job. However, sometimes medical help is not enough to save lives, and it is then that the organization will speak out to raise awareness, so that some action can be taken. The point of speaking out is to improve conditions for the population in danger. In some situations, volunteers may give testimony at the United Nations; or they may openly criticize mass violations of human rights such as genocide, forced displacement of refugees, and war crimes. In 1994, Doctors Without Borders volunteers were among the peacekeepers sent to Bosnia. Volunteers witnessed great suffering. One doctor testified before the U.S. Congress about what he had learned: Shots were fired at random into a group of some 230 people who were being kept in a small room, and then the dead and the injured were buried together. The testimony of the doctor led the United Nations to call these incidents "crimes against humanity."

Doctors Without Borders is independent and flexible in its operation because it is not funded by any government. Although the organization has its origins in France, it receives less than 1 percent of its total budget from the French government. It is a nonprofit organization that gets its funds from donations by the public. Some corporations, agencies, and other nonprofit organizations give financial support, too. Because it is not tied to government funding, it can maintain its independence and live up to its ideals.

In 1999, Doctors Without Borders won the Nobel Peace Prize for its "pioneering humanitarian work on several continents," in the words of the Norwegian Nobel Committee. One of the organization's founders, Bernard Koucher, said, "I'm deeply moved, and I'm thinking of all the people who died without aid, of all those who died waiting for someone to knock on their door." Since the organization was founded, volunteers have worked in Nicaragua, Afghanistan, Ethiopia, Rwanda, Kosovo, Timor, and Iraq, as well as with the Kurds.

Today, Doctors Without Borders has operations in more than 80 countries. These operations are run by more than 2,500 volunteer doctors, nurses, medical professionals, sanitation engineers, and administrators from 45 countries. These people work with 15,000 people who are hired locally to provide medical aid in troubled areas. Doctors Without Borders continues to find and to confront some of the greatest challenges in the world today.

Vocabulary

A. Vocabulary in Context

Select the letter of the answer that is closest in meaning to the **bold** word or phrase.

1. Political **affiliation** does not matter to Doctors Without Borders.
   a. power   c. relatives
   b. association   d. problems

2. It realized it needed **funds**.
   a. money   c. advertising
   b. time   d. investments

3. The organization began to give its doctors a **stipend**.
   a. value   c. payment
   b. loan   d. credit

4. The stipend was for doctors who worked on long-term **missions**.
   a. conditions   c. research
   b. experiments   d. projects

5. Doctors Without Borders is **impartial**.
   a. has many parts   c. does not reveal names
   b. treats all sides fairly   d. does not take risks

6. Volunteers may **give testimony** at the United Nations.
   a. give evidence   c. talk about their lives
   b. give their opinions   d. write tests

7. Shots were fired **at random**.
   a. without a plan   c. quickly
   b. deliberately   d. one by one

Word Partnership	Use **mission** with:
adj.	**dangerous** mission, **secret** mission, **successful** mission
n.	**combat** mission, **rescue** mission, **suicide** mission, **training** mission, **peacekeeping** mission
v.	**accomplish a** mission, **carry out a** mission

8. It gets its funds from **donations** by the public.

    a. services

    b. contributions

    c. employment

    d. operations

9. Because Doctors Without Borders is not tied to a government, it can **live up to** its ideals.

    a. achieve

    b. solve

    c. investigate

    d. save

10. Doctors Without Borders continues to find and to **confront** some of the greatest challenges in the world today.

    a. avoid

    b. understand

    c. experience

    d. face

B. Vocabulary Building

Match the parts of the following phrases as they were used in the context of the reading. Look back at the reading to check your answers.

1. give emergency aid to   _____   **a.** emergencies

2. take a   _____   **b.** victims of war

3. deal with   _____   **c.** its ideals

4. provide   _____   **d.** its independence

5. maintain   _____   **e.** medical assistance

6. live up to   _____   **f.** professional approach

C. Vocabulary in New Context

Use each of the phrases in Part B to make a question about Doctors Without Borders. Start your questions with **What, Why, Who,** or **How**. For example: *How does Doctors Without Borders maintain its independence?* With a partner, take turns asking and answering the questions.

Reading Comprehension

A. Looking for the Main Ideas

Some of the following statements from the reading are main ideas, and some are supporting statements. Write **M** in the blank in front of each main idea. Write **S** in front of each supporting statement.

_____ **1.** In 1971, a group of doctors got together in France and created an organization called *Médecins Sans Frontières*, or MSF.

_____ **2.** Other international organizations considered the volunteers from Doctors Without Borders to be "amateurs" or "tourists."

_____ **3.** After 1978, with the growth of refugee camps everywhere, the organization's activities spread like the roots of a tree.

_____ **4.** In 1987, a U.S. branch of Doctors Without Borders was established in New York to allow American doctors to become involved.

_____ **5.** Doctors Without Borders is very efficient and quickly comes to the aid of people in a crisis.

_____ **6.** The team then sends its information to one of the operational offices.

_____ **7.** Each mission is coordinated by one of the organization's sections.

_____ **8.** Another mission of the organization is to bear witness and speak out.

_____ **9.** In 1994, Doctors Without Borders volunteers were among the peacekeepers sent to Bosnia.

_____ **10.** Since the organization was founded, volunteers have worked in Nicaragua, Afghanistan, Ethiopia, Rwanda, Kosovo, Timor, and Iraq, as well as with the Kurds.

B. Skimming and Scanning for Details

Scan the reading quickly to complete the following sentences.

1. Doctors Without Borders believes that all people have the right to medical care, whatever their _____, _____, or _____.

2. Expanding from its origins in _____, the organization developed sections in other countries.

3. In 1987, a U.S. branch of Doctors Without Borders was established in _____ _____.

4. Volunteers sometimes give testimony at the _____

_____.

5. Doctors Without Borders is a _____ organization that gets its funds from donations by the public.

6. Today, the organization's operations are run by more than _____ volunteer doctors, nurses, medical professionals, sanitation engineers, and administrators.

7. Because Doctors Without Borders is not tied to government funding, it can live up to its _____.

8. Doctors Without Borders sends _____ _____, which include generators and operating rooms.

C. Making Inferences and Drawing Conclusions

Some of the following statements are facts taken from the reading. Other statements can be inferred from the reading. Write **F** in the blank in front of each factual statement. Write **I** in front of each inference.

_____ **1.** Doctors Without Borders volunteers have witnessed great suffering and crimes against humanity.

_____ **2.** Doctors Without Borders may speak out to raise awareness of a situation.

_____ **3.** Doctors Without Borders is an organization that is similar to the Red Cross.

_____ **4.** Doctors Without Borders sometimes gets to areas of crisis before other relief agencies.

_____ **5.** Doctors Without Borders volunteers put their lives in danger when they volunteer.

_____ **6.** Doctors Without Borders is a private, independent organization.

_____ **7.** Doctors Without Borders gives emergency medical aid to people to whom other relief agencies will not give aid.

_____ **8.** Doctors Without Borders has created unique emergency kits.

Discussion Questions

Discuss the answers to these questions with your classmates.

1. Why do people volunteer to work for organizations like Doctors Without Borders?
2. What do you think Doctors Without Borders is doing that other relief organizations are not?
3. What are some other relief organizations, and what do they do?
4. Do you think that these organizations should be funded by volunteers and private funds, or should governments take over this role?

Critical Thinking Questions

Discuss the answers to these questions with your classmates.

1. People who volunteer for organizations like Doctors Without Borders have certain characteristics in common. What are they? Do you have any of these character traits? Do you know someone who does?
2. Given the opportunity, would you like to work for Doctors Without Borders or a similar organization? Why or why not? In what ways can each and every one of us contribute to the welfare and happiness of others in our daily lives?
3. What are some of the natural and man-made causes of humanitarian disasters and crises around the globe? Could some of them be prevented? Why and how?

Reading 2

Inspired to Serve

CD 1,
Track 8

The following passage is from the John F. Kennedy Presidential Library and Museum's Web site.

1   **O**n October 14, 1960, Senator John F. Kennedy spoke to the students at the University of Michigan
5 in Ann Arbor during a campaign speech and challenged them to live and work in developing countries around the world,
10 thus dedicating themselves to the cause of peace and development. That idea inspired the beginning of the Peace Corps.

   The Peace Corps was designed to encourage mutual understanding
15 between Americans and other cultures of the world. It was established by executive order in 1961 and was approved by Congress as a permanent, U.S. federal agency within the State Department later that year. Robert Sargent Shriver, President Kennedy's brother-in-law, was appointed the first director of the U.S. Peace Corps in 1961. In 1981, the Peace Corps was made an
20 independent agency.

   The Peace Corps has now been operating for over 4 decades, and is still growing. In 44 years, the Peace Corps has had over 178,000 volunteers serving in over 138 countries and learning more than 200 languages and dialects. Volunteers serve 2-year periods helping to build a self-sustaining, better
25 future within their host country, along with establishing good will. Life as a Peace Corps volunteer is not easy and volunteers face many challenges from language barriers to poor living conditions. There is no salary. Volunteers

receive a monthly stipend for room, board and few essentials—"enough to be at a level sufficient only to maintain health and basic needs. Men and women will be expected to work and live alongside the nationals of the country in which they are stationed—doing the same work, eating the same food, talking the same language." Culturally, volunteers work to build trust within their communities and with their counterparts to be included within the community and their skills realized and utilized.

At a grass-roots level, volunteers teach and share their skills to help solve challenges that face developing communities. There are many different areas/sectors that volunteers work in. These sectors include: education/teaching; health and nutrition, including HIV/AIDS training, agriculture, business, community development and the environment/forestry.

The Peace Corps is always adapting to the times and to an ever-changing world, but has never wavered from its three original goals:

- To help the people of interested countries and areas in meeting their needs for trained workers
- To help promote a better understanding of Americans on the part of the peoples served
- To help promote a better understanding of other peoples on the part of Americans

Countries that are interested in hosting Peace Corps volunteers must meet certain requirements in order to participate in the Peace Corps program. These requirements are:

- A country must invite the Peace Corps
- Since there is a limited budget, the Peace Corps decides in which countries it can be active in and then prioritizes each country's needs
- The Peace Corps makes sure that the volunteers go to a country that is safe

To start a Peace Corps program, the Peace Corps announces its availability to foreign governments in countries that have met these established requirements. These governments determine areas in which the Peace Corps can be involved. The Peace Corps then matches the requested assignments to applicants with the appropriate skills who first made the request. The Peace Corps membership and funding have increased since the opening of Eastern Europe to American interests in 1990.

Today, the Peace Corps is still growing and is more vital than ever. From Kennedy's inspiration came an agency devoted to world peace and friendship and volunteers who continue to help individuals build a better life for themselves, their children, their community and their country.

⁶⁵

Vocabulary

A. Vocabulary in Context

Select the letter of the answer that is closest in meaning to the **bold** word or phrase.

1. On October 14, 1960, Senator John F. Kennedy spoke to students during a **campaign speech**.

a. a formal address given by someone who has just been elected

b. a lecture given by a teacher or professor

c. an address given by a person of authority

d. a talk given by a person trying to win political office

2. President Kennedy challenged them to live and work in **developing countries** around the world.

a. poor nations without many industries

b. nations with high standards of living

c. nations that are at war

d. nations with rapidly growing economies

3. The Peace Corps was designed to encourage **mutual** understanding between Americans and other cultures.

a. separate

b. shared

c. controlled

d. equal

4. Volunteers serve 2-year periods helping to build a **self-sustaining**, better future within their host country.

a. able to keep going without outside help

b. able to stay strong with the help of others

c. able to go back and start over

d. able to improve over time

5. Volunteers receive a monthly **stipend**.

    a. merchandise   c. payment

    b. agreement   d. bill

6. Volunteers work to build trust within their communities and with their **counterparts**.

    a. people in charge   c. people working for others

    b. people doing the same thing   d. people doing different jobs

7. Volunteers work with their counterparts to have their skills realized and **utilized**.

    a. repeated   c. used

    b. tested   d. praised

8. At a grass-roots level, volunteers teach and share their skills.

    a. by the side of people in the government   c. by the side of ordinary working people

    b. by the side of people with wealth and influence   d. by the side of people who farm

9. The Peace Corps has never **wavered** from its three original goals.

    a. progressed   c. profited

    b. taken from   d. changed

10. The Peace Corps then matches the requested assignments to applicants with the **appropriate** skills.

    a. suitable   c. admirable

    b. convenient   d. helpful

B. Vocabulary Building

Read the list of verbs below. Find verbs in the reading that have the same meaning.

1. intend (paragraph 2)   _design_

2. start (paragraph 2)   _____

3. work for (paragraph 3)   _____

4. encounter (paragraph 3)   _____

5. dedicate (final paragraph)   _____

C. Vocabulary in New Context

Make questions about the Peace Corps, using each of the verbs in Part B. For example, *What was the Peace Corps designed to do?* With a partner, take turns asking and answering questions.

Reading Comprehension

A. Looking for the Main Ideas

Answer the questions with complete sentences.

1. What is the main idea of this reading?
2. What is paragraph 4 mainly about?
3. What is the main idea of paragraph 6?
4. What is paragraph 8 mainly about?

B. Skimming and Scanning for Details

Scan the reading quickly to find the answers to the following questions.
Write complete sentences.

1. Where did Senator Kennedy give a speech challenging students to work in developing countries?
2. What was the Peace Corps designed to do?
3. Who was the first director of the U.S. Peace Corps?
4. How long do Peace Corps volunteers serve?
5. For what is the stipend given to volunteers?
6. What are the volunteers expected to do as they work and live alongside the nationals of the country in which they're stationed?
7. How do volunteers help solve challenges that face developing communities?
8. What is the first goal of the Peace Corps?
9. What is the first requirement that host countries must meet?
10. When did Eastern Europe become open to American interests?

C. Making Inferences and Drawing Conclusions

Circle the letter of the correct answer.

1. What can we infer about Kennedy's speech in 1960?
   a. It was a very moving speech.
   b. People didn't respond much to the speech.
   c. It was a rather boring speech.
   d. It was a good speech, but it didn't cause any major changes.

2. In paragraph 2, what can we conclude about Peace Corps volunteers?
   a. They are mostly from wealthy families.
   b. They live comfortably in their host countries.
   c. They are willing to endure hardships.
   d. They often don't understand the people with whom they live.

Complete the sentence.

3. From the three goals of the Peace Corps, we can conclude that the purpose of the Corps is not only to provide workers to a country but to _____.

Answer the question with a complete sentence.

4. From paragraph 7, what can we infer about a country that is at war or has internal strife?

Discussion Questions

Discuss the answers to these questions with your classmates.

1. What are some prominent volunteer organizations in your country? Who do they help? What are their goals and purpose?
2. Are there Peace Corps volunteers in your country? Do you think the Peace Corps has a positive effect on the countries that host its volunteers? Why or why not? If given the opportunity, would you like to be a Peace Corps volunteer? Why or why not?
3. Do you do any volunteer work? If yes, what is it? If not, would you like to do volunteer work one day? Why or why not? What kind of volunteer work would you do if you had the opportunity?

4. When natural disasters strike, countries from around the world send volunteers to help. What is a natural disaster that has occurred in your country? Describe what happened, and explain when and where it happened. What organizations came to the aid of the victims?

Critical Thinking Questions

Discuss the answers to these questions with your classmates.

1. Peace Corps volunteers are not sent to dangerous countries. However, Doctors Without Borders volunteers often stay in dangerous areas after all other organizations have left. Do you think this is foolish? Do you think Peace Corps volunteers should also serve in dangerous areas? Why or why not? Would you help save someone's life if it put your life in danger?
2. What are some of the neediest countries in the world today? What can the Peace Corps and other volunteer organizations do to help them? What can the countries do to help themselves?
3. Imagine yourself as a Peace Corps volunteer. In what country would you be working? What job would you be doing? What knowledge would you be sharing? What hardships might you be enduring? What challenges would you be facing?

Writing

Writing Skills

A. Organizing: *Description*

Description is often used to make a narration or exposition more lively and interesting. An exposition may rely on some narration and description, and a narration may include some exposition and description. A descriptive essay, therefore, does not have to be purely descriptive, but can use narration and exposition as well.

The Dominant Impression

A good description has two strong elements: a dominant impression and appropriate supporting details. The dominant impression is the main effect a place, an object, a person, or a group of people has on our feelings or senses. We create a dominant impression by selecting the most important characteristic or feature of the person or group of people or place and emphasizing that feature. We can then develop the dominant impression by providing details that support it.

Typically, the three elements of the dominant impression are clearly stated in the thesis. They are then developed in the body paragraphs. The reading on Doctors Without Borders focuses on how the doctors put their beliefs into practice. The second paragraph states, "These doctors believed that all people have the right to medical care, whatever their race, religion, or political affiliation—and that meeting their needs is more important than respecting national borders."

Examine paragraph 5 of the reading on Doctors Without Borders. How does it describe the organization's efficiency? Paragraph 6 describes how volunteers speak out about their beliefs. In what ways do they do this?

In the reading about the Peace Corps, the dominant impression that comes to mind is of how the Peace Corps carries out its goals. Which paragraph clearly describes the goals of the Peace Corps? Which paragraph describes how the volunteers put these goals into action? In what ways to they do this?

Figures of Speech

Writers often use figures of speech to make their descriptions more vivid. Figures of speech are colorful words and expressions that make some kind of comparison. We will look at two figures of speech: the simile and the metaphor.

Simile

Of the many types of figures of speech, the simile provides the most direct comparison. In a simile, one thing is compared with another to show similarity, typically by using the word *like* or *as*.

Examples:

Developing countries are *like* growing children.

The doctors worked together *as* smoothly *as* a fine orchestra.

Metaphor

A metaphor expresses a comparison more indirectly, without using *like* or *as*. A word or phrase is used to suggest the strong likeness between the people or things being compared.

Example:

The volunteer's kindness was a lamp, shining wherever she went.

(This is a metaphor comparing the volunteer's effect on others to that of someone carrying a lamp. A lamp brings light into our lives. In the same way, the volunteer brings hope and happiness to those she serves.)

B. Exercises

1. Complete the similes in the following sentences.
   1. The volunteers for the Big Brothers Big Sisters program are as devoted
      as _____.
   2. Sometimes Peace Corps volunteers have to be as tough
      as _____.
   3. The Red Cross worker was as brave as _____.
   4. A UNICEF worker can bring a smile to a child that is as bright
      as _____.

5. The Nature Conservancy believes plants and animals are as important as _____.

6. First-time volunteers are as enthusiastic as _____.

7. The medical team is as efficient as _____.

8. Their work is as desperately needed as _____.

2. Work with a partner or a group. Explain the comparisons being made in the following metaphors.

1. Rescuing the survivors was a Herculean effort.

2. The arrival of the rescue team was a ray of sunshine.

3. After the war began, night descended on the country.

4. The volunteers lift the loads from the backs of the villagers.

5. Through their testimony, they hold a torch to the suffering of people everywhere.

6. Their knock on the door has saved the lives of many who had lost hope.

Writing Model: The Descriptive Essay

Read the following descriptive essay written by a student.

Vegans

1   A vegetarian is someone who does not eat meat. However, there are many kinds of vegetarians. Some vegetarians don't eat meat, but they drink milk and eat cheese and eggs. Strict vegetarians are called vegans. Vegans make an effort to avoid all forms of animal exploitation and live their lives accordingly.

5   Most vegans can be characterized by their avoidance of consuming animal foods and their derivatives, their avoidance of using products derived from animals, and their support for animal rights groups.

    Vegans do not eat meat, fish, poultry, eggs, or animals' milk and its derivatives such as yogurt, cheese, and butter. Vegans think it is cruel to make

10   a cow produce milk all the time, and therefore they avoid any derivatives from milk. They avoid using gelatin, which comes from the bones of animals. Gelatin is used in many desserts; it is also used in photography, but vegans have not found a substitute for this use yet. Most vegans avoid eating honey because bees are often killed when they produce honey. As for eggs, chickens

15   suffer as they are put in cages all their lives to lay eggs continuously. Vegans

eat substitutes for these foods, which they can get in vegan stores. These may be vitamins or derivatives from seaweed or soy.

Vegans avoid using any products derived from animals. For their clothes, they do not wear leather or fur. They also do not wear wool or silk. There are many ingredients from animals in many household items such as soap or shampoo. Vegans buy products that have the label "Cruelty Free" or "Not Tested on Animals." Even when they buy plates, they do not buy bone china because bone china really contains bones. There are vegan stores where vegans can buy foods and household items that are animal-free.

Most vegans support animal rights groups. People who support animal rights believe that animals feel pain in the same way as humans do. Therefore, causing pain to an animal is the same as causing pain to a human. If animals have the same right to be free from pain and suffering as humans, then we can't eat them, take off their skins, experiment on them, or use them cruelly for our entertainment. These ideas are shared by most vegans, who do not want to cause suffering to animals, and therefore many vegans become supporters of animals' rights.

In conclusion, vegans can be generally characterized by their avoidance of consuming animal foods and their derivatives, their avoidance of using any products derived from animals, and their support for animal rights groups. However, this does not mean to say these are their only beliefs. Many vegans have strong beliefs in human rights and the environment. Being a vegan is a whole way of life.

Domenico
Ecuador

Student Essay Follow-Up

1. Underline the thesis statement.
2. What 3 characteristics of vegans does the writer focus on?
3. Is each of these characteristics then developed in the body paragraphs?
4. Examine paragraph 2. Do all the ideas support the main idea? Are descriptive words used to strengthen the dominant impression?
5. Underline the dominant aspect or impression in each of the 3 body paragraphs.

Writing Practice

A. Write a Descriptive Essay

Write an essay on one of the following topics. In your essay, try to include **3** or more vocabulary words from the readings in this chapter.

1. Write a descriptive essay on an organization, a society, or a club that you are familiar with or would like to research. Use 2 or 3 adjectives to give the dominant impression.
2. Write a descriptive essay on a tribe or group of people that you are familiar with or would like to research. Use 2 or 3 adjectives to give the dominant impression.
3. Write a descriptive essay on a person you know. Use 2 or 3 adjectives to give the dominant impression.

B. Pre-Write

1. Work alone, with a partner, or in a group.
2. Brainstorm the topic. Look at pages 254–256 to find out about brainstorming. Choose a pre-writing technique you prefer.
3. Brainstorm ideas for descriptive adjectives and supporting details.
4. Work on a thesis statement.

C. Outline

1. Organize your ideas.

   Step 1: Write your thesis statement.

   Step 2: Select two or three of the best descriptive adjectives from your brainstorming activity.

   Step 3: Find relevant descriptive details to support your dominant impression.

2. Make a more detailed outline. The essay form on page 21 will help you.

D. Write a Rough Draft

Look at page 257 to find out about writing a rough draft.

E. Revise Your Rough Draft

Use the Revision Checklist on page 258.

F. Edit Your Essay

Use the Editing Checklist on page 259. Check your work for the following type of error, known as a *dangling modifier*. The modifier (*visiting*) does not refer to the subject of the main clause.

Example:

Error:	<u>Visiting</u> Pennsylvania some years ago, my friends told me about a group of people called the Amish.	*dm*
Correct:	When I was visiting Pennsylvania some years ago, my friends told me about a group of people called the Amish.	

When you find a mistake of this type, you can write the symbol "dm" (dangling modifier). Look at page 260 for other symbols to use when editing your work.

G. Write Your Final Copy

When your rough draft has been edited, you can write the final copy of your essay.

Additional Writing Practice

A. Summarize

Write a one-paragraph summary of Reading 1. Compare your summary to the Summary Checklist on page 269.

B. Paraphrase

Paraphrase paragraph 5 in Reading 2. Look at pages 264–267 to find out about paraphrasing. Begin with either "According to the historical resources at the John F. Kennedy Presidential Library and Museum, . . ." or "Based on the historical resources at the John F. Kennedy Presidential Library and Museum, ..."

C. Research

Choose a particular group of people, and find 2 or 3 dominant characteristics particular to them. Consult appropriate sources in the library, and/or use your own experience or that of your friends to gather information.

The following are suggested topics:

- The Amish
- The Boy Scouts/Girl Scouts
- Greenpeace
- The Mormons
- The Masons
- The Quakers
- The Red Cross
- The Salvation Army
- The Shakers

Weaving It Together

⏱ Timed Writing

Choose one of the following topics that you have not already written about in "Writing Practice," or choose the topic that you have researched. You have 50 minutes to write an essay.

1. Write a descriptive essay on an organization, a society, or a club that you are familiar with or would like to research. Use 2 or 3 adjectives to give the dominant impression.
2. Write a descriptive essay on a tribe or group of people that you are familiar with or would like to research. Use 2 or 3 adjectives to give the dominant impression.
3. Write a descriptive essay on a person you know. Use 2 or 3 adjectives to give the dominant impression.
4. Write a descriptive essay on the topic you researched.

Connecting to the Internet

A. Use the Internet to find out about one of these international organizations: UNICEF, Oxfam, AfriCare, MercyCorps, Greenpeace, Friends of the Earth, WaterAid. Describe what the organization does. Does it provide volunteer opportunities in your area? If so, which ones would you like to participate in?

B. Use the Internet to find volunteer organizations in your city, region, or country. Write 2 short descriptions of the work of 2 local or national organizations. Include when they were established, their purpose and goals, and the work they do.

What Do You Think Now?

Refer to page 90 at the beginning of this chapter. Do you know the answers now? Complete the sentence or circle the best answer.

1. Doctors Without Borders started in _____.
2. Doctors Without Borders is/is not completely funded by governments.
3. Doctors Without Borders has operations in _____ countries.
4. Peace Corps volunteers serve for a _____ period.
5. Peace Corps volunteers receive/do not receive a monthly salary even for basic food and board.

5 Psychology

What Do You Think?

Answer the questions with your best guess. Circle **Yes** or **No**.

Do you think . . .

1. there is proof that the shape of your body and your character
   are connected?   **Yes   No**
2. muscular people are always dominant?   **Yes   No**
3. introverts are more responsive to caffeine than extraverts?   **Yes   No**
4. extraverts do not like crowded social gatherings?   **Yes   No**
5. extraverts are bored with soft music?   **Yes   No**

Pre-Reading

Discuss the answers to these questions with your classmates.

1. Look at the picture of the muscular man on the previous page. What do you think he is like? Check the box beside the adjectives that you think describe this man.
   - ☐ athletic
   - ☐ bold
   - ☐ imaginative
   - ☐ outgoing
   - ☐ quiet
   - ☐ reserved
   - ☐ sensitive
   - ☐ shy
   - ☐ studious
   - ☐ tough-minded

2. Now look at the thin man. Check the box beside the adjectives that you think describe him.
   - ☐ active
   - ☐ aggressive
   - ☐ anxious
   - ☐ calm
   - ☐ easygoing
   - ☐ intellectual
   - ☐ outgoing
   - ☐ passive
   - ☐ talkative
   - ☐ thoughtful

3. On what basis did you characterize these people?
4. Is it possible that the thin man is outgoing and athletic and the muscular man is shy? Describe an incident in which you were wrong when you judged a person based on physical appearance.
5. Do people expect their leaders to look a certain way?

Reading 1

What Our Bodies Say About Us

CD 1,
Track 9

1   "Let me have men about me that are fat," says Julius Caesar to Marcus Antonius in Shakespeare's play *Julius Caesar*. In Julius Caesar's opinion, fat people were more trustworthy than thin ones—that is, those with a "lean and hungry look" who "are dangerous."

5   Shakespeare wasn't the first person to categorize personality according to body type. And if you've ever reacted to people based on the way they look, you know he wasn't the last. The relationship between physical characteristics and personality has been explored for thousands of years and used to predict and explain the actions of others. Although prehistoric man probably had

10 his own ideas about the skinny guy in the cave next door, the ancient Greeks historically have been responsible for Western theories about body and character.

    The Greeks believed the body was composed of four humors, or fluids: blood, black bile, yellow bile, and phlegm. The one someone had the

15 most of determined his or her temperament or personality type—sanguine (hopeful), melancholic (sad), choleric (hot-tempered), or phlegmatic (lazy or slow). Although this ancient theory eventually lost its popularity, it was replaced over the next few thousand years by

20 all kinds of other ways to identify and catalog people by type. One of the most popular modern theories was proposed

25 by William Sheldon in the late 1940s and early 1950s. He suggested a relationship between body shape and temperament

30 (see the figure). According

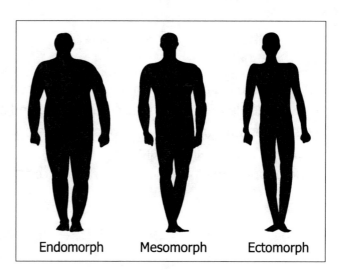

Endomorph   Mesomorph   Ectomorph

to Sheldon's system, the endomorph—with an oval-shaped body and large, heavy stomach—is slow, sociable, emotional, forgiving, and relaxed. The mesomorph—with a triangular shape and a muscular, firm, upright body, is confident, energetic, dominant, enterprising, and at times hot-tempered. The ectomorph—with a thin, fragile body—is tense, awkward, and meticulous.

A number of researchers since Sheldon have contributed their own ideas to the basic theory that body shape and personality are somehow connected. Going one step beyond basic shape is the idea of "body splits." This theory looks at the body in sections—top to bottom, front to back, torso and limbs— with the idea that each part of the body tells its own story. For example, the upper half of the body, consisting of the chest, head, and arms, is expressive and conveys our feelings to others through gestures and facial movements. The lower body, on the other hand, is associated with more deeply felt emotions—particularly those about family, children, and self-image.

According to this theory, someone with a well-developed upper body will be active and outwardly confident. However, if this same person has noticeably thinner legs and narrow hips, he or she might have trouble expressing himself or herself to others, lack self-confidence, and find it difficult to think about deep emotions. A person with a small chest but large hips will have opposite traits, such as being shy in public, but emotional and loving towards friends and family. Look for many clues to personality: weight distribution (heaviness or thinness in different parts of the body), muscular development, grace and coordination, and general health. For example, does one half of the body seem healthier, or more tense, or more relaxed than the other? Look for tense shoulders or stiff legs and hips.

Backs and fronts are different, too. The front of the body is associated with our conscious self, the one we think about and show to others. The back, which is hidden from us most of the time, is associated with our unconscious self—that is, the feelings we hide from both ourselves and others. Many times, we don't want to think about or show emotions such as anger and fear, and we tend to store these feelings in the back. If you're feeling stress, your back is likely to be tense. People who find it hard to deal with problems without losing their temper are likely to have some kind of back trouble. Look around you at the stories backs tell. A stooped back is weighed down by burdens or troubles. A stiff and rigid back is hiding anger or stress. A straight and graceful spine is strong and flexible. Do you know what kind of back you have?

Finally, there is the split between the torso, or body, and the limbs, or arms and legs. You express yourself with your arms and hands, and even your legs
70 in the way you move about. People who are outgoing often use their hands and arms to gesture when they talk. They also walk with long, confident strides. Shy people hold their hands and arms quietly close to them and walk with small steps. Energetic people often tap their feet and move around a lot because it's hard for them to sit still. They can sometimes be impatient and
75 are not the best listeners.

There is no end to theories about body shape and personality, and there is no doubt that certain people with certain bodies often have very predictable characters. However, there are some researchers who believe that the many instances in which body and personality go together are due to stereotyping;
80 that is, we expect a certain type of person to have certain traits, so we see those traits whether they are there or not. For example, muscular people are believed to be dominant and forceful, so we treat them as leaders. But sometimes they are actually shy and timid. Fat people are supposed to be happy and warmhearted, but in reality they can just as easily be depressed or
85 mean. Sometimes people will even act the way they think others expect them to act. By doing that, people fill the role in which we picture them.

No matter how you look at it, bodies and personalities are related, whether by chance or by choice. However, there are always exceptions to the rule—and whenever that happens, there goes the theory. After all, we're only human;
90 and that means we have a mind of our own—whether we're fat, skinny, or something in between.

Vocabulary

A. Vocabulary in Context

Select the letter of the answer that is closest in meaning to the **bold** word or phrase.

1. According to Shakespeare's Julius Caesar, people with a "**lean** and hungry look" are dangerous.
   a. wild   c. weak
   b. thin   d. angry

2. The Greeks believed a choleric person was **hot-tempered**.
a. lively
b. romantic
c. easily angered
d. enthusiastic

3. The person with a triangular shape is confident, dominant, and **enterprising**.
a. possessing the courage to start new and difficult things
b. ready to attack at any time
c. possessing special skills in business
d. fond of being in control

4. The person with a thin, fragile body is tense and **awkward**.
a. not friendly to people
b. not very active or worried
c. lacking in ability to make decisions
d. lacking in skill in moving his or her body

5. The thin, fragile ectomorph is also **meticulous**.
a. concerned about details
b. concerned about spending money
c. unable to decide
d. unable to relax

6. Each section of the body—top to bottom, front to back, **torso** and limbs—tells its own story.
a. the head and shoulders
b. the body without the head, legs, and arms
c. the front of the head and body
d. the body with the head, but without the legs and arms

7. Look for clues to personality such as weight distribution, muscular development, **grace** and coordination, and general health.
a. beauty and harmony in movement
b. beauty of physical features
c. healthy color of physical features
d. straight and flexible body

8. A **stooped** back is weighed down by troubles.
a. hardened
b. painful
c. tense
d. bent

9. People who are outgoing walk with long, confident **strides**.
a. movements
b. steps
c. gestures
d. manners

10. Fat people can just as easily be depressed or **mean**.
a. unkind
b. moody
c. anxious
d. gloomy

B. Vocabulary Building

1. Find words in the reading that go together with the words below to make phrases.

1. active and ___confident___

2. burdens and _____

3. anger and _____

4. dominant and _____

5. shy and _____

6. happy and _____

2. Complete the sentences with the words you found in Exercise 1.

1. A person who is _____ likes to talk a lot.

2. A _____ person is afraid of everything.

3. A _____ person is very generous.

4. A person who uses strength to get his or her own way is _____.

5. Someone with a stooped back usually has a lot of _____.

6. If you are under a lot of _____, you will get sick more often.

C. Vocabulary in New Context

Do you agree with the definitions above? Make your own definitions, using the words you found in Part B, Exercise 1.

Reading Comprehension

A. Looking for the Main Ideas

Circle the letter of the best answer.

1. What is the main idea of paragraph 4?
   a. The Greek theory of personality lost its popularity over the years.
   b. Many personality theories had been developed by the 1940s and 1950s.
   c. William Sheldon's theory relates body shape to personality.
   d. Large, heavy people are usually sociable and emotional.

2. Paragraph 7 is mostly about _____.
   a. the difference between a person's front and back
   b. how stress and anger can cause back problems
   c. how we hide our feelings from ourselves and others
   d. what a person's back can reveal about him or her

3. Paragraph 9 is mainly concerned with _____.
   a. the many theories that exist about body shape and personality
   b. how stereotyping affects the way we see ourselves and others
   c. how muscular people tend to be leaders
   d. how some people have very predictable characters

B. Skimming and Scanning for Details

Scan the reading quickly to find the answers to these questions. Write complete sentences.

1. According to the reading, how has the relationship between physical characteristics and personality been used?
2. What are the four fluids and their related personality types, as defined by the Greeks?
3. What are the three shapes into which William Sheldon divided people?
4. In paragraph 5, sentence 1, to what does the word *their* refer?
5. In the theory of "body splits," what is the significance of the upper body?
6. In paragraph 6, line 1, to what do the words *this theory* refer?
7. What are four clues to personality that you should look for, according to the theory of "body splits"?

8. With which part of the personality is the front of the body associated?

9. According to the reading, what type of person may not be a good listener? Why?

10. What is the stereotype of fat people?

C. Making Inferences and Drawing Conclusions

The answers to these questions are not directly stated in the reading. Circle the letter of the best answer.

1. The reading implies that _____.

a. ancient people didn't know enough to understand personality theories

b. very few theories that categorize people by their appearance have been popular

c. it's natural for people to look for relationships between physical characteristics and personality

d. it takes a scientific mind to identify and categorize people according to body type

2. From the reading, it can be concluded that _____.

a. our emotions and attitudes can affect our health and appearance

b. a person with a pleasant personality is most likely to be pear-shaped

c. the shape of the body as a whole tells the most about personality

d. it's easy to hide our emotions from others

3. It can be inferred from the reading that _____.

a. people have lost interest in theories linking personality to looks

b. when we expect people to behave in a certain way, we're often disappointed

c. there is nothing to support theories about body shape and personality

d. stereotyping can make it difficult for us to see others as they really are

4. The author's attitude toward theories that categorize people according to body type is _____.

a. disbelieving

b. interested

c. shocked

d. disappointed

Discussion Questions

Discuss the answers to these questions with your classmates.

1. Which physical characteristics do you use to categorize people?
2. Do you like or trust certain people on the basis of their physical features? What type of personality are you most attracted to? Do you seek out people with certain personalities to be your friends?
3. How can gestures and body movement be used to classify people?
4. Give some examples of how people are stereotyped.

Critical Thinking Questions

Discuss the answers to these questions with your classmates.

1. What do you think of Sheldon's theory of relating body type to personality? Is his theory valid? Do you agree or disagree with him? Why or why not?
2. Since ancient times, people have tried to classify humans by personality type. Why do you think people have always been so fascinated with this subject? What does categorizing people allow us to do? How can it be a benefit? How can it be harmful?
3. Develop your own theory of personality types based on your own experiences and observations.

Reading 2

Why We Are What We Are

CD 1,
Track 10

The following passage is taken from a college psychology text called Personality, *written by Jerry Burger and published by Wadsworth, a division of Thomson Learning, Belmont, CA, 2000. In Chapter 9, The Biological Approach, Hans Eysenck's theory of personality is described. Eysenck claims that differences in personality are based on biological differences.*

1   **E**ysenck's research strategy begins by dividing the elements of personality into various units that can be arranged hierarchically. The basic structure in

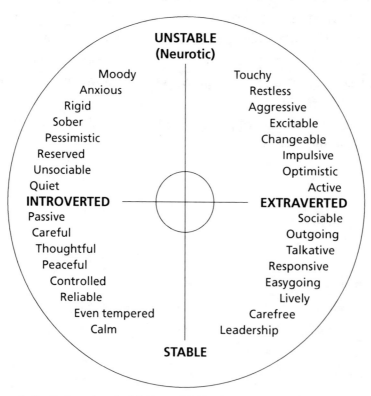

Figure 1: Traits Associated with Eysenck's Two Major Personality Dimensions[1]

---

[1]**Figure 1**: Adapted from Eysenck and Eysenck (1968); reprinted by permission of Educational and Industrial Testing Service

this scheme is the *specific response* level, which consists of specific behaviors. For example, if we watch a man spend the afternoon talking and laughing with friends, we would be observing a specific response. If this man spends many afternoons each week having a good time with friends, we have evidence for the second level in Eysenck's model, a *habitual response*. But it is likely that this man doesn't limit himself to socializing just in the afternoon and just with these friends. Suppose this man also devotes a large part of his weekends and quite a few evenings to his social life. If you watch long enough, you might find that he lives for social gatherings, discussion groups, parties, and so on. You might conclude, in Eysenck's terms, that this person exhibits the *trait*[2] of sociability. Finally, Eysenck argues that traits such as sociability are part of a still larger dimension of personality. That is, people who are sociable also tend to be impulsive, active, lively, and excitable. All these traits combine to form the *supertrait* Eysenck calls extraversion.

How many of these supertraits are there? Originally, Eysenck's factor analytic research yielded evidence for two basic dimensions that could subsume[3] all other traits: *extraversion-introversion* and *neuroticism*. Because the dimensions are independent of one another, people who score on the extraversion end of the first dimension can score either high or low on the second dimension. Further, as shown in Figure 1, someone who scores high on extraversion and low on neuroticism possesses different traits than does a person who scores high on both extraversion and neuroticism.

Where do you suppose you fall in this model? If you are the prototypic[4] extravert, then Eysenck describes you as "outgoing, impulsive and uninhibited, having many social contacts and frequently taking part in group activities. The typical extravert is sociable, likes parties, has many friends, needs to have people to talk to, and does not like reading or studying by himself." An introvert is "a quiet, retiring sort of person, introspective, fond of books rather than people; he is reserved and distant except to intimate friends." Of course, most people fall somewhere between these two extremes, but each of us is perhaps a little more of one than the other.

Eysenck argues that extraverts and introverts differ not only in terms of behavior but also in their *physiological*[5] makeup. Eysenck originally

---

[2]**trait:** characteristic
[3]**subsume:** include within its larger categories
[4]**prototypic:** very typical; original after which others are modeled
[5]**physiological:** biological; concerned with how the body works

maintained that extraverts and introverts have different levels of *cerebral cortex arousal*[6] when in a nonstimulating, resting state. Although it may sound backward at first, he proposed that extraverts generally have a *lower* level of cortical arousal than do introverts. Extraverts seek out highly arousing social behavior *because* their cortical arousal is well below their desired level when doing nothing. In a sense, highly extraverted people are simply trying to avoid unpleasant boredom. Their problem is feeding their need for stimulation. Introverts have the opposite problem. They typically operate at an above-optimal cortical arousal[7] level. These people select solitude and nonstimulating environments in an effort to keep their already high arousal level from becoming too aversive. For these reasons, extraverts enjoy a noisy party that introverts can't wait to leave.

Unfortunately, a great deal of research has failed to uncover the different levels of base-rate cortical arousal[8] proposed by Eysenck. For example, introverts and extraverts show no differences in brain-wave activity when at rest or when asleep (Stelmack, 1990). But this does not mean that Eysenck's original theorizing was entirely off base. Rather, there is ample evidence that introverts are more sensitive to stimulation than extraverts are (Stelmack, 1990). That is, introverts are more quickly and strongly aroused when exposed to loud music or the stimulation found in an active social encounter. Introverts are even more responsive than extraverts when exposed to chemical stimulants, such as caffeine or nicotine.

Consequently, many researchers now describe extraverts and introverts in terms of their different sensitivity to stimulation, rather than the different base rate of cortical activity Eysenck proposed. However, the effect is essentially the same. Because of physiological differences, introverts are more quickly overwhelmed by the stimulation of a crowded social gathering, whereas extraverts are likely to find the same gathering rather pleasant. Extraverts are quickly bored by slow-moving movie plots and soft music because they are less likely to become aroused by these subtle sources of stimulation than introverts are.

---

[6]**cerebral cortex arousal:** level of activity in the part of the brain that is responsible for language, memory, and thinking
[7]**above-optimal cortical arousal:** higher-than-desirable level of activity in the cerebral cortex
[8]**base-rate cortical arousal:** low-degree activation of the brain

Vocabulary

A. Vocabulary in Context

Select the letter of the answer that is closest in meaning to the **bold** word or phrase.

1. Eysenck divided the elements of personality into units that can be arranged **hierarchically**.
   a. evenly
   b. randomly
   c. from higher to lower
   d. in groups

2. Traits are part of a larger **dimension** of personality.
   a. subject
   b. aspect
   c. division
   d. range

3. People who are sociable also tend to be **impulsive**.
   a. kind
   b. arrogant
   c. hasty
   d. cautious

4. Eysenck describes extraverts as "outgoing, impulsive and **uninhibited**."
   a. generous with money
   b. free and open
   c. unimaginative
   d. undependable

5. An introvert is "a quiet, **retiring** sort of person."
   a. possessing an excellent memory
   b. attending to duties willingly
   c. not fond of work
   d. tending to avoid the company of others

6. Eysenck thinks introverts are **introspective** and fond of books.
   a. thoughtful
   b. tolerant
   c. patient
   d. easygoing

7. Highly extraverted people try to feed their need for **stimulation**.
   a. excitement
   b. relaxation
   c. knowledge
   d. success

Word Partnership	Use **dimension** with:
adj.	**different** dimension, **important** dimension, **new** dimension, **spiritual** dimension

8. Introverts select nonstimulating environments in an effort to keep their already high arousal level from becoming too **aversive**.
   a. unimportant
   b. unpleasant
   c. unnecessary
   d. unsafe

9. There is **ample** evidence that introverts are more sensitive to stimulation than extraverts are.
   a. less than might be expected
   b. incomplete
   c. more than enough
   d. exactly enough

10. Extraverts are less likely to become aroused by **subtle** sources of stimulation than introverts are.
   a. hardly noticeable
   b. very unusual
   c. extremely displeasing
   d. constant

B. Vocabulary Building

1. Read the list of verbs below. Find verbs in the reading that have the same meaning.

   1. watch   _observe_
   2. have or own   _____
   3. claim   _____
   4. suggest   _____
   5. look for   _____
   6. choose   _____

2. Complete the sentences with the words you found in Exercise 1. Then look back at the reading to check your answers.

   1. An extravert _____ different personality traits than an introvert does.
   2. Extraverts tend to _____ noisy situations.
   3. Introverts usually _____ solitude.
   4. Eysenck _____ typical behavior of different personality types.
   5. Eysenck _____ that people have different levels of cerebral cortex arousal.
   6. Eysenck _____ a theory to explain the connection between cerebral cortex arousal and personality.

B. Vocabulary in New Context

1. Now make a question using each of the verbs you found in Part B, Exercise 1. With a partner, take turns asking and answering questions.

2. The phrases below can all be used to describe people. Make each adjective negative by filling in the blank with the most appropriate one of the following prefixes: ir   im   in   un

1. ____ offensive person
2. ____ flexible boss
3. ____ practical way
4. ____ discreet manner
5. ____ fallible judge of character
6. ____ efficient worker
7. ____ reproachable character
8. ____ rational thinker
9. ____ patient onlooker
10. ____ enlightened colleague

11. ____ sincere woman
12. ____ consistent behavior
13. ____ corruptible officer
14. ____ decisive child
15. ____ elegant posture
16. ____ judicious judgment
17. ____ responsible person
18. ____ personal judge
19. ____ bending father
20. ____ pretentious millionaire

Reading Comprehension

A. Looking for the Main Ideas

Write complete answers to the following questions about the reading.

1. What is the main idea of paragraph 1?
2. Which lines state the main idea of paragraph 2?
3. What is paragraph 3 mostly about?
4. Which sentence contains the main idea of paragraph 4?

B. Skimming and Scanning for Details

Scan the reading quickly to complete the following sentences. Circle the letter of the best answer.

1. According to the reading, the basic structure in Eysenck's scheme for determining someone's personality type is _____.
   a. habitual response level
   b. supertraits
   c. specific response level
   d. extraversion

2. If a person often does the same activity, then that behavior is considered
_____.

    a. not unusual   c. a habitual response

    b. trait   d. model behavior

3. According to the reading, a man who enjoys parties, gatherings, and
discussion groups is exhibiting the trait of _____.

    a. sociability   c. optimism

    b. leadership   d. neuroticism

4. _____ is *not* an element of the supertrait "extraversion."

    a. Impulsiveness   c. Liveliness

    b. Activeness   d. Restlessness

5. Eysenck's original theory divided personality into _____.

    a. three basic dimensions   c. impulsive and outgoing behavior

    b. several supertraits   d. extraversion-introversion and
                                     neuroticism

6. According to Eysenck's theory, an introvert _____.

    a. has many friends   c. goes to parties several times a week

    b. likes books more than people   d. is impulsive

7. According to Eysenck, extraverts and introverts differ _____.

    a. only in their behavior   c. only in their physiological makeup

    b. both behaviorally and   d. mostly in the way they think
       physiologically

8. Eysenck was interested in comparing levels of cerebral cortex arousal in
extraverts and introverts when _____.

    a. they were resting   c. they were alone

    b. they were meeting other people   d. they were feeding their need for
                                      stimulation

9. Eysenck thought that, compared to introverts, extraverts had _____.

    a. a higher level of cortical arousal   c. a lower level of cortical arousal

    b. nearly the same level of cortical   d. a different kind of cortical arousal
       arousal

10. According to Eysenck, extraverted people like busy, noisy places because
_____.

    a. they're lonely without other people   c. they're shy

    b. they're not very emotional   d. they need the stimulation

C. Making Inferences and Drawing Conclusions

Some of the following statements can be inferred from the passage, and others cannot. Circle the number of each statement that can be inferred.

1. Eysenck didn't spend enough time studying people to come up with a good personality theory.

2. People who don't have many friends are unhappy.

3. You can't categorize a person according to his or her behavior in a single situation.

4. An extravert isn't easily embarrassed.

5. Introverts are more intelligent than extraverts.

6. An introvert would like a museum better than a crowded movie theater.

7. An extravert likes people more than he or she needs them.

8. An introvert's discomfort might be mistaken for unfriendliness.

9. It's difficult to categorize people because their personalities are too complex to fit into defined categories.

10. You're likely to find more extraverts than introverts at a packed, high-energy nightclub.

Discussion Questions

Discuss the answers to these questions with your classmates.

1. Do you see yourself as an extravert or an introvert? Why?
2. To what extent is personality hereditary? What other factors do you think affect the development of someone's personality?
3. Do you think people look for a partner whose personality type is like theirs? Do relationships between opposites work well?
4. Have you ever been in a situation in which you felt uncomfortable while others were happy and at ease? What aspect of your personality didn't match the situation? Do you find yourself trying to avoid situations because they don't "fit" your personality?

Critical Thinking Questions

Discuss the answers to these questions with your classmates.

1. Do you think most people are happy with the personality they have? Do you think it's possible to change our personality? If you could change your personality, what kind of person would you become?
2. Do you think Eysenck's theory makes sense? Why? What would you add to either support Eysenck's theory or to prove it wrong?
3. In what ways does personality affect a person's behavior, lifestyle, and choice of profession? Create an imaginary day in the life of an introvert and in that of an extravert.

Writing

Writing Skills

A. Organizing: *Classification*

Classification means dividing people, objects, places, or ideas into various groups so that members of each group share similar characteristics. With this method, we give order to the many things in this world. Sociologists classify people into different classes; biologists classify plants or animals into species; and psychologists classify people's personalities into various types.

The Principle of Classification

To be clear, a classification should be based on a single principle. This means that you must choose one criterion on which to make your classification. In Reading 1 on body language, Sheldon classified people into three types—the endomorph, the mesomorph, and the ectomorph—based on the principle of body type. In Reading 2, Eysenck classified people into extraverts and introverts based on the principle of personality. In your classroom, you could classify the students according to their ethnicity: Hispanic, Asian, European. You could also classify the same students according to their age: under 20, between 20 and 25, over 25. Another classification of the same students could be according to their work in class: hardworking students, average students, lazy students. Yet another classification could be made based on where they sit in class: in the front rows, in the middle, in the back rows. As you can see, many principles can be used; however, you must choose *one* principle of classification in your essay.

Once you have chosen a principle of classification, make sure that the classification includes all members of the group. For example, suppose you have decided to classify the students in your class by race. All the students fit nicely into the categories of Asian, Hispanic, and European except for one, who is Arabic and does not fit. You must either add another category so that this student will fit or look for another principle of classification.

To avoid omitting members, it's usually a good idea to divide the group into more than two categories. Most classification essays have three or four categories.

Introduction in the Classification Essay

In your thesis statement, introduce the categories of classification you will be using.

Examples:

The students in my class can be classified according to their level of intelligence: those who are intelligent, those who are average, and those who are below average.

People can be classified according to the shape of their chin: those who have a pointed chin, those who have a round chin, those who have a broad chin, and those who have a small chin.

Wrinkles fall into two categories: horizontal and vertical.

Fish fall into three basic classes: jawless fish, bony fish, and cartilaginous fish.

When stating your categories in the thesis statement, remember to use parallel structure, or words of the same grammatical form, in the series.

Examples:

Teachers can be classified as *those who dress formally, those who dress semiformally,* and *those who dress casually.* (clauses)

In terms of body language, people can be classified according to *movements, posture,* and *facial expression.* (nouns)

The Greeks categorized people as *melancholic, phlegmatic, sanguine,* and *choleric.* (adjectives)

Transitions in the Classification Essay

For your classification essay, you will need several types of transitions:

Type of Transitions	Transitions		Examples
transitions that introduce categories	besides finally first in addition second	the first the last the last third	*The first* group consists of students who are intelligent. *The next* category includes students who are average.
transitions that show comparison and contrast	different from in contrast to like	whereas while unlike	*Unlike* the slow endomorph, the mesomorph is energetic. The temperament of the sanguine type, *in contrast to* that of the melancholic type, is hopeful.
transitions that show examples	a good example one example typical		*A good example* of an extravert is the director of our company. Your tennis coach is a *typical* mesomorph.

B. Exercises

1. Identify one item in each of the following groups, and say how it is different from the others in that group. The first one is done for you.

   1. Vehicles: car, truck, van, jeep, motorcycle
      Motorcycle does not belong. All the others have four wheels.

   2. Sports: football, baseball, tennis, volleyball, swimming

   3. Literature: poetry, newspaper article, short story, drama, novel

   4. Transportation: by land, by air, by sea, by bus

   5. Teachers: bachelor's degree, master's degree, Ph.D., brilliance

   6. Style of clothes: formal, semiformal, casual, beachwear

   7. Sports: hiking, skiing, swimming, ice skating, tennis

   8. Animals: tortoise, crocodile, snake, lizard, monkey

   9. Food: protein, carbohydrates, fats, minerals, sugar

 10. Drugs: stimulants, depressants, hallucinogens, sedatives

2. Look at the following subjects and categories. Identify the principle of classification being used. The first one is done for you.

  1. Students: intelligent, average, below average
  Principle of classification: _____level of intelligence_____

  2. Teachers: tough graders, fair graders, easy graders
  Principle of classification: _____

  3. People: round faces, diamond-shaped faces, rectangular faces, square faces, triangular faces
  Principle of classification: _____

  4. People: dark hair, blond hair, red hair
  Principle of classification: _____

  5. Drivers: very careful, careful, careless, reckless
  Principle of classification: _____

  6. Bats: plant eaters, blood eaters, fish eaters
  Principle of classification: _____

  7. Burns: first-degree, second-degree, third-degree
  Principle of classification: _____

  8. People: U.S. citizens, permanent legal residents, illegal residents
  Principle of classification: _____

3. Fill in the blanks using the following transition words. Each word can be used only once.

a good example	in addition to	third
besides	last	typical of
first	next	whereas
fourth	on the other hand	

According to Dr. Li Tao in his book *How to Read Faces*, people can be divided into two broad categories: those who are mentally inclined and those who are firmly practical. Mind-oriented people have balanced faces that can be divided into three roughly equal sections. **1.**_____, physical types tend to have larger jaws and shorter faces. **2.**_____ these two broad categories, Dr. Tao divides faces into five basic shapes. The **3.**_____ is the round face with strong bone structure. It is **4.**_____ a mentally active person with self-confidence, resistance to illness, and a potentially long life. **5.**_____ is the diamond-shaped face, which indicates a generally warm, strong-willed, and lucky person. **6.**_____ is the rectangular face, and **7.**_____ is the square face. **8.**_____, the rectangular face indicates creativity, intelligence, and self-control, the square face belongs to an honest, well-balanced person with leadership qualities. **9.**_____ is the triangular face, with its wide forehead, prominent cheekbones, and pointed chin. **10.**_____ having a brilliant and sensual temperament, the triangular-faced person is intelligent and ambitious. **11.**_____ of such a person is the famous Elizabeth of Austria.

Writing Model: The Classification Essay

Read the following classification essay written by a student.

Classifying Personalities by Way of Astrology

1   The ancient Greek scientists observed the dazzling stars in the sky
and created basic astronomy. They named each constellation after the
characteristics of Greek gods. They used the 12 signs that appear in different
periods in a year cycle to represent 12 human personalities. The 12 signs
5   are Aries, Taurus, Gemini, Cancer, Leo, Virgo, Libra, Scorpio, Sagittarius,
Capricorn, Aquarius, and Pisces. Each sign projects the character and
personality of one specific Greek god. The person born under a certain sign
has a personality related to the characteristics of that Greek god. These 12
astrological signs can be classified into the four elements in this world, which
10   are wind, earth, fire, and water.

The three signs in the first category are Gemini, Libra, and Aquarius. The
characteristics of this element are just like the name of the element, wind.
The people in this category are natural-born debaters. Their skills allow them
to have more advantages than others in their careers and enable them to
15   overcome difficulties easily. A lot of people in this element are often important
people in big companies. They are remarkable people compared to other
groups. People in this category do not like steady jobs; they like work with
challenges and prefer exciting jobs. Nobody knows what is going on inside
their heads, just as you cannot catch the wind.

20   The second element, earth, includes the signs of Taurus, Virgo, and
Capricorn. People born in this element have a rooted mind. They do not
change their minds after making decisions. Their personality can be described

as solid or immovable. Earth people usually exhibit a lot of patience. They can keep doing the same thing for years and often manage their lives into routines. Since they prefer doing stable tasks, they can often be found working for the government. These people are obstinate as stones, but show higher loyalty to what they are doing than other groups. Earth people are often reliable partners in life.

Fire, the third element, includes the astrological signs of Aries, Leo, and Sagittarius. People born under this element tend to hurry and do not have a lot of patience. In the battle of their lives, they like to charge ahead and take their enemy's position. They also have a strong desire for success. Because of their personalities, they become leaders of groups. Also, since they are not afraid of taking risks, they often become pioneers in new fields such as explorers and inventors. Fire people are fighter types.

The last in the four elements is water, which includes the signs of Cancer, Scorpio, and Pisces. People in these three astrological signs have sensitive feelings in the areas of emotions and love. They are born with talent in the field of art. Many artists, poets, sculptors, and musicians belong to one of these three signs. They use their natural-born skills to create many delicate articles of brilliance unequaled by their contemporaries. The way they express themselves is as soft and tender as water. Water people often may be the closest friends or relatives in one's life. They are often perfect lovers, and there are many romantic stories about water people.

Classifying personality by using the four elements is not a foolproof method, and there are many exceptions. A person with the element water may have an impatient personality as in the element fire; a fire person may be interested in the field of art or music; a person in the element of wind may enjoy working in a steady job; and an earth person may have multiple lifestyles. Psychiatrists use many techniques to classify human personality. Although using astrological signs and the elements is a way of classifying human personality, there is not much evidence to support it since we have multiple personalities in general—but it is a fun way of classifying personality.

Hsing Chueh
Taiwan

Student Essay Follow-Up

1. Underline the thesis statement.
2. How does the writer classify astrological signs?
3. What signs are in the first category, and what are the characteristics of the first category? What signs are in the second category, and what are the characteristics of the second category? What signs are in the third group, and what are the characteristics of the third group? What signs are in the fourth group, and what are the characteristics of the fourth group?
4. Does the writer use supporting examples for each element?
5. Do all the members of your class fall under one of the elements?

Writing Practice

A. Write a Classification Essay

Write a classification essay on one of the following topics. In your essay, try to include **3** or more vocabulary words from the readings in this chapter.

1. Write an essay about major types of food, using a principle of classification.
2. Write an essay classifying people by the way they dress. Establish your principle of classification and give examples of each group.
3. Write an essay classifying your friends into 3 or 4 major categories.

B. Pre-Write

Work alone, with a partner, or in a group.

1. Brainstorm the topic. Look at pages 254–256 to find out about brainstorming. Choose a pre-writing technique you prefer.
2. Brainstorm for a principle of classification that includes all the members of the group. Do not have more than 5 categories, since you need to write a paragraph on each.
3. Work on a thesis statement.

C. Outline

1. Organize your ideas.

   Step 1: Write your thesis statement using parallel structure.

   Step 2: Identify each category, defining or describing it.

   Step 3: Give examples and specific details for each category.

2. Make a more detailed outline. The essay form on page 21 will help you.

D. Write a Rough Draft

Look at page 257 to find out about writing a rough draft.

E. Revise Your Draft

Use the Revision Checklist on page 258.

F. Edit Your Essay

Use the Editing Checklist on page 259. Check your work for faulty parallel structures.

Example:

//st

Error:	There are three main skills a writer has to learn: <u>to organize ideas correctly, logical thought, and clear expression of ideas</u>.
Correct:	There are three main skills a writer has to learn: to organize ideas correctly, to think logically, and to express ideas clearly.

When you find a mistake of this type, you can write the symbol "//st" (faulty parallel structure). Look at page 260 for other symbols to use when editing your work.

G. Write Your Final Copy

When your rough draft has been edited, you can write the final copy of your essay.

Additional Writing Practice

A. Summarize

Write a one-paragraph summary of Reading 1. Compare your summary to the Summary Checklist on page 269.

B. Paraphrase

Paraphrase paragraph 4 in Reading 2. Look at pages 264–267 to find out about paraphrasing. Begin with either "According to Burger,…" or "Based on Burger's chapter,…."

C. Research

Choose a particular subject that can be classified into 3 to 5 groups. Consult appropriate sources in the library, and/or use your own experience or that of your friends to gather information.

The following are suggested topics:

- Blood groups
- Personality types
- People's looks
- Political groups
- Socioeconomic groups
- Types of emotions
- Types of pollution
- Types of TV shows
- Types of wars

You may use your research later to write a classification essay.

Weaving It Together

⏱ Timed Writing

Choose one of the following topics that you have not already written about in "Writing Practice," or choose the topic that you have researched. You have 50 minutes to write a classification essay.

1. Write an essay about major types of food, using a principle of classification.
2. Write an essay classifying people by the way they dress. Establish your principle of classification and give examples of each group.
3. Write an essay classifying your friends into 3 or 4 major categories.
4. Write a classification essay on the topic you researched.

Connecting to the Internet

A. Find a "free personality test" on the Internet. What type of personality do you have, according to the test?

B. Look up "personality theories" on the Internet. Find additional theories about the classification of personalities (for example, type A and type B; Carl Jung's Psychological Types; David Keirsey's "temperament sorter"; Katherine Benziger's Brain Type Theory; and the "Big Five" personality model, etc.). Write about how personalities are classified in one of these theories.

What Do You Think Now?

Refer to page 116 at the beginning of this unit. Do you know the answers now? Complete the sentence or circle the best answer.

1. There is/isn't proof that the shape of your body and your character are connected.
2. Muscular people are/are not always dominant.
3. Introverts are/aren't more responsive to caffeine than extraverts.
4. _____ do not like crowded social gatherings.
5. _____ are bored with soft music.

6 Gender

What Do You Think?

Answer the questions with your best guess. Circle **Yes** or **No**.

Do you think . . .

		Yes	No
1.	men talk more than women?	Yes	No
2.	men and women have different ways of communicating online?	Yes	No
3.	women send more e-mails than men do?	Yes	No
4.	in Russia, most doctors are men?	Yes	No
5.	in traditional societies in sub-Saharan Africa and South America, women do most of the heavy work?	Yes	No

Pre-Reading

1. Discuss the answers to these questions with your classmates.

    1. What are some ways in which males and females think and act differently?

    2. Do you think boys and girls are born different, or taught to be different?

    3. Do you think most people have set ideas about male and female characteristics? Do you?

2. Which of these stereotypes are commonly associated with men and which with women? Write **M** in the blank if you think it is a trait characteristic of men. Write **F** in the blank if you think it is characteristic of women.

_____ aggressive

_____ ambitious

_____ dependent

_____ direct

_____ gentle

_____ logical

_____ self-confident

_____ tactful

_____ talkative

_____ unemotional

Reading 1

Males and Females: What's the Difference?

CD 2, Track 1

1   **I**s it true that men don't ask for directions? Do women talk more than men? Are men more jealous than women? Who likes the color red? Is there more to the difference between males and females than meets the eye? The answers are *yes, no, yes, males,* and a resounding yes! Of course, these are
5   generalizations. They don't apply to all men or all women. However, after decades of study, scientists and researchers have concluded that there are important differences in the way males and females think, speak, and act; in their values and habits; in what makes them laugh and what makes them cry. And they know that these differences are true across countries, cultures,
10   ages, and other factors.

Does this sound like something you've known all along? It may, but not everyone has agreed with that. Over the years, there have been varying opinions on this subject. In the 1960s and 1970s, when women were fighting for equality, many people said that males and females were not different
15   beyond the physical. They gave dolls to boys and trucks to girls. They said that society taught girls and boys to behave differently. In one way, they were right. Males and females are basically alike. We're all human, after all. And society certainly does affect our thinking and behavior. Nevertheless, researchers now know that there are distinct differences between males and
20   females that are not just social. They know for sure that not only are men's and women's brains different but that they use their brains differently as well!

If you think that boys and girls are different from birth, you're right. From the time they're born, boys and girls differ in the way they function and the way their brain works. Boy babies are more interested in objects than in
25   people. Girl babies respond to the human voice more than boys do. At play, little girls naturally practice carrying infants. On the other hand, little boys play more actively and aggressively. Researchers agreed a long time ago that girls have better language abilities than boys. But now they know that

it's all in their heads—that is, their brains. Both areas of the brain that deal with language work harder in girls than in boys. Also, girls use different parts of the brain when performing language tasks. Boys, however, are better at solving technical problems and have better math skills.

Recently, scientists and researchers have come up with a number of interesting differences between males and females. These differences are in ways as simple as color preferences and as complicated as memory. If you're a female who likes pink or a male who likes yellow, you won't be surprised to hear that it comes naturally. As it turns out, men prefer bright-colored things like yellow and red, whereas women prefer soft colors like pink and aqua. But if you've always thought that women talk more than men, you're wrong. Most men probably wouldn't agree with this statement. But after decades of study, research has shown that men talk more than women overall. And while a woman talks to create a relationship with the listener, men on the other hand try to influence the listener. Men, it seems, are always trying to make their point! And they probably think they're right, too, because men are more self-assured, more self-centered, and more satisfied with their performance than women. Women are more critical of themselves and less self-assured. But all that self-doubt doesn't seem to make them sick. While women worry more about their health, men actually get sick twice as often. As to who is more forgiving, studies show that men are more vengeful and less forgiving than women. That's in spite of the fact that a woman is more likely to remember the wrongdoing! Whereas women are better at remembering faces and events, men can remember more symbolic and spatial things, such as how to find their way back from a place they've driven to. It's amusing to think about how some of these studies have proven what men and women have known all along. While men are better at finding their way or fixing a car, women are better at fixing friendships.

One of the biggest ways in which men and women are different is in how they communicate. Girls use language to get closer to others, to make friends. Language is used in a cooperative way. However, boys use language to establish their position among others. Language is used for competition. Both males and females carry these ways of using language into adulthood. This is true for all situations: in the home, at work, in personal and formal situations, in meetings, or at social functions. Women cooperate to bring about understanding. In contrast, men use power to negotiate their status. Recently, researchers were surprised to discover that this difference carries over into e-mail communication and Internet postings in chat rooms.

At first, researchers thought that language differences would be less or even disappear in an Internet environment. After all, there's no physical interaction. Writers don't hear or see one another. So the playing field is quite equal. But as it turned out, they discovered that women and men have very different online ways of communicating. And these ways reflect exactly how they use language in their lives.

The language of males is adversarial. They use put-downs, like "Get a life," or "You must be dreaming!" or "Have you lost it?" They make strong statements, too: "It's a fact that . . . ," or "Here's what I know." They send more e-mails than women and they're longer. Men also use language that is self-promoting, such as, "I happen to be an expert on this subject." And they often use sarcasm, like "Yeah, right," or "Sure, and the moon's made of cheese."

On the other hand, females generally use language that is supportive, like "I'm sure you can do it." They express gratitude, such as, "Thanks for all your much-appreciated help," or "Thanks so much for the great advice." Not only do women apologize more, such as, "I'm sorry I haven't been in touch," or "I apologize if I sounded harsh," but they also express doubt and make self-conscious statements like: "I'm not sure I'm right about this, but . . ." Women ask more questions. And when they offer an idea or opinion, it's usually in the form of a suggestion, such as, "I think it might help you if . . .," or "I suggest you . . ."

After extensive study, researchers have concluded that all in all, men use language that is aggressive, competitive, and dominating, whereas women offer support and friendship. Furthermore, they believe that the different ways in which men and women use language in e-mails is a result of their different goals. Men see Internet technology as a way to influence others and extend their authority and respect. On the other hand, women use it to strengthen existing friendships and make new ones.

Men and women have always known they are different. Men have thought long and hard about that, just as women have. It's what brings them together—and also gives them headaches! Knowing that boys and girls learn and communicate differently helps educators to teach more effectively. Studying how men and women respond to drugs, pain, and infections can help doctors treat them better. And, of course, knowing how the male and female brains differ can help everyone to understand each other better.

Vocabulary

A. Vocabulary in Context

Select the letter of the answer that is closest in meaning to the **bold** word or phrase.

1. The answers are *yes*, *no*, *yes*, *males*, and a **resounding** *yes*!
   a. deep
   b. loud
   c. exciting
   d. demanding

2. Scientists and researchers have **come up with** a number of interesting differences.
   a. created
   b. determined
   c. furnished
   d. designed

3. Research has shown that men talk more than women **overall**.
   a. most likely
   b. preferably
   c. generally
   d. undoubtedly

4. Men, it seems, are always trying to **make their point**!
   a. assert their ideas and opinions
   b. give purpose to their actions
   c. give directions to a place
   d. hold others to blame

5. Men can remember more symbolic and **spatial** things.
   a. something in a physical location
   b. something in a period of time
   c. an idea or attitude
   d. something in the mind or imagination

6. Women cooperate to **bring about** understanding.
   a. suggest
   b. take on
   c. prevent
   d. cause

7. Men use power to negotiate their **status**.
   a. duty or occupation
   b. ability or talent
   c. character or personality
   d. rank or position

Word Partnership	Use **status** with:
v.	achieve status, maintain/preserve one's status,
n.	celebrity status, wealth and status, change of status
adj.	marital status, tax status, current status, economic status, financial status

8. This difference carries over into e-mail communication and **Internet postings**.
   a. personal communications between two people on the Internet
   b. statements put on the Internet for the everyone to read
   c. work-related statements among workers on company computers
   d. government-controlled information on the Internet

9. The language of males is **adversarial**.
   a. supportive
   b. uncertain
   c. competitive
   d. friendly

10. They use **put-downs**.
   a. statements meant to confuse
   b. statements meant to shame
   c. statements meant to be helpful
   d. statements meant to entertain

B. Vocabulary Building

1. A compound adjective is often made by joining a past participle, or adjective ending in –ed, to another word using a hyphen, such as a *level-headed woman*. Complete the sentences, using a compound adjective from the reading.

   1. A person who is concerned only with his own wants and needs is self-_____.
   2. A person who is nervous because she thinks everyone is looking at her is self-_____.
   3. A person who is confident because he is sure of his own abilities is self-_____.
   4. If you recognize something for its good qualities, it is much-_____.
   5. Things with strong, noticeable colors are bright-_____.

2. Make two more compound adjectives starting with these words:

   bright-_____   bright-_____
   much-_____   much-_____
   self-_____   self-_____

C. Vocabulary in New Context

Make sentences using the compound adjectives in Part B, Exercise 2.

Reading Comprehension

A. Looking for the Main Ideas

Answer the following questions with complete sentences.

1. What is the main idea of paragraph 2?
2. Which line states the main idea of paragraph 3?
3. Which sentences contain the main idea of paragraph 4?
4. What is paragraph 6 mainly about?

B. Skimming and Scanning for Details

Scan the reading quickly to complete the following sentences. Circle the letter of the best answer.

1. According to the reading, many people in the 1960s and 1970s believed that _____.

   a. society had very little influence on girls and boys
   b. boys and girls had vast differences in their abilities
   c. boys and girls were not different physically
   d. boys and girls should not be treated equally

2. The reading states that men prefer _____.
   a. bright colors
   b. pale colors
   c. aqua
   d. green

3. According to the reading, researchers have long agreed that girls have better _____ than boys.
   a. language abilities
   b. memories
   c. math skills
   d. technical skills

4. According to the reading, women talk in order to _____ the listener.
   a. find out their status with
   b. give forceful opinions to
   c. influence
   d. create a relationship with

5. The reading states that men are better at remembering _____.
   a. faces
   b. emotions
   c. locations
   d. events

6. According to the reading, women tend to _____ others more than men do.
   a. forget
   b. convince
   c. take revenge against
   d. forgive

7. The writer states that both males and females _____.
   a. change the way they use language as they get older
   b. carry their use of language into adulthood
   c. use language in the same ways
   d. use their brains in the same way when processing language

8. According to the reading, researchers thought that differences in language use would _____ in an Internet environment.
   a. be greater
   b. not exist
   c. not matter
   d. cause problems

9. The reading states that when women write e-mails, they _____ more than men.
   a. make jokes
   b. use strong language
   c. apologize
   d. use sarcasm

10. Researchers have reached the conclusion that in general, men use language that _____.
   a. is aggressive and competitive
   b. is supportive of others
   c. makes and strengthens friendships
   d. shows respect

C. Making Inferences and Drawing Conclusions

Some of the following statements are facts from the reading. Other statements can be inferred from the reading. Circle the number of each statement that can be inferred.

1. A man in Denmark and a man in Athens would both use language in the same way.
2. The parts of the brain that deal with language work harder in girls than in boys.
3. A boy would probably learn to calculate miles per gallon more quickly than a girl.
4. Men talk more than women in most situations.
5. Women are more likely to remember the details of their best friend's wedding.

6. Differences in language use don't change in an Internet setting.

7. Men are less apt to send short thank-you notes in e-mails than women are.

8. Men regard Internet technology as a means of influencing others.

9. Women offer their ideas and opinions in the form of suggestions.

10. Advertisers would benefit from knowing how male and female brains differ.

Discussion Questions

Discuss the answers to these questions with your classmates.

1. Do you think that ideas about what men and women are like have changed over time? If yes, give examples of how they have changed and note whether the changes have been positive or negative for each gender. If you think ideas have not changed, explain why they haven't and if that is good or bad.

2. Do you think that studies of gender differences are helpful or harmful? Why?

3. What are some ways in which schools and businesses could use recent knowledge about the differences between men and women?

4. What can men and women learn from each other's differences?

Critical Thinking Questions

Discuss the answers to these questions with your classmates.

1. How can stereotypes about males and females negatively affect a child's life? Can they have a positive effect as well? How?

2. How has technology affected the way males and females think and act? Do you think there are fewer differences between males and females now than compared to 200 years ago? Why or why not? What changes do you think the future will bring?

3. What is gender discrimination? What are some common forms of gender discrimination in society, the workplace, and in schools? How can gender discrimination affect both males and females?

4. If you could create the "perfect" male and female, what character traits would they have, and why?

Reading 2

CD 2,
Track 2

Society and the Sexes

The following reading is reprinted from the college text Sociology, *by Craig Calhoun, Donald Light, and Suzanne Keller, McGraw-Hill Inc., Copyright 1994, pages 270–271. It compares and contrasts the roles of men and women in different cultures.*

1   **I**f gender characteristics were
simply a matter of biology, then
one would expect to find that
gender roles do not vary very

5   much from one culture to another.
But that is not the case. What
people consider masculine or
feminine behavior is actually quite
variable. Americans, for instance,

10   think of men as naturally stronger
and tougher than women and
better suited to perform the most
strenuous physical labor. In many
traditional societies, however,

15   particularly in sub-Saharan Africa
and South America, women do
most of the heavy work—carrying
goods to market, hauling firewood,
and constructing houses. Men

20   hunt—and spend a lot of time
talking. Similarly, in the United States, most doctors are men; in Russia most
are women. Among some people men are the main storytellers; among
others women are. Among some peoples agriculture is restricted to men,
in some societies farming is regarded as women's work, and in still others

men and women work in the fields side by side. Whatever innate biological differences exist between men and women, they allow for wide variation in actual social life.

The anthropologist Margaret Mead (1935–1963) was one of the first to study societies whose gender arrangements differ from our own. In three neighboring New Guinea tribes, she found evidence of aggression in women, passivity in men, and minimal differences in roles of men and women. According to Mead, the mild-mannered Arapesh expected both sexes to be gentle, cooperative, and maternal. In contrast, the neighboring Mundugumor believed both sexes were fierce, combative, and selfish. Both men and women exhibited exaggerated machismo, or compulsive masculinity, involving posturing, boasting, and an exploitative attitude. In the third tribe, the Tchambuli, ideals of masculinity and femininity were the opposite of ours. Women were the primary food providers for their families, shaved their heads, wore no ornaments, and dominated their men. The men were preoccupied with beauty and romance, and spent their days primping and gossiping.

Mead took a relatively extreme position on the issue of social construction of gender. As she wrote, "Many, if not all, of the personality traits which we have called masculine or feminine are as lightly linked to sex as are the clothing, the manners, and the form of head-dress that a society at a given period assigns to either sex . . . [T]he evidence is overwhelming in favor of the strength of social conditioning" (in Chafetz, 1970, p. 260). While no sociologist believes that biology completely determines gender roles, many believe that there is more cross-cultural consistency in male and female roles than Mead indicated. In hunting and gathering societies all over the world, for example, men are nearly always the hunters (Lenski, Lenski, and Nolan, 1991).

Furthermore, in nearly every culture gender roles are structured so that the skills and traits that are considered masculine are valued more highly than those considered feminine (Chafetz, 1984). Mead (1968) recognized this and summed it up nicely: There are societies where men farm and women fish, and societies where men fish and women farm; but whatever form the division of labor takes, the man's jobs are considered vitally important and the woman's tasks are viewed as routine and mundane. For example, before the Industrial Revolution in England, spinning was seen as women's work and weaving was men's work; weaving was better paid. When spinning machines were introduced, however, men claimed the right to operate them because they were the high technology of the day and their operators were paid better than hand spinners or weavers. As weaving was devalued, more women became weavers (Pinchbeck, 1930; Thompson, 1968).

65   Cross-cultural comparisons, thus, show that there is a wide range of variation in what different cultures consider to be "male" or "female," "masculine" or "feminine." At first men were able to dominate women because they were physically stronger—a biological difference. The longer this domination went on, however, the more resources men could accumulate
70   and thus the greater the inequality between men and women became. Male dominance became part of the social structure, supported by cultural norms and values as well as physical force, or power.

Vocabulary

A. Vocabulary in Context

Look at the reading to help you choose the best answer to each of the following questions.

1. Which adjective in paragraph 1 means "involving a lot of energy or effort"?

2. What does the word **hauling** in paragraph 1 mean?
a. carrying
b. cutting
c. pressing
d. pushing

3. Which word is closest in meaning to **innate** in paragraph 1?
a. strange
b. native
c. natural
d. learned

4. Which of these statements is true?
a. A *combative* person is eager to fight.
b. *Combative* means rough.
c. A *combative* person is always noisy.
d. *Negative* has the same meaning as *combative*.

5. What is another way of saying **boasting**?
a. showing off one's body
b. praising oneself
c. being violent
d. making fun of others

6. Which of these statements is true?

   a. *Exploitative* means self-satisfied.

   b. An *exploitative* person is someone who travels to unknown places.

   c. An *exploitative* person uses others to his/her advantage.

   d. *Exploitative* has the same meaning as *cheerful*.

7. Which word is closest in meaning to **primping** in paragraph 2?

   a. grooming themselves

   b. giggling

   c. getting together

   d. preparing food

8. What does the phrase **preoccupied with** in paragraph 2 mean?

   a. getting away from

   b. making fun of

   c. always thinking about

   d. taking chances with

9. Which of the following could substitute for **assigns** in paragraph 3?

   a. attaches

   b. designates

   c. details

   d. hires

10. Which word in paragraph 4 means "ordinary" or "commonplace"?

B. Vocabulary Building

1. Match the adjectives with nouns as they were used in the context of the reading. Look back at the reading to check your answers. Add two more nouns that may be used with each adjective.

   a. traits   c. life   e. roles

   b. societies   d. norms   f. force

1. __c__ social   ____life____   _____   _____

2. ____ gender   _____   _____   _____

3. ____ cultural   _____   _____   _____

4. ____ personality _____   _____   _____

5. ____ traditional _____   _____   _____

6. ____ physical   _____   _____   _____

2. Use the adjectives and nouns you listed in Exercise 1 to complete these sentences about men and women. Then look back at the reading to help you check your answers.

1. Since _____ change from one culture to another, sociologists believe that male and female characteristics are not only a matter of biology.

2. In many _____ women do most of the hard work, such as farming and making houses.

3. Physical differences don't prevent a wide diversity in the _____ of men and women.

4. _____ was an early cause of the dominance of males over females.

5. Mead believed that masculine and feminine _____ were not strongly linked to the physical differences between the sexes.

6. _____ and values supported the idea of male dominance as part of the social structure.

C. Vocabulary in New Context

Now make new sentences using the adjective and noun combinations you chose in Part B, Exercise 1.

Reading Comprehension

A. Looking for the Main Ideas

Some of the following statements from the reading are main ideas, and some are supporting statements. Write **M** in the blank in front of each main idea. Write **S** in front of each supporting statement.

_____ **1.** What people consider masculine or feminine behavior is actually quite variable.

_____ **2.** Americans think of men as naturally stronger and tougher than women.

_____ **3.** Among some peoples, agriculture is restricted to men; in some societies farming is regarded as women's work.

_____ **4.** According to Mead, the mild-mannered Arapesh expected both sexes to be gentle, cooperative, and maternal.

_____ **5.** In the third tribe, the Tchambuli, ideals of masculinity and femininity were the opposite of ours.

_____ **6.** Mead took a relatively extreme position on the issue of social construction of gender.

_____ **7.** In nearly every culture gender roles are structured so that the skills and traits that are considered masculine are valued more highly than those considered feminine.

_____ **8.** Before the Industrial Revolution in England, spinning was seen as women's work and weaving was men's work; weaving was better paid.

_____ **9.** Cross-cultural comparisons show that there is a wide range of variation in what different cultures consider to be "male" or "female," "masculine" or "feminine."

_____ **10.** Male dominance became part of the social structure, supported by cultural norms and values as well as physical force, or power.

B. Skimming and Scanning for Details

Scan the reading quickly to complete the following sentences.

1. In many traditional societies, women do most of the heavy work, such as _____ and _____.

2. In the United States, most doctors are men; in _____, most are women.

3. Margaret Mead was one of the first anthropologists to study societies whose _____.

4. Mead studies three neighboring tribes in _____.

5. In the Mundugumor tribe, men and women exhibited compulsive masculinity, involving _____, _____, and an _____.

6. The Tchambuli men were preoccupied with _____ and _____.

7. In hunting and gathering societies around the world, men are nearly always the _____.

8. Mead wrote that whatever form the division of labor takes, the man's jobs are considered vitally important and the woman's tasks are viewed as _____ and _____.

9. When _____ were introduced in England, men claimed the right to operate them.

10. The longer male domination went on, the more _____ men could accumulate.

C. Making Inferences and Drawing Conclusions

Some of the following statements are facts taken from the reading. Other statements can be inferred from the reading. Write **F** in the blank in front of each factual statement. Write **I** in front of each inference.

_____ 1. Depending on the culture, storytellers can be men or women.

_____ 2. In America, you would be more likely to find a man working in construction than a woman.

_____ 3. In many traditional societies, physical strength isn't the most important factor in the division of labor between men and women.

_____ 4. Physical environment doesn't appear to have much influence on gender arrangements among various cultures.

_____ 5. In the Tchambuli tribe, women dominated the men.

_____ 6. Mead would disagree with the idea that male and female brains cause differences in their behavior.

_____ 7. Sociologists do not believe that the biology of males and females completely determines gender roles.

_____ 8. With the introduction of spinning machines, men left weaving to the women.

_____ 9. The acceptance of male domination in society has allowed inequalities to exist for millennia.

_____ 10. Cross-cultural comparisons indicate that there is wide variation in what different cultures consider to be masculine or feminine.

Discussion Questions

Discuss the answers to these questions with your classmates.

1. In your country, what are the gender arrangements? What is considered masculine and feminine behavior, and what tasks are traditionally done by men and women?
2. Is society better off with distinct roles and differences between the sexes, or is it better when the sexes are treated more equally?
3. *Vive la difference!* is a French expression that means we should accept, even celebrate, the differences between men and women. Do you agree or disagree with this idea? Why or why not?
4. In which New Guinea tribe would you prefer to live? Why? If you could create an ideal world, what would the gender arrangements be?

Critical Thinking Questions

Discuss the answers to these questions with your classmates.

1. How do the two readings compare in terms of what they say about gender differences? Does one disprove the other? Which position do you agree with more: Mead's idea that social conditioning determines male and female behavior, or recent ideas that our brains influence male and female thoughts and actions? Why?
2. Historically when women did a job, it was valued less highly than when men did it. Does this attitude still prevail today? What are some examples of jobs that men once did that became "women's work"? Why are women often paid less for doing the same job as men? Do you believe in laws that guarantee "equal pay for equal work"? Why or why not?
3. We live in an age in which women are astronauts, research scientists, and heads of state in some countries, while being denied basic rights, such as voting and education, in others. What are the beliefs and traditions that account for these differences among countries and cultures? Do you believe these differences will always exist? Why or why not?

Writing

Writing Skills

A. Organizing: *Comparison and Contrast*

Comparison and contrast is a very useful and common method of essay organization. Many college essay assignments require you to compare and contrast ideas, theories, facts, characters, principles, and so on. In your personal life, too, you find similarities and differences in a whole array of things, from the products you buy to the friends you make and the jobs you get.

When you *compare* two items, you show how aspects of one item are similar to aspects of another. A comparison tells you what features are *similar*.

When you *contrast* two items, you show the differences between them. You point out the features that are not alike or are *different*.

Finding Two Comparable Items

To make a comparison, you need to choose two items that share a similar feature or have the same function. In Reading 1, the way men and women think, speak, and act are compared. In Reading 2, gender roles in different societies are compared. It would not be a good idea to compare a soldier with a homemaker. However, two kinds of homemakers could be compared and contrasted.

Basis of Comparison

The basis of comparison is an important aspect of the organization and development of a comparison-and-contrast essay. When comparing two items, you must compare the same aspects of each. For example, in comparing two people, the basis of comparison could be appearance, behavior, or personality. Whatever bases of comparison you choose, you must use the same ones to discuss each person. You cannot compare the personality of one person to the appearance of the other.

As an example, here are some of the possible bases for comparing two universities:

Basis of Comparison	University A	University B
size	large	small
location	rural	urban
reputation	affordable	expensive
specialty	engineering	the arts

Thesis Statement

In a comparison-and-contrast essay, you may want to compare and contrast two items to show that one is better than the other, that the two are totally different, or that they have some similarities and some differences. Purposes will vary.

The thesis statement for a comparison-and-contrast essay should include the names of the two items being compared and the dominant impression of each item.

Example:

University A is a better choice for me than University B because of its size, location, reputation, and specialty.

Organizing a Comparison-and-Contrast Essay

There are two basic ways to organize a comparison-and-contrast essay:

1. Block organization
2. Point-by-point organization

In block organization, one item, such as University A, is discussed in one block (one or more paragraphs), and the other is discussed in another block.

In point-by-point organization, similarities and differences on the same point are discussed together: In Reading 1, boys' and girls' brains are discussed in paragraph 3; and in paragraph 5, how men and women communicate is discussed. In Reading 2, gender roles are compared in tribes in New Guinea, and so on.

Imagine you were going to write a comparison-and-contrast essay about two male or female acquaintances or friends. The following outlines show how you might organize your essay using either the block or the point-by-point approach.

Block Organization Outline

Topic: A comparison and contrast of two female best friends, Nancy and Karen

Thesis Statement: Nancy and Karen are best friends and have similarities and differences in their looks, personality, and physical strength.

   I. Nancy
      A. Looks
      B. Personality
      C. Physical Strength
  II. Karen
      A. Looks
      B. Personality
      C. Physical Strength

Conclusion

Point-by-Point Organization Outline

Topic: A comparison and contrast of two female best friends, Nancy and Karen

Thesis Statement: Nancy and Karen are best friends and have similarities and differences in their looks, personality, and physical strength.

   I. Looks
      A. Nancy (tall, dark, strong)
      B. Karen (blond, not tall, frail)
  II. Personality
      A. Nancy (not afraid, very friendly)
      B. Karen (very shy, afraid to talk)
 III. Physical Strength
      A. Nancy (strong, plays sports with the boys)
      B. Karen (not strong, afraid of any physical sports)

Conclusion

As you can see, the block organization is simpler because fewer transitions are required and one subject is discussed completely before going on to the other. The point-by-point organization, in which similarities and differences of each point are discussed together, requires repeated use of comparison-and-contrast indicators.

Comparison-and-Contrast Indicators

A good comparison-and-contrast essay is sprinkled with comparison-and-contrast indicators, or structure words. The following is a list of some of these structure words.

Comparison Indicators

Sentence Connectors	Clause Connectors	Others
also	and	(be) similar to
likewise	as	(be) the same as
similarly	just as	both . . . and
		just like (+ noun)
		like (+ noun)
		not only . . . but also
		similar to (+ noun)

Contrast Indicators

Sentence Connectors	Clause Connectors	Others
however	although	but
in contrast	even though	despite (+ noun)
nevertheless	whereas	in spite of (+ noun)
on the other hand	while	yet
on the contrary		

B. Exercises

1. Underline all the comparison indicators in Reading 1 and Reading 2. Then, circle all the contrast indicators in Reading 1 and Reading 2.

2. Work with a partner. Write the names of two examples for each group. Say why the examples could be compared.

1. fast-food restaurants: _____ _____

2. amusement parks: _____ _____

3. computers: _____ _____

4. cars: _____ _____

3. Join the two sentences using the comparison or contrast word indicated. Make any necessary changes. The first one is done for you.

1. *although*

Most people think women talk more than men. Research has shown that men actually talk more than women overall.

Although most people think women talk more than men, research has shown that men actually talk more than women overall.

2. *whereas*

Boys use language for competition. Girls use language to make friendships.

3. *likewise*

Gender studies help educators teach more effectively. Gender studies help doctors treat patients better.

4. *just as*

Girls naturally practice carrying infants. Boys naturally play more aggressively.

5. *however*

Males and females are basically alike. Researchers have found some real and distinct differences between the sexes.

6. *in contrast*

The online language of males is adversarial. Females use language that is supportive.

7. *on the other hand*

Men are good at remembering symbolic and spatial things. Women are good at remembering faces and events.

8. *while*

Girls have an ability for language. Boys are good at solving technical problems.

9. *nevertheless*

Society does influence the thinking and behavior of males and females. Research has shown that gender differences are not just social.

10. *in contrast*

Women use the Internet to strengthen or make new friendships. Men use Internet technology to influence others and extend their authority.

Writing Model: The Comparison-and-Contrast Essay

Read the following comparison-and-contrast essay written by a student.

Comparing and Contrasting Male and Female Family Members

1   In my family, there are three women and three men. The three women are my mother, my sister, and me. The men are my father and my two brothers. From my own experience and observations, there are similarities and differences in the behavior of males and females in my family in regard to how

5   they communicate, what they communicate, and the way they shop.

When it comes to communicating, there are similarities and differences. Both the males and females go online to communicate with their friends. However, I noticed that the males are always looking at their messages and sending messages much more than the women. When communicating by

10   phone, it seems the women like to talk on the phone more than the men, especially my teenage sister. It's rare to find her not talking to her friends on the phone. Also, when men talk, they communicate more directly, almost like giving orders. Whereas, the women in the family we are much more indirect. Instead of "yes," my mother will write or say, "I think so."

15   The content of the conversations on the phone has similarities and differences too. Both the male and female members of my family talk to their friends on the phone. The women, I think, have a need to talk to a friend on the phone when they have the slightest problem. They talk about how they feel and show understanding if their friends have a problem. The women talk

20   about friends, their weight, food, clothes, and other women. On the other hand, my father or my brothers don't talk to their male friends for emotional support. When they have a conversation with a friend, they always joke a lot, and talk about things like sports, work, or politics.

Males and females in our family shop differently too. When my mother, sister, or I go shopping, it is like an outing; it's a fun thing to do just like for some men it is exciting and fun to go to a sports event. We, the females, love to shop. We go all around the stores and look and try everything, even if we don't buy anything. We go shopping not to buy, but just to look around as if it is a kind of entertainment, while the men in our family only go shopping when they need something. They go in the store, pick out the thing they need, and then leave right away.

In conclusion, there are similarities and differences in the way the male and female members of my family do things such as how and what they communicate and the way they shop. These are my own, personal observations of male and female differences in my family and may not be the same in other families or for others around the world. No matter what, it is good that we are different. *Vive la difference!*

Miranda
Peru

Student Essay Follow-Up

1. Underline the thesis statement.
2. Underline the topic sentences.
3. In which format did Miranda organize her essay?
4. How do women and men differ in the online communication styles and in the telephone communication styles?
5. Find 3 comparison indictors and 3 contrast indictors used in the essay.

Writing Practice

A. Write a Comparison-and-Contrast Essay

Choose one of the following topics. In your essay, try to include **3** or more vocabulary words from the readings in this chapter.

1. Write a comparison-and-contrast essay about 2 people you know or know something about. Use 3 or 4 bases of comparison.
2. Write an essay about a place you know, comparing and contrasting the way it was at some time in the past to the way it is now.
3. Compare and contrast 2 groups of people in your native country. Compare their lifestyles, social status, and feelings toward each other.

B. Pre-Write

Work alone, with a partner, or in a group.

1. Brainstorm the topic. Look at pages 254–256 to find out about brainstorming. Choose a pre-writing technique you prefer.
2. Brainstorm for your bases of comparison and supporting ideas.
3. Work on a thesis statement.

C. Outline

1. Organize your ideas.

   Step 1: Write your thesis statement.

   Step 2: Select 3 or 4 bases of comparison from your brainstorming activity.

   Step 3: Find relevant supporting details for each point.

2. Make a more detailed outline. Choose between the block and point-by-point organization outlines on page 165.

D. Write a Rough Draft

Look at page 257 to find out about writing a rough draft.

E. Revise Your Draft

Use the Revision Checklist on page 258.

F. Edit Your Essay

Use the Editing Checklist on page 259. Check your work for faulty shifts in verb tense. These happen when you change tense within a sentence or paragraph for no significant reason.

Example:

Error:	Men and women <u>have always known</u> they are different. Men, just like women, <u>thought</u> long and hard about that.	*tns*
Correct:	Men and women have always known they are different. Men, just like women, have thought long and hard about that.	

When you find a mistake of this type, you can write the symbol "tns" (shift in verb tense). Look at page 260 for other symbols to use when editing your work.

G. Write Your Final Copy

When your rough draft has been edited, you can write the final copy of your essay.

Additional Writing Practice

A. Summarize

Write a one-paragraph summary of Reading 1. Check your summary against the Summary Checklist on page 269.

B. Paraphrase

Paraphrase paragraph 5 of Reading 2. Look at pages 264–267 to find out about paraphrasing. Begin paraphrasing with either "According to Calhoun, Light, and Keller, . . ." or "Based on Calhoun, Light, and Keller, . . ."

C. Research

Choose one of the topics suggested below. Choose 2 or 3 points of comparison. Use the library, the Internet, your own experience, or your friends' experience to gather information on the topic.

- Communication between men and women
- Shopping behavior of men and women
- Women in the 19th century and women in the 21st century
- Compare and contrast 2 famous men/women in the same field (such as Leonardo da Vinci and Michelangelo)

You may use your research later to write a comparison-and-contrast essay.

Weaving It Together

⏱ Timed Writing

Choose one of the following topics that you have not already written about in "Writing Practice," or choose the topic you researched. You have 50 minutes to write a comparison-and-contrast essay.

1. Write a comparison-and-contrast essay about 2 people you know or know something about. Use 3 or 4 bases of comparison.
2. Write an essay about a place you know, comparing and contrasting the way it was at some time in the past to the way it is now.
3. Compare and contrast 2 groups of people in your native country. Compare their lifestyles, social status, and feelings toward each other.
4. Write a comparison-and-contrast essay, using 3 points of comparison and contrast, about the topic you researched.

Connecting to the Internet

A. Use the Internet to do your own survey of text and e-mail messages among your friends, relatives, and acquaintances. Compare the language between the writings of males and females. Does your research agree with the findings in the first reading? Write about your findings.

B. Use the Internet to look up "gender roles" in various countries. Write a brief article comparing gender roles in two different cultures/countries. For example, compare an African and a Scandinavian country, the United States and a South American nation, an Asian and a European country, or a Middle Eastern and a North American culture.

What Do You Think Now?

Refer to page 145 at the beginning of this chapter. Do you know the answers now? Complete the sentence or circle the best answer.

1. Men talk/don't talk more than women.
2. Men and women have/don't have different ways of communicating online.
3. Women send/don't send more e-mails than men do.
4. In Russia, most doctors are _____.
5. In traditional societies in sub-Saharan Africa and South America, _____ do most of the heavy work.

7 Nutrition

INGREDIENTS: CRUST: ENRICHED FLOUR (FLOUR, NIACIN, FERROUS SULFATE, THIAMINE MONONITRATE, RIBOFLAVIN), WATER, HYDROGENATED SOYBEAN OIL, CONTAINS LESS THAN 2% OF THE FOLLOWING: DRY YEAST, SOY FLOUR, SALT, BAKING POWDER (MONOCALCIUM PHOSPHATE, BAKING SODA), DEXTROSE, SORBITAN MONOSTEARATE. **TOPPINGS:** COOKED PORK SAUSAGE (PORK, SALT, SPICE, NATURAL FLAVOR), MOZZARELLA AND PASTEURIZED PROCESS AMERICAN CHEESE SUBSTITUTES (MADE FROM WATER, CASEIN, HYDROGENATED SOYBEAN OIL, MALTODEXTRIN. CONTAINS LESS THAN 2% OF THE FOLLOWING: SODIUM ALUMINUM PHOSPHATE, SALT, LACTIC ACID, SODIUM CITRATE, SODIUM PHOSPHATE, ARTIFICIAL COLOR, SORBIC ACID (PRESERVATIVE), CITRIC ACID, ZINC OXIDE, FERRIC ORTHOPHOSPHATE, VITAMIN A PALMITATE, RIBOFLAVIN, FOLIC ACID, MAGNESIUM OXIDE, VITAMIN B6 HYDROCHLORIDE, NIACIN, THIAMINE MONONITRATE), PEPPERONI (PORK, MECHANICALLY SEPARATED PORK, BEEF, SALT, WATER, DEXTROSE, SPICE AND COLORING, LACTIC ACID STARTER CULTURE, GARLIC POWDER, SODIUM NITRITE, BHA AND BHT AND CITRIC ACID ADDED TO PROTECT FLAVOR, SMOKE FLAVOR. MAY ALSO CONTAIN BEEF STOCK), GREEN PEPPERS, ONIONS, COOK CHEESE (SKIM MILK, CHEESE CULTURE, CALCIUM CHLORIDE, ENZYMES), TEXTURED VEGETABLE PROTEIN (SOY FLOUR, CARAMEL COLOR), HYDROGENATED SOYBEAN OIL. **SAUCE:** TOMATO PUREE (WATER, TOMATO PASTE), WATER, SUGAR, MODIFIED CORN STARCH, SALT, SPICE, HYDROGENATED SOYBEAN OIL, BEET POWDER, XANTHAN GUM, NATURAL FLAVOR, ARTIFICIAL COLOR.

What Do You Think?

Answer the questions with your best guess. Circle **Yes** or **No**.

Do you think . . .

1. food in the old days was always pure?	**Yes**	**No**
2. artificial sweeteners are not dangerous to our health?	**Yes**	**No**
3. the average American eats 2 pounds of food additives per year?	**Yes**	**No**
4. Canada and the United States use BST, a growth hormone for cows to produce more milk?	**Yes**	**No**
5. Europe and the United Kingdom do not use BST, because it can be dangerous to humans?	**Yes**	**No**

Pre-Reading

1. Discuss the answers to these questions with your classmates.

   1. Why do products have labels?
   2. Do you know why it is important to read the labels on products?
   3. Do people use additives in food in your country?
   4. How long do you think additives have been used in food?

2. Match the labels to the products.

1.
MADE WITH WATER, ENRICHED FLOUR (BARLEY
MALT, NIACIN, IRON (FERROUS SULFATE) THIAMIN
MONONITRATE, RIBOFLAVIN), HIGH FRUCTOSE CORN
SYRUP, WHEAT GLUTEN, SOY FIBER, COTTONSEED FIBER,
CONTAINS 2% OR LESS OF: YEAST, CALCIUM SULFATE,
SALT, CORN BRAN, FLAVORS (NATURAL), SOY FLOUR,
CORN GRITS, ETHOXYLATED MONO- AND DIGLYCERIDES,
CELLULOSE GUM, MALTODEXTRIN, SODIUM STEAROYL
LACTYLATE, MONO- AND DIGLYCERIDES, YEAST
NUTRIENTS (AMMONIUM SULFATE), STARCH, VINEGAR,
SOY PROTEIN, PRESERVATIVES (CALCIUM PROPIONATE).

2.
CURED WITH WATER, HONEY, POTASSIUM LACTATE,
SALT, CARRAGEENAN, DEXTROSE, SODIUM PHOSPHATE,
SODIUM ERYTHROBATE, SODIUM NITRATE.

3.
INGREDIENTS: WATER, CANOLA OIL, PARTIALLY
HYDROGENATED CORN OIL, MALTODEXTRIN, SALT,
VEGETABLE MONOGLYCERIDES (EMULSIFIER), POTASSIUM
SORBATE AND CALCIUM DISODIUM EDTA AND CITRIC
ACID TO PRESERVE FRESHNESS, ARTIFICIAL FLAVOR,
COLORED WITH BETA CAROTENE (SOURCE OF VITAMIN
A), VITAMIN A PALMITATE AND VITAMIN D3 ADDED.

4.
INGREDIENTS: WATER, CORN SYRUP, LIQUID SOYBEAN
OIL, MODIFIED FOOD STARCH, EGG WHITES, VINEGAR,
MALTODEXTRIN, SALT, NATURAL FLAVORS, GUMS
(CELLULOSE GEL AND XANTHAN GUM), ARTIFICIAL
COLORS, SODIUM BENZOATE AND CALCIUM DISODIUM
EDTA USED TO PROTECT QUALITY.

Reading 1

What's Really on Your Dinner Plate

CD 2,
Track 3

1 **W**hat's that on your pizza? You can bet it's not just the extra cheese and onions you ordered. As a matter of fact, you can count on at least a dozen other "extras" that you never asked for, including dextrin, mono- and diglycerides, potassium bromate, sodium aluminum phosphate,

5 sodium citrate, sodium metabisulfate, and xanthan gum. These common food additives make your pizza—among other things, lighter, tastier, and generally more pleasing to the palate. Because we like our pepperoni[1] without mold, our crackers crispy, our peanut butter smooth, and our tomatoes red, chemicals are added to just about everything we eat. They make food more

10 flavorful and easier to prepare; they make it last longer, look more appetizing, and feel better in our mouths (no lumps!).

Today's additives read like a chemistry book, so many people believe they're a modern invention. However, additives are nothing new, and neither is the controversy surrounding them. London in the eighteenth century could

15 have been called the "adulterated[2] food capital of the world," though it's likely that other cities in other countries were just as guilty of the practice of food adulteration. One might think that food in the "old days" was pure and simple; but in many cases, what people paid for was not what they were getting. Pepper, for example, was adulterated with mustard husks,[3] pea flour,

20 fruit berries, and sweepings from the storeroom floor. Tea, which was very expensive and brought all the way from China, was mixed with dried leaves from ash trees.[4] China tea was green, so fake China tea was often made from dried thorn leaves[5] colored with a poisonous substance called verdigris. When black Indian tea became popular, it was common for manufacturers to buy

25 up used tea leaves, which they stiffened with a gum solution and then tinted

---

[1]**pepperoni:** a very spicy pork or beef sausage often put on pizzas
[2]**adulterated:** made impure or of poorer quality by adding other substances
[3]**mustard husks:** the dry outer coverings of mustard seeds
[4]**ash trees:** trees belonging to the olive family
[5]**thorn leaves:** the dry, hard, pointed leaves from thorn bushes

with lead, another dangerous substance. Even candy was contaminated with highly poisonous salts of copper and lead to give it color. These practices eventually came to the public's attention, and in 1860 the first British Food and Drug Act was passed. Despite the regulations on food purity that currently exist in almost every country, there are still problems. One of the most alarming cases occurred in 1969, when an Italian gentleman was charged for selling what was supposed to be grated parmesan[6] cheese, but turned out to consist of grated umbrella handles!

Believe it or not, food adulteration is not all bad. Salt has been used as a preservative for thousands of years, and, thanks to some basic and other quite complicated substances, we have "fresh" vegetables in January, peanut butter that doesn't stick to the roof of the mouth, stackable potato chips, and meat that doesn't turn green on the way home from the grocery store. But as they say, there's a price to pay for everything.

In the case of vegetables and fruits, the price is taste. Bred[7] for looks and long hauls,[8] plump, red tomatoes have fine body and perfect skin but offer very little for our taste buds[9] to smile about. The reason is that the tomatoes are picked green and then "gassed" along the way; that is, they're treated with ethylene gas, the same gas tomatoes give off internally if allowed to ripen on the vine.[10] The artificial gassing tricks the tomatoes into turning red. They don't really ripen; they just turn a ripe color.

The federal government recognizes about 35 different categories of additives, which are used for various purposes. Antioxidants are added to oil-containing foods to prevent the oil from spoiling. Chelating agents stop food from discoloring. Emulsifiers keep oil and water mixed together. Flavor enhancers improve the natural flavor of food. Thickening agents absorb some of the water present in food and make food thicker. They also keep oils, water, and solids well mixed. About 800 million pounds of additives are added to our food every year.

What happens when we consume this conglomeration of chemicals? The average American ingests about five pounds of food additives per year. The good news is that the majority of the hundreds of chemicals that are added to

---

[6]**parmesan:** a hard, dry, strong-flavored cheese that is often sold grated
[7]**bred:** produced by selecting parent plants with certain characteristics
[8]**long hauls:** transportation over long distances
[9]**taste buds:** small groups of receptor cells on the tongue that distinguish different tastes
[10]**the vine:** the plant

food are safe. In some cases, they're even good for us, such as when vitamins are added. The bad news is that some of them are not safe, and these are the ones with which we need to concern ourselves.

The first of the unsafe additives is artificial sweeteners. The sugar substitute aspartame is sold commercially as Equal or NutraSweet and is used in many diet beverages.[11] However, studies have shown that about one out of 20,000 babies cannot metabolize one of the two substances that aspartame is made from and that toxic levels of that substance, called phenylalanine, can result in mental retardation.[12] Some scientists also believe that aspartame can cause problems with brain function and behavior changes in people who consume it. Some people who have consumed aspartame have reported dizziness, headaches, and even seizures.[13] Another controversy over aspartame involves its possible link to an increased risk of brain tumors. Aspartame is still widely added, although many lawsuits have been filed to block its use. Another sugar substitute, called saccharin, has been linked to cancer in laboratory animals.

The additives sodium nitrite and sodium nitrate are two closely related chemicals that have been used for centuries to preserve meat. These additives keep meat's red color, enhance its flavor, and stop the growth of dangerous bacteria. Nitrate by itself is harmless, but it is quickly changed into nitrite by a chemical reaction that occurs at high temperatures and may also occur to some degree in the stomach. During this chemical reaction, nitrite combines with other chemicals to form some very powerful cancer-causing agents. Bacon is a special problem because it is thinly sliced and fried at a high temperature. Other processed meats, such as hot dogs, ham, and bologna, are less of a risk. Nitrite has been considered an important cause of stomach cancer in the United States, Japan, and other countries. In the United States, in fact, the rate of stomach cancer has been declining for a number of years because of reduced use of nitrite and nitrate preservatives.

Artificial colorings, often used in combination with artificial flavorings, replace natural ingredients that are more costly to produce. Lemon-flavored "lemonade" is much cheaper to make than a real lemon product. Artificial colorings are synthetic dyes such as Blue No. 1, Blue No. 2, Citrus Red No. 2,

---

[11]**beverages:** drinks other than water, alcohol, or medicine—for example, coffee and tea

[12]**mental retardation:** underdevelopment of mental ability

[13]**seizures:** sudden or violent attacks, such as those associated with epilepsy

Green No. 3, Red No. 3, Red No. 40, Yellow No. 5, and Yellow No. 6. They are widely used in foods to make them look more natural and more attractive. All those colored breakfast cereals for kids are loaded with food dyes, as are ice cream, cakes, and other tasty treats. For decades, questions have been asked
95   about the safety of synthetic food dyes, and many dyes have been banned for being toxic or cancer-causing. There are still questions of safety about the dyes that are currently in use. Yellow No. 5, for example, causes allergic reactions in some people. Red No. 3 has been banned for some uses because it caused tumors in rats. Other dyes are also under investigation.

100   It's good to know that no single food additive poses a severe danger to the entire population. But several additives, such as those we have mentioned, do pose some risks to the general public and should be avoided as much as possible. Fortunately, people are more aware than ever of the dangers of pesticide residues on fruits and vegetables and of additives in our processed
105   foods. There is intense pressure on the federal government to ban unsafe substances. But it is also our responsibility as consumers to read labels and be aware of what we're putting into our bodies, and to learn how to eat safe and healthy food for long and healthy lives.

Vocabulary

A. Vocabulary in Context

Select the letter of the answer that is closest in meaning to the **bold** word or phrase.

1. We like to have pepperoni without **mold**.
   a. yellow fat   c. greenish growth
   b. strange spices   d. reddish color

2. The **controversy** surrounding additives is nothing new.
   a. purpose   c. idea
   b. debate   d. judgment

3. **Fake** China tea was often made from dried thorn leaves colored with a poisonous substance.
   a. Imitation   c. Ordinary
   b. Cheap   d. Light

4. Even candy was **contaminated** with highly poisonous salts.
   a. injured   c. diseased
   b. destroyed   d. made impure

5. What happens when we consume this **conglomeration** of chemicals?
   a. arrangement   c. discovery
   b. collection   d. preference

6. The average American **ingests** about five pounds of additives per year.
   a. cleans in the body   c. takes in as food
   b. changes to liquid   d. discharges from the body

7. Studies have shown that some babies cannot **metabolize** one of the
   substances that aspartame is made from.
   a. change into energy   c. sleep with
   b. grow with   d. live on

8. All the colored breakfast cereals for kids are **loaded with** food dyes.
   a. made out of   c. improved with
   b. destroyed by   d. packed with

9. No single food additive **poses** a severe danger to the entire population.
   a. transmits   c. presents
   b. maintains   d. donates

10. People are aware of the dangers of pesticide **residues** on fruits and
   vegetables.
   a. remainders   c. trash
   b. samples   d. portions

B. Vocabulary Building

Read the list of nouns below. Match one item from each column to make
sentences similar to those used in the reading.

Noun	Verb Phrase	Object
1. chemicals	**a.** are added to	**g.** cancer
2. pepper	**b.** are loaded with	**h.** copper salts
3. tea	**c.** has been linked to	**i.** dried leaves
4. candy	**d.** was adulterated with	**j.** everything we eat
5. saccharin	**e.** was contaminated with	**k.** food dyes
6. breakfast cereals	**f.** was mixed with	**l.** mustard husks

1. chemicals   _a_   _j_   <u>Chemicals are added to everything we eat.</u>

2. pepper   _____   _____   _____

3. tea   _____   _____   _____

4. candy   _____   _____   _____

5. saccharin   _____   _____   _____

6. breakfast cereals   _____   _____   _____

C. Vocabulary in New Context

1. Now make a question out of each of the sentences in Part B. For example, *What is added to everything we eat?* With a partner, take turns asking and answering these questions.

2. Use the verb phrases from Part B to make your own sentences about food additives.

Reading Comprehension

A. Looking for the Main Ideas

Circle the letter of the best answer.

1. What is the main idea of paragraph 2?
   a. Food additives are chemical substances.
   b. Some suppliers adulterate food to save money.
   c. Food adulteration has a long and sometimes dangerous history.
   d. Even something as innocent-looking as candy can be dangerous if it has additives.

2. Paragraph 7 is mostly about _____.
   a. how phenylalanine can cause brain problems and behavior changes
   b. the fact that lawsuits have failed to block the use of aspartame
   c. the uses of the sugar substitute aspartame
   d. the dangers posed by the substances in some artificial sweeteners

3. Paragraph 9 is mainly concerned with _____.
   a. the questionable safety of food dyes
   b. the money-saving value of artificial flavorings and colorings
   c. the banning of toxic and cancer-causing food dyes
   d. the most popular foods in which dyes are used

B. Skimming and Scanning for Details

Scan the reading to find the answers to these questions. Write complete sentences.

1. What are five reasons why additives are put into food?
2. According to the reading, why was tea adulterated in eighteenth-century London?
3. What negative effect does gassing have on tomatoes?
4. What are five categories of food additives and their uses?
5. In the last sentence of paragraph 6, to what does the word *these* refer?
6. What is a common use of NutraSweet?
7. To what does the word *its* in paragraph 8, sentence 2, refer?
8. Why does the use of nitrite in bacon pose a special problem?
9. Give two reasons why dyes are widely used in foods.
10. Why has Red No. 3 been banned for some uses?

C. Making Inferences and Drawing Conclusions

The answers to these questions are not directly stated in the reading. Circle the letter of the best answer.

1. The reading implies that _____.
   a. today's food additives are more dangerous than those used in the past
   b. economics has always played a role in the use of food additives
   c. food additives have more to do with making food look good than anything else
   d. regulations on food purity have eliminated most problems with food adulteration

2. From the reading, it can be concluded that _____.
   a. the health risks posed by some additives must be weighed against their positive values, such as food preservation
   b. Americans gain weight as a result of the large amount of food additives they consume
   c. most food additives are bad for us and should be banned
   d. there is no evidence to prove that banning certain additives reduces the risk of cancer

3. It can be inferred from the reading that _____.
   a. when questions of safety are involved, getting a substance banned is a quick and easy process
   b. there is no reason to be concerned about the safety of food additives because the government is doing all it can to protect consumers against unsafe substances
   c. the goal of some consumer groups is to pressure the government to ban all forms of food adulteration
   d. in spite of the government's role in regulating food additives, our health and safety also depend on our own education and awareness

4. The author's purpose is to _____.
   a. entertain
   b. inform
   c. persuade
   d. argue

Discussion Questions

Discuss the answers to these questions with your classmates.

1. Are there some foods that you think are safer than others?
2. What are some of your favorite foods? Say why you like them.
3. Have you ever been sick as a result of eating or drinking a particular type of food? Describe what it did to you and list the possible causes.
4. If you had a choice between (a) food that didn't look very appetizing, was more expensive, but was healthy; or (b) food that looked good and appetizing but was chemically treated, which would you choose and why?

Critical Thinking Questions

Discuss the answers to these questions with your classmates.

1. Health food stores seem to be popping up everywhere. Do you think these stores provide healthier foods for their customers? What do the terms *health food* and *organic food* mean? What are the controversies surrounding the use of those terms? Do you go to health-food stores? Why or why not?
2. Are you health conscious in your own life? Do you exercise and eat a healthy diet? Do you try to eat foods without chemicals? Do you think it's possible to remove all chemicals from foods and still have a safe diet? Do you think we should be concerned about additives?
3. Do you think food is safer today than it was 100 years ago? Do you think there will be more or less additives in our food 100 years into the future? How does your diet differ from that of your grandparents and great grandparents? How do you think people's diets will change in the future?

Reading 2

**CD 2,
Track 4**

More Than Milk in Your Glass

The following article by Nigel Collins was published in the journal Catalyst: GCSE
Science Review *(volume 12, issue 3, February 1, 2002). This journal is published
by Philip Allan Updates as an educational resource providing articles on key science
topics for the General Certificate of School Education in the United Kingdom.*

1   **P**esticides and growth-
promoting chemicals are
used to improve crop yields.
Farm animals may also be
5   treated with chemicals to
improve yield. There are both
advantages to and justified
concerns about the use of
such substances. You will
10   study these in your GCSE

science course. In this 'For debate' we look at the science involved and the
issues raised by the use of a hormone to improve milk yield in cattle.

Somatotropins are hormones involved in the growth and development
of mammals. Bovine somatotropin (BST) is a growth hormone produced by
15   cows. It is secreted into a cow's blood from the pituitary gland at the base of
the brain. Cows with a naturally high milk yield often have high BST levels.
In the 1930s it was found that injecting a lactating cow (one producing
milk) with BST increased its yield. BST is injected because it is a protein, like
insulin.[1] If proteins are given by mouth they are broken down by digestion in
20   the gut.

Injecting BST looks like a useful way of increasing the milk yield from
herds of dairy cows. BST is made by biotechnology using genetic engineering

------

[1]**insulin:** a hormone that regulates glucose in the blood

or recombinant DNA technology. The gene encoding BST is inserted into a
bacterium, a strain of E. coli. The bacteria grow rapidly in a fermenter[2] and,
because they carry the BST gene, they make lots of BST.

25

> **Hormones** are substances made by endocrine glands. They are released
> into the bloodstream in minute amounts. The blood circulates them to
> target organs where their effects are slow, widespread and often long-lasting.

HOW DOES BST WORK?

One effect of BST is to cause the liver to secrete another substance, insulin-
like growth factor (IGF). Human and bovine ST differ in structure, but IGF is
the same in both cow and human. It is not clear how IGF causes increased
milk production but increased blood flow to the mammary glands, and

30   increase in the number of mammary cells or an increase in mammary cell
activity could be involved. Cows need to eat more if they are making more
milk, and it has been shown that they consume 10–20% more food—grass,
hay or corn.

A cow will produce milk for about 300 days after calving,[3] providing it is

35   milked regularly after the calf[4] is taken away. Peak production is reached at
about 7–9 weeks. BST maintains milk yields at higher levels for longer and so
could improve yield by around 10% or more.

WHERE IS BST USED?

BST was approved for use in the USA in 1994 and in many countries
around the world since. Cows that give a lower milk yield are injected every

40   14–28 days after their natural lactation[5] has peaked. Canada and the
European Union (EU), including the UK, do not allow the use of BST. The
EU stated that if BST was allowed it should be by prescription, with veterinary
advice on which animals could be treated. Why doesn't the EU allow BST
while other countries do?

---

[2]**fermenter:** scientific equipment designed to exclude oxygen and encourage the
 growth of bacteria
[3]**calving:** giving birth to a baby cow
[4]**calf:** a young cow
[5]**lactation:** production of milk by cows

CONCERNS

There are four areas of concern:

Human Health

Could BST or IGF pass into milk from cows, and could they be harmful to people drinking the milk? Both hormones are proteins and should be digested, not absorbed, so there should not be a problem.

Cattle treated with BST have a slightly higher chance of mastitis which is a painful bacterial disease of the udder.[6] BST does not cause mastitis directly but the disease is more likely in high-yielding cows. The treatment for mastitis includes using antibiotics. Increased antibiotic use is undesirable because it might increase the incidence of antibiotic-resistant strains of bacteria, and reduce the usefulness of antibiotics in treating human disease.

In the UK it was felt that, because BST increases IGF levels to above normal and IGF is a hormone active in humans whose effects are widespread and difficult to measure, BST should continue to be banned. Many people feel that we should not introduce things until we are certain there will be no untoward effects.

IGF levels in milk from BST-treated cows rise by between 25 and 70%. This sounds dramatic, but in fact we produce IGF all the time and the levels in our own saliva[7] are greater than that in milk. However there are concerns about possible increased risks of some forms of cancer when IGF levels are higher.

An expert panel in Canada in 1999 felt there was 'no significant risk to human safety from eating products from BST treated animals.'

Animal Health and Welfare

Another expert panel in Canada felt that BST presented 'a sufficient and unacceptable threat to the safety of dairy cows.' This was based on the increased incidence of mastitis. There also appear to be increased foot problems in treated cattle. On these grounds, BST use was still not allowed. Europe takes a similar position, though this runs counter to an assessment made by the European Commission's Committee for Veterinary Medicinal Products.

---

[6]**udder:** part of cow where milk is stored
[7]**saliva:** liquid in the mouth which helps us to swallow food

Labelling

Many people think that milk from BST-treated cows should be labelled. In the USA it has been argued that milk in cartons is from many different sources, some using BST and some not, so labelling would be too difficult and is not justified. This same argument has been used about labelling genetically modified maize or soy products, but such foods are appropriately labelled and customers can make their choice. Small-scale farmers producing cartons of milk from untreated cows are allowed to label them, but only if the information is 'truthful and not misleading.'

Socioeconomic Aspects

The debate centres[8] on the effects of BST on farm organisation and whether farmers with small herds would be better or worse off if BST were used. BST is not authorised in Europe at the time of writing. If the USA were to ship dairy products to Britain on a large scale it is likely that commercial pressure would be applied to allow the import of milk from treated cows. This in turn would put pressure on European farmers.

In the meantime—what do you think? Should cows in Britain and the rest of Europe be injected with BST to increase milk production?

---

[8]Note the small differences in spelling and punctuation between the British English used in this article and American English.

Vocabulary

A. Vocabulary in Context

Look at the reading to answer the following questions.

1. Which word is closest in meaning to **yield** in paragraph 1?
   a. manufacture   c. production
   b. income   d. arrival

Word Partnership	Use **yield** with:
n.	yield **to pressure**, yield **to temptation**, yield **a profit**, yield **information**, yield **results**
v.	**refuse to** yield
adj.	annual yield, **expected** yield, **high/higher** yield

2. In paragraph 1, what does **concerns** mean?

a. fears

b. matters

c. ideas

d. restrictions

3. Which word in paragraph 2 means "intestines"?

4. Which word in paragraph 3 means "groups of cows"?

5. Which of these words is similar in meaning to **inserted** as used in paragraph 3?

a. started

b. introduced

c. contained

d. included

6. What does the word **peak** in paragraph 5 mean?

a. better

b. top

c. helpful

d. nice

7. Which word in paragraph 6 refers to a doctor who takes care of animals?

8. Which of these words is closest in meaning to **incidence** as used in paragraph 9?

a. total

b. frequency

c. cause

d. power

9. Which of these words is similar in meaning to **counter** as used in paragraph 13?

a. parallel

b. similar

c. unequal

d. opposite

10. Which word in paragraph 13 means "evaluation"?

B. Vocabulary Building

1. The reading contains several compound adjectives. Match the pairs below. Then look back at the reading to check your answers.

1. long-_____

2. insulin-_____

3. high-_____

4. antibiotic-_____

5. small-_____

a. like

b. lasting

c. scale

d. yielding

e. resistant

2. Use one-half of each compound above with a different word to complete each sentence below.

    1. A crop that is resistant to insects is _____.

    2. Something that is like a human is _____.

    3. Farms that have large quantities of land and crops are _____.

    4. A tradition or custom that has stood for a long time is _____.

    5. An official with a high rank is _____.

C. Vocabulary in New Context

Use the compound adjectives from Part B, Exercise 1 to make your own sentences about BST.

Reading Comprehension

A. Looking for the Main Ideas

Circle the letter of the answer that best completes the sentence.

1. BST _____.
    a. improves the quality of milk
    b. increases milk production
    c. is a hormone that is not produced by cows
    d. helps cows digest

2. BST is used _____.
    a. in Canada and the United States
    b. in the United States and some other countries
    c. in Europe
    d. in Canada and Europe

3. A panel in Canada thinks that BST _____.
    a. is not safe for cows
    b. makes cows healthier
    c. gives people mastitis
    d. has no effects on cattle or people

4. Milk from BST-treated cows is _____.
   a. difficult to label
   b. always labeled
   c. impossible to label
   d. labeled only in the United States

B. Skimming and Scanning for Details

Scan the reading quickly to find the answers to these questions. Write complete sentences.

   1. What is one effect of BST?
   2. How long does a cow produce milk after calving?
   3. When does a cow produce the most milk naturally?
   4. When did they find that injecting cows with BST increased milk production?
   5. How often are cows injected with BST after their natural lactation?
   6. By how much could BST improve milk yields?
   7. When was BST approved for use in the United States?
   8. What is used to treat mastitis in cows?
   9. Why does the United States think it is too difficult to label milk cartons?
   10. Who is allowed to label cartons of milk from untreated cows?

C. Making Inferences and Drawing Conclusions

Some of the following statements can be inferred from the reading, and others cannot. Circle the number of each statement that can be inferred.

   1. There isn't enough evidence against BST to stop its use completely.
   2. Milk from the United States is more likely to have BST than is milk from Europe.
   3. Europeans are more concerned about food safety than Americans.
   4. Cows treated with BST are more likely to have mastitis than are those not treated with BST.
   5. The use of BST can indirectly affect the health of humans.
   6. The question of the safety of BST has caused worldwide debate.
   7. Giving cows antibiotics will make humans safer from disease.
   8. Europeans are more concerned about animal welfare and safety than Americans are.

9. It is not in the interest of large-scale U.S. dairy farms to label food containing BST.
10. People in the United Kingdom believe that until the effects of BST are known for sure, it should be banned.

Discussion Questions

Discuss the answers to these questions with your classmates.

1. Do you know of any other animals that are harmed by methods used to make them more productive?
2. What do you think the government should do to control the safety of our food supply?
3. Why do you think that substances like BST and pesticides are allowed to be used?

Critical Thinking Questions

Discuss the answers to these questions with your classmates.

1. The author asks the reader: "Should cows in Britain and the rest of Europe be injected with BST to increase milk production?" Artificial hormones are also given to cattle in the United States to fatten them up and make them grow faster. Should Britain and the European Union allow either of these? Why or why not? Why do you think the use of BST and other hormones is allowed in the United States? Would you like to see it banned?
2. Given the problem of world hunger, do you believe that any plants and animals that are genetically modified to produce more food should be allowed? Should all uses of growth-promoting chemicals be banned? Do you think there are ways to provide more food without using chemicals?
3. If a chemical hurts an animal but benefits humans, should it be allowed? Why or why not?
4. Farmers are allowed to label their products as free of BST, but only if the information is "truthful and not misleading." There is a lot of controversy about food labeling today. What are some of the areas of controversy? Do you believe that food labels are always truthful and accurate? How can we ensure "truth in labeling"?

Writing

Writing Skills

A. Organizing: *The Cause-and-Effect Essay*

Another popular type of essay is the cause-and-effect essay. This form is frequently used in academic writing. In college, your history teacher may ask you to write about the causes of the American Civil War; your biology teacher may ask you to write on the three effects of a snake bite; your psychology teacher may ask you to explain the high rate of alcoholism among American Indians.

There are three types of cause-and-effect essays:

1. The cause analysis essay explains causes.
2. The effect analysis essay explains effects.
3. The causal chain essay explains causes that lead to effects in a chain.

The Cause Analysis Essay

Very few situations can be traced back to a single cause. Something usually has several causes or a combination of causes that lead to an effect.

For example, consider this question: Why do some children have a low IQ? For some, it may be a result of early malnutrition, which slows brain growth; for others, it may be a result of exposure to toxins, such as lead, which damage the nervous system. It may be caused by the lack of a stimulating environment. It may also be caused by parents who do not encourage their children or spend time with them. If you examined the topic further, you might find that family size could also be a cause.

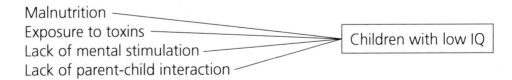

Malnutrition
Exposure to toxins
Lack of mental stimulation   Children with low IQ
Lack of parent-child interaction

The Thesis Statement

The thesis statement should state the causes to be discussed.

Example:

> Low IQ in children is generally caused by the following factors: malnutrition in childhood, lack of a stimulating environment, and lack of interaction with their parents.

Then you might go on to comment on the causes.

Example:

> Although there are other causes for low IQ in children, these were picked out as the more important causes and the ones that could be easily supported.

The Body Paragraphs

Each body paragraph should discuss one of the causes mentioned in the thesis statement.

The Conclusion

The conclusion should restate the thesis and provide a general comment on the topic.

The Effect Analysis Essay

Just as there can be many causes for something, a cause can have several effects. For example, many people consume caffeine in one form or another, which has the effect of making them alert. However, addiction to caffeine can have many negative effects such as restlessness, insomnia, heartbeat irregularities, and even high blood pressure, which may lead to other serious problems.

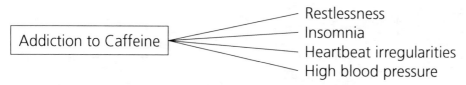

In the student essay "The Negative Sides of Fast Food" on page 199, you can see the two negative effects of eating fast food regularly. In Reading 1, the effects of food additives are explained. Notice that reference is made to the cause before explaining the effect. It is important to understand which is the cause and which is the effect. Look at the following examples:

Cause: The additives sodium nitrite and sodium nitrate are two closely related chemicals that have been used for centuries to preserve meat.

Effect: Nitrite has been considered an important cause of stomach cancer in the United States, Japan, and other countries.

Cause: The sugar substitute aspartame is sold commercially as Equal or NutraSweet and is used in many diet beverages.

Effect: About one out of 20,000 babies cannot metabolize one of the two substances that aspartame is made from, and toxic levels of that substance can result in mental retardation.

Effect: Some people who have consumed aspartame have reported dizziness, headaches, and even seizures.

Effect: Aspartame may be linked to an increased risk of brain tumors.

The Thesis Statement

As in the causal analysis essay, the thesis statement of an effect analysis essay should state the effects to be discussed.

Example:

Eating fast food regularly may cause our bodies to be deficient in vitamins and minerals we need to maintain good health; also, eating fast food can be very addictive, and people accustomed to it rarely change their eating habits.

The Body Paragraphs

As for a cause analysis essay, select two or three major effects. In the thesis statement above, two effects have been selected. Therefore, the first body paragraph will explain the effects on health of eating fast food, and the second body paragraph will explain the addictive effect of eating fast food regularly. Support each effect with relevant examples and/or facts.

The Conclusion

The conclusion should restate the thesis and provide a general comment on the topic.

The Causal Chain Essay

In the causal chain type of cause-and-effect essay, one cause leads to an effect, which leads to another cause, and so on, creating a chain of causes and effects.

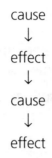

cause
↓
effect
↓
cause
↓
effect

For example, bad weather conditions such as excessive rainfall may affect farmers' vegetable crops, causing the vegetable crops to die. This makes vegetables scarce, causing prices to rise in the supermarkets. This results in people not buying very many vegetables, because they are so expensive. Since people eat fewer vegetables, their health is affected.

excessive rainfall
↓
damage to vegetable crops
↓
vegetable prices go up
↓
people eat less vegetables
↓
people are not as healthy

In Reading 2, a causal chain may be implied: Cows are given BST to increase their production of milk. The BST causes the cows to get infections, so the cows are given antibiotics. The antibiotics in turn get into our milk supply, creating cause for alarm.

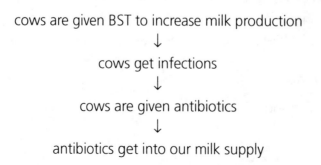

cows are given BST to increase milk production
↓
cows get infections
↓
cows are given antibiotics
↓
antibiotics get into our milk supply

The most frequent use of this type of essay is in the sciences—for example, in essays about biological or weather cycles.

Plan the causal chain for one of the topics below or for another topic from geography or biology.

1. The cutting of forests in the Amazon
2. The killing of elephants for ivory

The Thesis Statement

The thesis statement should state the three or four steps in the chain.

Example:

The use of BST to increase milk production indirectly affects human health, since the cows that are given BST get infections and are treated with antibiotics, which then get into our milk supply.

The Body Paragraphs

It is important to break the chain into three or four major steps. Each body paragraph should describe one step in the chain stated in the thesis statement. Each step should be supported with details.

The Conclusion

The conclusion should restate the main points in the chain and provide a comment on the topic.

B. Exercises

1. Identify which is the cause **(C)** and which is the effect **(E)**.

   1. _____ Accident death rates dropped by 30 percent.
      _____ A seat belt law was passed.
      _____ Motorists were required to wear seat belts.

   2. _____ Carla burned 500 calories per week.
      _____ Carla's blood pressure was lower.
      _____ Carla exercised 45 minutes each day.

   3. _____ Social and work-related pressures have increased in modern times.
      _____ People are more at risk for stress-related illnesses, such as heart attacks.

4. _____ The sun's ultraviolet rays penetrate the deeper layer of the skin.
   _____ Skin cancer is one of the most common forms of cancer in the United States.
   _____ The protective ozone layer in the atmosphere is decreased by pollutants.

5. _____ Most American women over the age of 50 consume half of their daily calcium requirements.
   _____ Calcium in bones is gradually depleted, leaving them weak and brittle—a condition called osteoporosis.
   _____ In this country, older women suffer approximately 5 million fractures each year.

6. _____ People who walk daily have healthier cardiovascular systems.
   _____ Aerobic exercises allow the heart and lungs to utilize oxygen more efficiently.

7. _____ Flu viruses are highly contagious and are spread through close contact with infected persons.
   _____ Flu epidemics spread rapidly through the workplace.

8. _____ Antibiotics have been overprescribed by doctors for decades.
   _____ Over a period of time, bacteria can become resistant to antibiotics when repeatedly exposed to them.
   _____ A medical crisis exists because many antibiotics are no longer useful for combating diseases.

2. In each sentence of the paragraph, underline the cause **once** and the effect **twice**.

1. Ear pain occurs when there is a buildup of fluid and pressure in the middle ear. Often during a cold or an allergy attack, particularly in small children, the ear tube becomes swollen shut, preventing the normal flow of fluid from the middle ear. Fluid begins to accumulate, causing stuffiness and decreased hearing. Sometimes a bacterial infection starts in the fluid, resulting in pain and fever. Ear pain and ear stuffiness can also result from high altitudes, such as when flying in an airplane or driving in the mountains. Swallowing will frequently relieve the pressure in the ear tube.

2. Eating candy can produce acids in the body. Consuming carbohydrates can even produce an alcoholic condition in your body. One of our great orators, William Jennings Bryan, gave speeches nationwide about the

bad effects of drinking alcohol, causing more than one person to change his drinking habits. Ironically, Bryan himself died of an alcoholic stomach as a result of eating 13 pancakes with syrup for breakfast. Eating the pancakes, which are full of carbohydrates, and the sugary syrup created a kind of alcoholic brew in his stomach. This innocently consumed brew produced alcohol poisoning, which in turn led to his death.

3. Exercise is the central ingredient of good health because it tones the muscles, strengthens the bones, makes the heart and lungs work better, and prevents disease. It increases energy and vitality and gives you a good feeling about yourself. This sense of well-being helps you deal better with stress, eases depression, and aids sleep. There are three kinds of exercises, of which *strengthening* is the least important because it builds more bulky muscles, although it increases general *strength*. Stretching exercises keep the muscles loose and are a bit more important than weight lifting. Stretching before doing other kinds of exercises warms up the muscles and makes them looser and less susceptible to injury. *Aerobic* exercises are the key to fitness because they improve your heart and lungs. Your heart speeds up to pump larger amounts of blood. You breathe more frequently and more deeply to increase the oxygen transfer from the lungs to the blood. As a result of these efforts, the heart becomes larger and stronger and your lungs healthier.

Writing Model: The Cause and Effect Essay

Read the following cause-and-effect essay written by a student.

The Negative Sides of Fast Food

With today's fast lifestyle, it is very hard to keep up with the traditional way of taking care of all human needs. Eating habits are no exception. According to an article in *Success* magazine (November 1994), America today eats more fast food than ever before. Ninety-six out of every one hundred Americans eat fast food on some kind of regular basis. There are many side effects related to this popular eating habit, most of which are damaging to our health and personal care. Eating fast food regularly may cause our bodies to be deficient in the vitamins and minerals we need to maintain good health; also, eating fast food can be very addictive, and people accustomed to it rarely change their eating habits.

The food sold in most fast food restaurants may not be all that good for us. The majority of those restaurants are franchises, which means that everything has to look, taste, and smell the same way in all the restaurants of a particular franchise. A franchise controls this by having a main food distribution center, which implies that the food has to go through a long frozen storage period, then a transportation period before it gets to the consumer. In order for the food to still taste fresh after all this time, a lot of artificial preservatives have to be added. As if that were not enough, the main element that the fast food market advertises and competes for is not good food or fresh ingredients, but lowest prices, and we all know what that means.

People who have the habit of eating fast food rarely even try to change their diet. Instead, people tend to get more and more used to the convenience and taste of fast food. According to a survey in *Industrial and Labor Relations Review* magazine (October 1992), out of every ten fast food eaters, only four will eat the same amount or less, and the other six will double their "loads" of fast food within four years; and out of every ten people who finally get to control their eating disorder, six will come back to eating fast food within six years. These alarming figures seem to be in contradiction with today's convenient ways of cooking at home. Easy-to-make dishes like those for microwaves, soups, etc., would appear to be the solution for the fast food problem, but obviously the real problem is not the trouble of cooking at home, but the addicting simplicity of fast food.

In conclusion, eating fast food is not only an unhealthy habit but also a corrupting one. Chances are most of us will have to eat some kind of fast food over a period in our lives, but this would not be a problem if we planned a diet that could be combined with fast food. Simple meals such as cereals, yogurts, and dishes for microwave ovens can make a big difference and are just as fast and affordable as food from any of the popular franchises. All it takes is a little conscience and responsibility.

Pedro
Dominican Republic

Student Essay Follow-Up

1. Underline the thesis statement.
2. What two effects of eating fast food is the writer considering?
3. What is the topic sentence of paragraph 2? Is it clearly supported?
4. What effect is the writer considering in paragraph 3? What evidence of the effect does he give?
5. In the conclusion, does the writer restate the thesis statement in other words?

Writing Practice

A. Write a Cause-and-Effect Essay

Write a cause-and-effect essay on one of the following topics. In your essay, try to include **3** or more vocabulary words from the readings in this chapter.

1. Write an effect analysis essay on eating junk food regularly, focusing on 3 effects.
2. Write an essay on the causes or effects of pollution.
3. Write an essay on the causes or effects of the use of pesticides.

B. Pre-Write

Work alone, with a partner, or in a group.

1. Brainstorm the topic. Choose a pre-writing technique you prefer.
2. Brainstorm for 3 causes or 3 effects.
3. Work on a thesis statement.

C. Outline

1. Organize your ideas.

   Step 1: Write your thesis statement. Include the 3 causes or effects.

   Step 2: Order the causes or effects.

   Step 3: Provide supporting ideas and details for each cause or effect.

2. Make a more detailed outline. The essay form on page 21 will help you.

D. Write a Rough Draft

Look at page 257 to find out about writing a rough draft.

E. Revise Your Rough Draft

Use the Revision Checklist on page 258.

F. Edit Your Essay

Use the Editing Checklist on page 259. Check your work for fragments (sentences that are not complete).

Example:

Error:	Although I try to eat fresh food.	frag
Correct:	Although I try to eat fresh food, it is easier to buy prepackaged food.	

When you find a mistake of this type, you can use the symbol "frag" (fragment). Look at page 260 for other symbols to use when editing your work.

G. Write Your Final Copy

When your rough draft has been edited, you can write the final copy of your essay.

Additional Writing Practice

A. Summarize

Write a one-paragraph summary of Reading 1. Check your summary with the Summary Checklist on page 269.

B. Paraphrase

Paraphrase the last paragraph (The debate . . .) in Reading 2. Look at pages 264–267 to find out about paraphrasing. Begin paraphrasing with either "According to the *Catalyst,* . . ." or "Based on an article in the *Catalyst,* . . . ."

C. Research

Choose a particular food or drink additive and find out 3 effects it has, or choose a disease and find 3 causes of it.

The following are suggested topics:

- Causes of anorexia
- Causes of obesity
- Effects of caffeine
- Effects of DDT use
- Effects of lead poisoning
- Effects of vitamin supplements

You may use your research later to write a cause-and-effect essay.

Weaving It Together

⏱ Timed Writing

Choose one of the following topics that you have not already written about in "Writing Practice," or choose the topic you researched. You have 50 minutes to write a cause-and-effect essay.

1. Write an effect analysis essay on eating junk food regularly, focusing on 3 effects.
2. Write an essay on the causes or effects of pollution.
3. Write an essay on the causes or effects of the use of pesticides.
4. Write a cause-and-effect essay on the topic you researched.

Connecting to the Internet

A. Use the Internet to find two different Web sites that offer information on "organic food." Who created the Web sites, and what information do they provide? How are the two Web sites different in content and presentation? Which Web site did you think was more reliable, and why?

B. Use the Internet to research healthy foods. Write a short article on 10 great health foods and the benefits attributed to these foods. Which Web site provided the best information?

C. Use the Internet to research food additives. Write a short article on why and how ancient people used food additives, how food additives have changed over time, and why our modern lifestyles are causing the increased use of food additives. Indicate which Web sites you used to find your information.

What Do You Think Now?

Refer to page 174 at the beginning of this chapter. Do you know the answers now? Complete the sentence or circle the best answer.

1. Food in the old days was/was not always pure.
2. Artificial sweeteners are/are not dangerous for our health.
3. The average American eats _____ pounds of food additives per year.
4. _____ uses BST, a growth hormone for cows to produce more milk.
5. Europe and the UK use/do not use BST, because it can be dangerous to humans.

Issues for Debate

What Do You Think?

Answer the questions with your best guess. Circle **Yes** or **No**.

Do you think . . .

1. the U.K. passed laws to protect animals from abuse before they did so for children?   **Yes**   **No**
2. an American wrote the first book on animal rights?   **Yes**   **No**
3. Germany gives rights to animals in its constitution?   **Yes**   **No**
4. the key genes in humans and chimpanzees are 99.4 percent the same?   **Yes**   **No**
5. in the United States chickens are cloned?   **Yes**   **No**

Pre-Reading

1. Discuss the answers to these questions with your classmates.

> **1.** How do animals help humans?
> **2.** Are all animals the same, or are some more important than others?
> **3.** Do you agree with society's treatment of animals?

2. Look at the photos and answer the questions.

> **1.** Which of the animals shown above do you think is the most intelligent, and why?
> **2.** Which animal is the most useful to humans?
> **3.** Which animal is the friendliest?
> **4.** Describe some other ways in which humans use animals.

Reading 1

Do Animals Have Rights?

CD 2,
Track 5

1   The American Declaration of Independence said that "all men are created
equal, that they are endowed . . . with certain inalienable rights, that among
these are Life, Liberty and the pursuit of Happiness." This was one of the first
statements of human rights. Back in 1776, this was a new idea, but today we
5   are used to the idea that as humans we have certain basic rights.

Our right to equal treatment also means that we have to treat other people
as equals. In the beginning, equal rights and responsibilities were limited
to certain groups. Over time, justice prevailed, and with the civil rights
movement came the modern belief that it is not acceptable to discriminate on
10   the grounds of sex, race, or religion.

Does the belief in equality, freedom, and the right to be treated in a certain
way apply to animals as well? Do animals also have "certain inalienable
rights" among which are "Life, Liberty and the pursuit of Happiness"? This
issue is at the heart of the debate about animal rights.

15   Animal welfare societies started in Britain and the United States in the
early 1800s. In fact, the United Kingdom passed laws to protect animals from
abuse before there were any laws to protect children. The Royal Society for the
Prevention of Cruelty to Animals (RSPCA) was founded in 1824 to find and
punish people who deliberately harmed animals. The first book on animal
20   rights was written by an Englishman, Henry Salt, in 1892. His book and the
animal rights movement that he started were based on two ideas: that human
beings are not made to eat meat and that we have a moral duty to treat
animals "like us." This means we should behave toward animals just as we
behave toward other human beings. Not everybody supported Salt's ideas, but
25   he made people think about animals and their rights.

In 1948, human rights became universal with the United Nations
Declaration of Human Rights, which stated that "recognition of the inherent
dignity and of the equal and inalienable rights of all members of the human
family is the foundation of freedom, justice and peace in the world." But it is

30   only since the 1970s that the idea of animals having rights just as humans do has developed. It started with an essay written by Peter Singer in which he used the term "animal liberation." In his article in the *New York Review of Books*, Singer wrote about how animals should be treated, and this started the debate that continues up to now.

35   How similar are animals to humans? Can some animals feel and think in ways similar to humans? Scientists have discovered that chimpanzees have many similarities with humans. Researchers who work with chimpanzees say they experience almost every emotion we do. They use tools, think ahead, and take care of one another. At Central Washington University in the United

40   States, a chimpanzee named Washoe has learned American Sign Language; he uses it to communicate with humans and has even taught it to another chimpanzee called Loulis. Researchers also claim that other creatures, such as gorillas, whales, and dolphins, are more like us than we think. On May 20, 2003, the BBC reported on a study published in the U.S. journal *Proceedings*

45   *of the National Academy of Sciences*, which claims chimpanzees are so closely related to humans that they should properly be considered members of the human family. Scientists from Wayne State University's School of Medicine in Detroit, Michigan, examined key genes in humans and several ape species and found them to be 99.4 percent the same as those of chimpanzees.

50   A British animal welfare group called Compassion in World Farming (CIWF) started campaigning in the 1980s to win a new status in law for animals. They wanted animals to be given the status of "sentient beings" (i.e., possessing a level of conscious awareness and able to have feelings). After years of petitions, the concept that animals are sentient was finally

55   recognized by the European Union in 1997. A statement was added to the treaty that established the EU, recognizing animals as sentient beings and requiring that their welfare be properly taken into account in the development of the Community's policies on agriculture, transport, the internal market, and research. Compassion in World Farming accepts that

60   farm animals will be killed for their meat, but argues that they should be treated humanely. As reported by the BBC on May 9, 2003, the group believes that animals that live in communities "often exhibit signs of morality that resemble human behavior. There is evidence that some animals do have some level of morality and some concern over other animals. Living within

65   a group requires a moral code of behavior. Zoologists who have spent their professional lives studying animal behavior, either by observation or by

experiments to test their mental capacities, believe that many animals feel and think." Joyce D'Silva, chief executive of CIWF, told BBC *News Online,* "This has huge implications for the ways we use animals and implies that all
70 farm animals are entitled to humane lives and deaths." If it is true that some creatures have a capacity for consciousness similar to that of human beings, then there is justification for giving them rights like those of humans.

Germany has become the first European nation to vote to guarantee animal rights in its constitution. Before the vote, animals in Germany were
75 already protected by laws governing the conditions under which they could be held in captivity. The issue of animal rights had been debated among German politicians for years. Then, in 2002, lawmakers in Germany voted to add "and animals" to a clause that obliges the state to respect and protect the dignity of humans. With this new law, there will be tighter restrictions on the
80 use of animals for testing cosmetics and nonprescription drugs. Lawmakers in Germany said that they would give more funding to projects that look at alternatives to using animals for experiments.

Today, animal welfare groups around the world continue with their work to change laws to protect animals and make their existence more humane.

Vocabulary

A. Vocabulary in Context

Select the letter of the answer that is closest in meaning to the **bold** word or phrase.

1. All men are **endowed with** certain inalienable rights.
   a. gifted with
   b. intelligent enough to have
   c. capable of
   d. lacking in

2. All men have the right to "Life, Liberty and the **pursuit of** Happiness."
   a. search for
   b. judgment of
   c. answer to
   d. decision for

3. Over time, justice **prevailed**.
   a. failed
   b. succeeded
   c. existed
   d. lived

4. This **issue** is at the heart of the debate about animal rights.
   a. question   c. danger
   b. doubt   d. answer

5. The United Kingdom passed laws to protect animals from **abuse**.
   a. anger   c. mistreatment
   b. attack   d. worry

6. The RSPCA was founded to punish people who **deliberately** harmed animals.
   a. intentionally   c. accidentally
   b. forcefully   d. strongly

7. Chimpanzees have a richly developed **consciousness**.
   a. knowledge   c. memory
   b. awareness   d. order

8. Compassion in World Farming started campaigning to win a new **status** in law for animals.
   a. purpose   c. position
   b. degree   d. level

9. CIWF argues that animals should be treated **humanely**.
   a. politely   c. generously
   b. cruelly   d. caringly

10. With this new law, there will be tighter **restrictions on** the use of animals for testing.
   a. limitations on   c. areas for
   b. methods for   d. systems for

B. Vocabulary Building

1. Find at least one adjective that was used in the reading before each noun in **bold** below. Add some more of your own.

1. rights

_____human_____ rights   _____ rights
_____ rights   _____ rights

2. treatment

_____ treatment   _____ treatment
_____ treatment   _____ treatment

3. duty

_____ duty   _____ duty

_____ duty   _____ duty

4. code

_____ code   _____ code

_____ code   _____ code

5. needs

_____ needs   _____ needs

_____ needs   _____ needs

2. Using the phrases above, take turns asking and answering questions about the reading.

C. Vocabulary in New Context

Use the phrases from Part B to make your own sentences about animal rights.

Reading Comprehension

A. Looking for the Main Ideas

Answer the following questions. Write complete sentences.

1. Which paragraph describes the main issue affecting the debate about animal rights?

2. What was Henry Salt's philosophy?

3. How have developments in human rights influenced ideas and opinions about animal rights?

4. What aspects of our treatment of animals are called into question by animal rights groups?

B. Skimming and Scanning for Details

Scan the reading to find the answers to these questions. Write complete sentences.

1. What were the aims of the RSPCA?

2. How did the issue of animal rights start to become discussed?

3. In what ways have researchers tried to compare animals and humans?

4. In what ways has Germany done more than other countries to protect animals?

C. Making Inferences and Drawing Conclusions

The answers to these questions are not directly stated in the article. Write complete sentences.

1. What conclusion do you draw from the fact that, in Britain, laws protecting animals preceded laws protecting children?
2. How is prevention of suffering to animals related to meat eating?
3. How might gorillas, whales, and dolphins be like humans?

Discussion Questions

Discuss the answers to these questions with your classmates.

1. Do humans have to eat meat?
2. How similar are animals to humans, in your opinion?
3. Should animals be used for medical research?
4. Do you think animals' rights should be protected by law?
5. Do you think the term *moral behavior* can be used to describe the behavior of animals? Why or why not?

Critical Thinking Questions

Discuss the answers to these questions with your classmates.

1. Do you have a pet or care for an animal of any kind? Do you have an emotional attachment to an animal? Do you believe that animals have feelings? Do you believe that animals have basic rights? Do you think people have gone too far, or not far enough, to protect the rights of animals? How would you respond if you saw an animal being abused?
2. What are some farming practices that are considered inhumane to animals? In what ways could farm animals be treated more humanely? Does it make sense to treat animals humanely and then eat them? Do you think humans will ever stop eating meat?
3. Do you think animals have human characteristics, and vice versa? In what ways are animals and humans commonly compared? Do you agree with Henry Salt that we have a moral duty to treat animals like us? What do you think he meant by that statement? Do you think that people who deliberately harm animals should be punished?

Reading 2

The Clone Factory

CD 2,
Track 6

The following article by Andrea Graves appeared in the New Scientist, *August 18, 2001.*

1   **B**illions of identical chickens could soon be rolling off production lines. Factory farming could soon
5   enter a new era of mass production. Companies in the US are developing the technology needed to "clone" chickens on a
10   massive scale.

Once a chicken with desirable traits has been bred or genetically engineered, tens of thousands of eggs, which will hatch into identical copies, could roll off the production lines every hour. Billions of clones could be produced each year to supply chicken
15   farms with birds that all grow at the same rate, have the same amount of meat and taste the same.

This, at least, is the vision of the US's National Institute of Science and Technology, which has given Origen Therapeutics of Burlingame, California, and Embrex of North Carolina $4.7 million to help fund research. The
20   prospect has alarmed animal welfare groups, who fear it could increase the suffering of farm birds.

That's unlikely to put off the poultry industry, however, which wants disease-resistant birds that grow faster on less food. "Producers would like the same meat quantity but to use reduced inputs to get there," says Mike
25   Fitzgerald of Origen.

To meet this demand, Origen aims to "create an animal that is effectively a clone", he says. Normal cloning doesn't work in birds because eggs can't

be removed and implanted. Instead, the company is trying to bulk-grow
embryonic stem cells taken from fertilised eggs as soon as they're laid. "The
trick is to culture the cells without them starting to differentiate, so they
remain pluripotent,[1]" says Fitzgerald.

Using a long-established technique, these donor[2] cells will then be injected
into the embryo of a freshly laid, fertilised recipient egg, forming a chick that
is a "chimera." Strictly speaking a chimera isn't a clone, because it contains
cells from both donor and recipient. But Fitzgerald says it will be enough if,
say, 95 per cent of a chicken's body develops from donor cells. "In the poultry
world, it doesn't matter if it's not 100 per cent," he says.

With its patent still at application stage, Origen is unwilling to reveal if it
can reliably obtain such chimeras. But it has occasionally created the ideal:
chicks that are 100 per cent donor-derived, or pure clones.

Another challenge for Origen is to scale up production. To do this, it has
teamed up with Embrex, which produces machines that can inject vaccines
into up to 50,000 eggs an hour. Embrex is now trying to modify the machines
to locate the embryo and inject the cells into precisely the right spot without
killing it. Automating the process will be tricky, admits Nandini Mandu of
Embrex. Even when it's done by hand, up to 75 per cent of the embryos die.

In [the] future, Origen envisages freezing stem cells from different strains[3]
of chicken. If orders come in for a particular strain, millions of eggs could be
produced in months or even weeks. At present, maintaining all the varieties
the market might call for is too expensive for breeders, and it takes years to
breed enough chickens to produce the billions of eggs that farmers need.

Fitzgerald insists that genetic modification isn't on Origen's menu. The
stem cells will come from eggs laid by unmodified pedigree[4] birds, he says.
All the same, Origen's website says the company has licenses for tools for
genetically engineering birds, and it talks about engineering birds that lay
eggs containing medical drugs.

Animal welfare groups say that it would be cruel if breeders used
technology to mass-produce the fastest-growing birds. Some birds already
go lame when bone growth doesn't keep pace with muscle growth. "The last
thing they should be doing is increasing growth rates," says Abigail Hall of
Britain's Royal Society for the Prevention of Cruelty to Animals.

---

[1]**pluripotent:** able to develop into many different kinds of cells
[2]**donor:** person or animal that gives something (in this case, cells)
[3]**strains:** breeds of animal within one species
[4]**pedigree:** record of the breed of a specific strain

There are other dangers. If one bird were vulnerable to a disease, all its clones would be too. But if one set of clones fell victim to a disease, the technology would allow farmers to "roll out" a resistant set rapidly.

65   There could also be benefits for consumers, as farmers could quickly adopt strains that don't carry food-poisoning bacteria such as *Salmonella*, for instance. Whether shoppers will buy meat from a clone, even if it's not genetically engineered, remains to be seen. And the FDA[5] has yet to decide whether meat and milk from cloned animals is fit for humans.

---

[5]**FDA:** stands for Food and Drug Administration, which is an agency that is part of the Department of Health and Human Safety Services responsible for protecting public health

Vocabulary

A. Vocabulary in Context

Select the letter of the answer that is closest in meaning to the **bold** word or phrase.

1. Factory farming could soon enter a new **era**.
   a. control   c. plan
   b. age   d. law

2. Companies are developing the technology needed to clone chickens on a **massive** scale.
   a. famous   c. small
   b. huge   d. modern

3. Chicken farms could have birds that all grow at the same **rate**.
   a. speed   c. rush
   b. slowness   d. size

4. The **prospect** has alarmed animal welfare groups.
   a. offer   c. idea
   b. test   d. preparation

Word Partnership	Use **prospect** with:
n.	prospect **for/of peace**, prospect **for/of war**,
v.	prospect **of being** *something*, prospect **of having** *something*

5. Another challenge for the company is to **scale up** production.
   a. discontinue   c. decrease
   b. develop   d. increase

6. To do this, the company has **teamed up** with another company.
   a. worked together with   c. put in order
   b. worked in small groups with   d. taken control of

7. The company is now trying to **modify** the machines.
   a. exchange   c. envisage
   b. adapt   d. replace

8. The company **envisages** freezing stem cells.
   a. is not considering   c. is fighting
   b. is planning on   d. is organizing

9. If one bird were **vulnerable to** a disease, all its clones would be too.
   a. without defense against   c. protected from
   b. hurt by   d. free from

10. Farmers could quickly **adopt** strains that don't carry food poisoning bacteria.
   a. take on   c. challenge
   b. object to   d. avoid

B. Vocabulary Building

1. Match the verbs with the nouns as they were used in the context of the reading. Look back at the reading to check your answers. Then add two more nouns that may be used with each verb.

   a. suffering   c. research   e. demand
   b. production   d. machines

   1. __c__ fund   ____research____ _____ _____

   2. _____ increase   _____ _____ _____

   3. _____ meet   _____ _____ _____

   4. _____ scale up   _____ _____ _____

   5. _____ modify   _____ _____ _____

2. Take turns asking and answering questions about the reading, using the phrases from above.

B. Vocabulary in New Context

Use the phrases from Part B, Exercise 1 to write your own sentences about animal cloning.

Reading Comprehension

A. Looking for the Main Ideas

Circle the letter of the best answer to the first question. Answer the other questions with complete sentences.

1. What is the main idea of the first paragraph?
   a. United States companies plan to clone chickens.
   b. Cloning chickens is the future of chicken farming.
   c. We now have the technology to clone chickens.
   d. Cloning chickens will increase chicken production.

2. Why is it desirable to have chickens that are all identical?
3. Why are animal welfare groups against mass production of chickens?
4. What are the advantages and disadvantages of mass-producing identical chickens?

B. Skimming and Scanning for Details

Scan the reading to find the answers to these questions. Write complete sentences.

1. In paragraph 3, line 4, what does *it* mean?
2. How is a chimera created?
3. What is the difference between a chimera and a clone?
4. How does Origen plan to scale up production of genetically engineered chickens?
5. The first sentence in paragraph 8 refers to "another challenge." What was the first challenge?
6. What discrepancy is noted between information on Origen's Web site and statements made by its spokesperson?

C. Making Inferences and Drawing Conclusions

The answers to these questions are not directly stated in the reading. Write complete sentences.

1. Why might some shoppers hesitate to buy meat from cloned chickens?
2. What can you deduce from the article about the motivation of chicken farmers?
3. Why might Origen be unwilling to reveal details of its results?
4. What did you deduce from the article about chicken farming in the United States?
5. Do you think the article presents a balanced view of the topic? What is the author's opinion?

Discussion Questions

Discuss the answers to these questions with your classmates.

1. Would you like all chickens to taste the same? Why or why not?
2. A welfare group says that the prospect of cloning billions of identical chickens could increase the suffering of farm birds. How do factory-farmed birds suffer now? How could they suffer more if cloned? How can farmers improve conditions for their farm birds?
3. What are the benefits of cloning chickens and other farm animals? What are the dangers?

Critical Thinking Questions

Discuss the answers to these questions with your classmates.

1. Do you think cloning animals is moral? Why or why not? Do you think there are purposes, such as saving endangered animals, for which cloning technology should be used? Do you think there are purposes for which cloning technology should not be used?
2. Scientific advances often come at the expense of animals. How do animals suffer for the sake of science and medicine? Should animals be used at all for the benefit of humans? What might happen if all animals were protected from scientific experiments and manipulation?

3. Origen talks about engineering birds to lay eggs containing medical drugs. Genetic engineering has been used mostly in food crops to make them hardier and pest resistant. Scientists have also genetically modified goats to produce an important clotting medicine in their milk. Some people believe that all genetic engineering is morally wrong because it goes against nature. Others are afraid that genetically modified plants or animals could enter the environment and have serious effects on the ecosystem. Do you agree with either (or both) of these groups? Why or why not? Are there positive aspects to genetic engineering? Why do cloning and genetic engineering spark such fierce debate? What do you predict for the future?

Writing

Writing Skills

A. Organizing: *The Argument Essay*

In an argument essay, just like an oral argument, you must win the person over to your way of thinking. You must appeal to the other person's sense of reason by being logical and by providing evidence.

Assume that the reader does not agree with you. If the reader did agree, then you would not have to write an argument. When arguing your point, remember not to insult the reader in any way just because his or her opinion may be different from yours. Insulting your reader with a statement such as "People who believe that handguns should not be banned are all killers" will weaken your argument. Always be respectful and logical.

Just presenting your own reasons is not sufficient to convince the reader. To convince the reader, you must understand your opponents' position and the reasons they would give to support their opinion. It is, therefore, essential to know both sides of the argument in order to make a strong case for your position.

Using Specific Evidence

Nothing will support your opinion better than pertinent facts and statistics. To find evidence, go to the library, where you will find facts, numbers, and data. These will make your argument more definite and harder to contest.

Look at the following examples of statements with and without support:

Examples:

Without support: Many Americans don't support human cloning.
With support: According to the 2002 Genetics and Public Policy Center survey, most Americans (76 percent) oppose allowing scientists to work on ways to clone humans.

Without support: Most Americans support giving animals the same rights as people.

With support: According to a 2003 Gallup News Service poll, 71 percent of Americans said animals deserved some protection, and a full 25 percent responded that animals deserve the same rights as people.

Use authority to support your argument. The authority you use must be recognized, reliable, and expert. In the above examples, the authority for cloning was the Genetics and Public Policy Center, and the authority for animal rights was the Gallup News Service, a famous polling service.

When using an authority, you should identify it by name and enclose the exact words of the authority in quotation marks. In Reading 2, an authority is used to make a convincing argument:

> "The last thing they should be doing is increasing growth rates," says Abigail Hall of Britain's Royal Society for the Prevention of Cruelty to Animals.

Avoid making vague references to authorities using phrases such as "authorities agree . . .," "people say . . .," and "research says . . .." These are not acceptable in a logical argument.

Organizing Your Argument

The Introduction

Introduce the topic by giving background information. It is important that the reader understand the issue to be argued. Define any terms that are unclear. If you were going to argue against animal testing, you would have to define animal testing very clearly before taking your stand.

The thesis statement in an argument essay is different from those in other types of essays. In the argument essay thesis, you have to be persuasive and take a stand or choose a side on an issue. Look back at the thesis statement of the student essay.

Body Paragraphs

The body paragraphs give reasons for your opinion and support them with evidence or facts. Each body paragraph relates to a point of the argument stated in your thesis. The body paragraphs should be ordered so that the strongest reason is last.

A characteristic of the argument essay is that it recognizes the opposing view and proves it wrong, or *refutes* it. This means that you start with one of your opponents' viewpoints and use your superior reasons to prove that it is wrong. Generally, the refutation occurs in the last body paragraph. Look back at the student essay to see how the student refutes the opposing argument.

Read the following argument about animal testing. Then read the sample refutation.

Argument:

Using animals for testing is wrong and should be banned. Animals feel pain in the same way as humans. Causing pain to an animal is the same as causing pain to a human being. If animals have the same right to be free from pain, we should not experiment on them. Each year in the United States, about 70 million animals are used in research. They are tortured, injured, and killed in the name of science by private companies, government agencies, and educational institutions. Animals are used to test the degree of harmfulness of certain household products and their ingredients. Sometimes animals are injected with infectious diseases such as AIDS. In most cases, the animals are left to die with no certainty that this suffering and death will save a single life or benefit humans in any way at all. There is no reason to make innocent animals suffer; other alternatives should be used.

Refutation:

While it is true that many animals suffer and die in scientific research, it is a fact that we need animal research for advances in medicine and product safety. Most of today's medical advances, such as vaccines, surgical procedures, and so on, would not have been possible without animal experimentation. Computer models or artificial substances cannot work in the same way as blood, bones, or organs can in a living system. It is not possible to predict the course of many diseases or the effects of treatments without testing them on living systems. At present, scientists do not know enough about living systems to replicate one on a computer. Until that day comes, animals are vital in research if medical progress is to continue.

The Conclusion

In the conclusion, summarize the main points of your argument or restate the thesis. End your conclusion with a strong statement, such as a demand for action or an alternative solution.

The following is a brief outline for an argument essay:

Introduction

Background information
Thesis: Take a stand

Paragraph 1

Argument that supports your opinion

Paragraph 2

Stronger argument that supports your opinion

Paragraph 3

Strongest argument that supports your opinion

Paragraph 4

Refutation

Conclusion

Restate thesis or summarize main points.
End with an alternative or demand for action

B. Exercises

1. Look at both sides of the issue. Read each thesis statement and then write two reasons for it and two reasons against it. The first one is done for you.

    1. Is it right to clone animals?

        For

        a. Cloning allows us to mass-produce animals that provide products that are desirable to humans.

        Against

        a. It violates animal rights.

b. It is possible for scientists to advance our knowledge of genetics by studying cloned animals.

b. Cloning is expensive. We could spend the money on more important things.

2. Animals should be used for scientific and medical research.

For

a. _____

_____

_____

b. _____

_____

_____

Against

a. _____

_____

_____

b. _____

_____

_____

3. It is a good idea to genetically engineer farm animals and fish for consumption.

For

a. _____

_____

_____

b. _____

_____

_____

Against

a. _____

_____

_____

b. _____

_____

_____

4. It is not right to kill animals for any reason.

For

a. _____

_____

_____

b. _____

_____

_____

Against

a. _____

_____

_____

b. _____

_____

_____

2. Which of these sentences do not use a reliable authority?

a. A 2002 poll from Johns Hopkins University shows that 76 percent of Americans are against scientific efforts to clone humans.

b. Research indicates that most Americans are against cloning humans.

c. A recent study shows that fish don't like fishermen.

d. According to PETA (People for the Ethical Treatment of Animals), fish farms make fish suffer by keeping them in overcrowded conditions.

Writing Model: The Argument Essay

Read the following argument essay written by a student.

Against Animal Rights

1   There has been a debate about animal rights for a long time. People who
support animal rights believe that animals should have the same rights as
humans, such as the right to equality and freedom. It is important that as
rational humans we protect all living things in order to keep our planet in
5   balance. However, it is my belief that this does not mean that animals should
have the same rights as humans. First, animals are not the same as humans;
they are different. If we give them the same rights as humans, we will not
be able to eat meat or keep animals for pleasure and entertainment, which
humans have done since the beginning of time.

10   Are animals like us? This is a complex problem. It is true that animals
feel pain like humans, but they cannot think like humans. Animals cannot
reason. Animals do not survive by making conscious decisions. Human rights
are about conscious decisions we make about how we live and how we behave
toward one another. Can animals make decisions like that? Animals cannot
15   tell you what their rights are. No animal can take you to court for violating its
rights. This does not mean we should treat them cruelly or in a way that is not
humane. On the contrary, we should treat them with respect because they are
different from us. We need to treat all living species with respect to keep our
planet in balance.

20   Secondly, if animals had the same rights as humans, then people who killed
animals for food would be murderers. Anyone who ate a steak or had turkey
for Thanksgiving would go to prison. What would happen if someone killed a
fly? Most people who support animal rights are vegetarians. They believe that
humans are supposed to be vegetarians, and that their teeth and stomachs
25   are designed to eat vegetables and not meat. However, there is historical and
biological proof that humans have always eaten meat. They hunted animals
for food and ate seeds and nuts. Humans are not different today. Not only
could we no longer eat meat, but we could not wear leather or fur. Humans
have been wearing the skins of animals since the beginning. If it was not
30   wrong then, why should it be wrong now?

My opponents say it is wrong for people to use animals in experiments or use them for entertainment. The Web page of PETA (People for the Ethical Treatment of Animals), an organization that supports animal rights, says, "Animals are not ours to eat, wear, experiment on or use for entertainment." People who support animal rights have such strong beliefs about this that they have set fire to or destroyed fur and leather stores and medical laboratories. They have even used violence to show their beliefs. Is this humane toward other humans? They believe that animals should not be used for research even if it would lead to cures for deadly diseases. Using animals for research has saved and will save human lives, but this does not matter to animal rights supporters. Is it better to experiment on humans rather than animals? They think so. They also believe that animals should not be used for entertainment. This means that we could not have zoos to go to, and we could not even have pets because to have pets would be a form of pleasure and entertainment.

In conclusion, I think people want to protect all species to keep the earth in balance. Some want to give animals the same rights as humans, while others, which I think are the majority, want to give animals the right to be free from cruelty and torture. Even if some animals are more conscious of the world than others, this does not mean animals are "like us." They are different and cannot have the same rights as humans. If they did, we could no longer eat meat, wear their skins, or use them for research. This does not mean we should be cruel to animals. We should respect them and treat them humanely.

Fernando
Brazil

Student Essay Follow-Up

1. Underline the thesis statement.
2. Is the student's argument for animal rights or against them? State his 3 reasons.
3. Are the 2 reasons developed in the body paragraphs?
4. Examine paragraph 1. Do all the ideas support the student's opinion?
5. Are the main points restated in the conclusion? Does the writer give a final comment on the topic?

Writing Practice

A. Write an Argument Essay

Write an essay on one of the following topics. In your essay, try to include **3** or more vocabulary words from the readings in this chapter.

1. Write an argument for or against using animals for medical research.
2. Write an argument for or against using animals for entertainment.
3. Write an argument for or against fish farms.

B. Pre-Write

Work alone, with a partner, or in a group.

1. Brainstorm the topic. Look at pages 254–256 to find out about brainstorming. Write 3 reasons for and 3 reasons against some aspect of the topic.
2. Select the strongest points. Which side do you want to take a stand on?
3. Work on a thesis statement.

C. Outline

1. Organize your ideas.

Step 1: Write your thesis statement, including the 3 reasons for or against some aspect of the topic.

Step 2: Order your reasons. Choose the opponents' arguments that you will refute.

Step 3: Decide what kinds of support would be relevant. Go to the library or use the Internet to get relevant facts.

2. Make a more detailed outline. The essay form on page 21 will help you.

D. Write a Rough Draft

Look at page 257 to find out about writing a rough draft.

E. Revise Your Rough Draft

Use the Revision Checklist on page 258.

F. Edit Your Essay

Use the Editing Checklist on page 259. Check your work for correct use of transition words.

Example:

Error: Some people want to save animals from cruelty and torture; others want to give animals the same rights as humans.   trans

Correct: Although some people want to save animals from cruelty and torture, others want to give animals the same rights as humans.

When you find a mistake of this type, you can write the symbol "trans" (incorrect use of transition word). Look at page 260 for other symbols to use when editing your work.

G. Write Your Final Copy

When your rough draft has been edited, you can write the final copy of your essay.

Additional Writing Practice

A. Summarize

Write a one-paragraph summary of Reading 1. Check your summary with the Summary Checklist on page 269.

B. Paraphrase

Paraphrase the last paragraph in Reading 2. Look at pages 264–267 to find out about paraphrasing. Begin with "As Graves reports . . .," or "Based on Graves's article . . .."

C. Research

Do research to find the name of an organization or group that is against eating meat. Find 3 arguments for and against the group's point of view. Use the library and the Internet to find facts to support your arguments. Use your own experience and that of your friends to gather information on this topic.

You may use your research later to write an argument essay.

Weaving It Together

⏱ Timed Writing

Choose one of the following topics that you have not already written about in "Writing Practice," or choose the topic you researched. You have 50 minutes to write an argument essay.

1. Write an argument for or against using animals for medical research.
2. Write an argument for or against using animals for entertainment.
3. Write an argument for or against fish farms.
4. Write an argument for or against eating meat, using the information you researched.

Connecting to the Internet

A. Go to the Web site of a well-known British or American news magazine or newspaper. Find a recent news article on the topic of animal rights. Summarize the article in about 50 words. Tell your class about the information you found. What Web sites did you use for your search? Which ones were most helpful? Did you encounter any problems when searching for this information? How did you solve them?

B. Use the Internet to research animal cloning. Write a short article on animal cloning that includes answers to these questions: What was the first cloned animal? What others have been clones since then? What reasons do scientists give for cloning? What are some their goals? What are some controversies involving animal cloning?

C. Use the Internet to research gorillas, whales, or dolphins. Find out how the animal you chose exhibits behavior similar to humans and then write about it.

What Do You Think Now?

Refer to page 205 at the beginning of this chapter. Do you know the answers now? Complete the sentence or circle the best answer.

1. The U.K. passed/did not pass laws to protect animals from abuse before they did so for children.
2. _____ wrote the first book on animal rights.
3. _____ gives rights to animals in its constitution.
4. The key genes in humans and _____ are 99.4 percent the same.
5. In the United States chickens are/are not cloned.

Chapter

9 Readings from Literature

What Do You Think?

Answer the questions with your best guess. Circle **Yes** or **No**.

Do you think . . .

	Yes	No
1. "Winterblossom Garden" is about a Japanese garden?	Yes	No
2. *the point of view* in literature means the opinions of the person?	Yes	No
3. there is only one point of view from which to tell a story?	Yes	No
4. a short story can be an autobiography?	Yes	No
5. the feeling of a story doesn't change if it is written in the first person (I) or third person (he/she)?	Yes	No

Pre-Reading

1. Discuss the answers to these questions with your classmates.

    1. Look at the picture. What is traditional and what is not traditional?

    2. How have traditional ways of preparing food changed?

    3. Which kind of food do you prefer to eat—freshly prepared food or prepackaged and ready-to-eat food?

2. Decide whether the following phrases are more likely to be said by a young adult or a parent, and put them in the proper column in the table. Then add some phrases of your own.

Why don't you eat your vegetables?   It's time you thought about the future.

I don't have time to go with you.   I'd like to buy my own.

Clean up your room!   Why don't we meet your friend?

That is so corny!

Parent	Young Adult

3. Discuss the answers to these questions with your classmates.

    1. What kind of things do your parents tell you to do?

    2. If your parents have different ideas or values than you do, how do you react?

4. How are your ideas different from your parents' ideas? Make short notes in the following categories:

	My Ideas	My Parents' Ideas
Education		
Marriage		
Work		
Responsibility		
Other		

**CD 2,
Track 7**

Winterblossom Garden *by David Low*

The following is an excerpt from an autobiographical short story. Born in 1952 in Queens, New York, David Low now lives in the East Village of New York City. The short story "Winterblossom Garden" appeared in the anthology Under Western Eyes *(Doubleday, New York, 1995), edited by Garrett Hongo.*

1   **M**y mother pours two cups of tea from the porcelain teapot that has always been in its wicker basket[1] on the kitchen
5   table. On the sides of the teapot, a maiden[2] dressed in a jade-green gown visits a bearded emperor at his palace near the sky. The maiden waves a
10   vermilion[3] fan.

"I bet you still don't know how to cook," my mother says. She places a plate of steamed roast pork buns before me.

15   "Mom, I'm not hungry."

"If you don't eat more, you will get sick."

I take a bun from the plate, but it is too hot. My mother hands me a napkin so I can put the bun down. Then she peels a banana in front of me.

20   "I'm not obsessed with food like you," I say.

"What's wrong with eating?"

---

[1]**wicker basket:** basket made of woven grass or twigs
[2]**maiden:** young unmarried woman (old English)
[3]**vermilion:** bright red

She looks at me as she takes a big bite of the banana.

"I'm going to have a photography show at the end of the summer."

"Are you still taking pictures of old buildings falling down? How ugly! Why don't you take happier pictures?"

"I thought you would want to come," I answer. "It's not easy to get a gallery."

"If you were married," she says, her voice becoming unusually soft, "you would take better pictures. You would be happy."

"I don't know what you mean. Why do you think getting married will make me happy?"

My mother looks at me as if I have spoken in Serbo-Croatian. She always gives me this look when I say something she does not want to hear. She finishes the banana; then she puts the plate of food away. Soon she stands at the sink, turns on the hot water and washes dishes. My mother learned long ago that silence has a power of its own.

She takes out a blue cookie tin from the dining room cabinet. Inside this tin, my mother keeps her favorite photographs. Whenever I am ready to leave, my mother brings it to the living room and opens it on the coffee table. She knows I cannot resist looking at these pictures again; I will sit down next to her on the sofa for at least another hour. Besides the portraits of the family, my mother has images of people I have never met: her father, who owned a poultry store on Pell Street and didn't get a chance to return to China before he died; my father's younger sister, who still runs a pharmacy in Rio de Janeiro (she sends the family an annual supply of cough drops); my mother's cousin Kay, who died at thirty, a year after she came to New York from Hong Kong. Although my mother has a story to tell for each photograph, she refuses to speak at all about Kay, as if the mere mention of her name will bring back her ghost to haunt us all.

My mother always manages to find a picture I have not seen before; suddenly I discover I have a relative who is a mortician[4] in Vancouver. I pick up a portrait of Uncle Lao-Hu, a silver-haired man with a goatee[5] who owned a curio shop on Mott Street until he retired last year and moved to Hawaii. In a color print, he stands in the doorway of his store, holding a bamboo Moon Man in front of him, as if it were a bowling trophy. The statue, which is actually two feet tall, has a staff in its left hand, while its right palm balances a peach, a sign of long life. The top of the Moon Man's head protrudes in

---

[4]**mortician:** person whose job is to take care of funerals; also called an undertaker
[5]**goatee:** small, pointed beard

the shape of an eggplant; my mother believes that such a head contains an endless wealth of wisdom.

"Your uncle Lao-Hu is a wise man, too," my mother says, "except when he's in love. When he still owned the store, he fell in love with his women customers all the time. He was always losing money because he gave away his merchandise to any woman who smiled at him."

I see my uncle's generous arms full of gifts: a silver Buddha, an ivory dragon, a pair of emerald chopsticks.

"These women confused him," she adds. "That's what happens when a Chinese man doesn't get married."

Mother shakes her head and sighs.

"In his last letter, Lao-Hu invited me to visit him in Honolulu. Your father refuses to leave the store."

"Why don't you go anyway?"

"I can't leave your father alone." She stares at the pictures scattered on the coffee table.

"Mom, why don't you do something for yourself? I thought you were going to start taking English lessons."

"Your father thinks it would be a waste of time."

While my mother puts the cookie tin away, I stand up to stretch my legs. I gaze at a photograph that hangs on the wall above the sofa: my parents' wedding picture. My mother was matched[6] to my father; she claims that if her own father had been able to repay the money that Dad spent to bring her to America, she might never have married him at all. In the wedding picture she wears a stunned expression. She is dressed in a luminous gown of ruffles[7] and lace; the train[8] spirals at her feet. As she clutches the bouquet tightly against her stomach, she might be asking, "What am I doing? Who is this man?" My father's face is thinner than it is now. His tuxedo[9] is too small for him; the flower in his lapel[10] droops. He hides his hand with the crooked pinky behind his back.

I have never been sure if my parents really love each other. I have only seen them kiss at their children's weddings. They never touch each other in public. When I was little, I often thought they went to sleep in the clothes they wore to work.

---

[6]**matched:** given in an arranged marriage
[7]**ruffles:** decorative frills on clothing; usually found around the neck, wrist, or hem
[8]**train:** long back part of a dress that trails along the ground
[9]**tuxedo:** formal suit worn by men
[10]**lapel:** part of the front of a coat or jacket that is attached to the collar and folds back on both sides

Vocabulary

A. Vocabulary in Context

Select the letter of the answer that is closest in meaning to the **bold** word or phrase.

1. His mother is **obsessed with** food.
    a. has problems with   c. thinks about all the time
    b. never thinks about   d. criticizes all the time

2. He cannot **resist** looking at the pictures.
    a. force himself to   c. accept
    b. stop himself from   d. insist on

3. His uncle held the Moon Man in front of him as if it were a **trophy**.
    a. flower   c. child
    b. prize   d. puppet

4. The statue's head **protrudes** in the shape of an eggplant.
    a. sticks out   c. gets smaller
    b. hangs down   d. sinks

5. He **gazes at** a photograph on the wall.
    a. talks about   c. points to
    b. mentions   d. looks at for a long time

6. She has a **stunned** expression.
    a. doubtful   c. clear
    b. surprised   d. positive

7. His mother is dressed in a **luminous** wedding gown.
    a. white   c. plain
    b. heavy   d. shiny

8. She **clutches** a bouquet against her stomach.
    a. holds tightly   c. shows
    b. opens up   d. hides

9. The flower in his lapel **droops**.
    a. looks fresh   c. hangs down
    b. shines   d. sticks out

10. He hides his hand with the crooked **pinky**.

    a. nail   c. thumb

    b. little finger   d. middle finger

B. Vocabulary Building

1. Read the list of verbs below. Find verbs in the reading that have the same meaning.

    1. manage _____run_____

    2. revive _____

    3. abandon _____

    4. stare _____

    5. hold tightly _____

    6. conceal _____

2. Use the verbs you found in Exercise 1 to complete these questions. Then, with a partner, take turns asking and answering these questions.

    1. Why is his mother _____ a bouquet in the picture?

    2. Why doesn't she want to _____ his father?

    3. What does the son think as he _____ at the wedding picture?

    4. Why does the father _____ his pinky?

    5. What kind of store does his cousin _____?

    6. What does the mother think will _____ the aunt's ghost?

C. Vocabulary in New Context

Use the verbs from Part B, Exercise 1 to make sentences of your own.

Reading Comprehension

A. Understanding the Story

    1. Describe the sequence of events in the story.

    2. What information does the son tell his mother?

    3. How does the mother respond?

    4. What does the son want his mother to do? Why?

    5. What does the mother want her son to do? Why?

B. Interpreting the Story

1. How do the actions of the people in the story express their values and feelings? Give examples.
2. Why is the blue cookie tin important to the son and as well as the mother?
3. What is the mother's idea of marriage? How might this be different from the son's idea?

C. Understanding the Characters

1. Describe the character of the mother. What are her values? Support your description with examples from the story.
2. Describe the character of the son. What are his values? Support your description with examples from the story.
3. Role-play the conversation between the writer and his mother. Continue the conversation with your own ideas.

D. Recognizing Style

1. From whose point of view is the story told? Does the writer want us to sympathize with or criticize this point of view?
2. Think about how the following images are used in the story. What do they symbolize?
   a. the teapot
   b. the blue cookie tin
   c. the parents' wedding picture
3. Find examples of similes and metaphors in the story. How do they help us to understand the characters?

Discussion Questions

Discuss these questions with your classmates.

1. What are some things that parents and children have different ideas about?
2. Do you think parents are usually right?
3. If you were a parent, what advice would you give your child?
4. If your values and your parents' values were different, how would this affect your relationship with them?
5. What advice would you give to the mother and son in the story?

Critical Thinking Questions

Discuss these questions with your classmates.

1. This story is about what seems to be a very mundane event in the life of the author. It is called a "slice of life" story. It doesn't have a complicated plot and it isn't exciting or suspenseful. Nevertheless, slice-of-life stories are very popular. Did you enjoy this reading? Why or why not? Why do you think people like "slice-of-life stories? What experiences and people in your life could you turn into a story?

2. What lessons can we learn from this excerpt from "Winterblossom Garden"?

3. What is the "generation gap"? Why are generational differences often more pronounced between immigrants and their children? What are some of the problems that immigrant parents and their children face at home? What are some problems they face outside the home?

4. The author's father thinks it's a waste of time for his wife to learn English. Why do you think he feels this way? Are there certain fears the father might have? What does he gain by not having his wife learn English? What does he lose? What does the mother gain and lose? Do you think that older people have less need to learn the language of a new country?

5. The son questions his mother's happiness in her arranged marriage. Do you think the mother is unhappy with her situation? What is affecting the son's perception of his mother and father? Arranged marriages still exist in many cultures. What are the advantages and disadvantages of arranged marriage? Do you think people can find happiness in an arranged marriage? Do you think arranged marriage will still exist 50 or 100 years from now?

Reading 2

CD 2,
Track 8

Mrs. Sen's *by Jhumpa Lahiri*

The following is an excerpt from a short story by Jhumpa Lahiri. Born in London in 1967 and raised in Rhode Island, the daughter of Bengali parents, Lahiri has a heritage and culture influenced by both India and the United States. "Mrs. Sen's" appeared in her collection of short stories entitled The Interpreter of Maladies *(Houghton Mifflin, Boston, 1999).*

1　　Eliot didn't mind going to Mrs. Sen's after school. By September the tiny beach house where he and his mother lived year-round was already cold; Eliot and his mother had
5　to bring a portable heater along whenever they moved from one room to another, and to seal the windows with plastic sheets and a hair dryer. The beach was barren and dull to play on alone; the only neighbors who stayed
10　on past Labor Day, a young married couple, had no children, and Eliot no longer found it interesting to gather broken mussel shells in his bucket, or to stroke the seaweed, strewn like strips of emerald lasagna on the sand.

An Indian woman preparing food.

15　Mrs. Sen's apartment was warm, sometimes too warm; the radiators continuously hissed like a pressure cooker. Eliot learned to remove his sneakers first thing in Mrs. Sen's doorway, and to place them on the bookcase next to a row of Mrs. Sen's slippers, each a different color, with soles as flat as cardboard and a ring of leather to hold her big toe.

20　He especially enjoyed watching Mrs. Sen as she chopped things, seated on newspapers on the living room floor. Instead of a knife she used a blade that curved like the prow[1] of a Viking ship, sailing to battle in distant seas. The blade was hinged at one end to a narrow wooden base. The steel, more

---

[1]**prow:** front part of a boat, which on some old ships curved up quite far

black than silver, lacked a uniform polish, and had a serrated[2] crest, she told
Eliot, for grating. Each afternoon Mrs. Sen lifted the blade and locked it into
place, so that it met the base at an angle. Facing the sharp edge without ever
touching it, she took whole vegetables between her hands and hacked them
apart: cauliflower, cabbage, butternut squash. She split things in half, then
quarters, speedily producing florets, cubes, slices, and shreds. She could peel
a potato in seconds. At times she sat cross-legged, at times with legs splayed,
surrounded by an array of colanders[3] and shallow bowls of water in which
she immersed her chopped ingredients.

    While she worked she kept an eye on the television and an eye on Eliot, but
she never seemed to keep an eye on the blade. Nevertheless she refused to let
Eliot walk around when she was chopping. "Just sit, sit please, it will take just
two more minutes," she said, pointing to the sofa, which was draped at all
times with a green and black bedcover printed with rows of elephants bearing
palanquins on their backs. The daily procedure took about an hour. In order
to occupy Eliot, she supplied him with the comics section of the newspaper,
and crackers spread with peanut butter, and sometimes a Popsicle, or carrot
sticks sculpted with her blade. She would have roped off the area if she could.
Once, though, she broke her own rule; in need of additional supplies, and
reluctant to rise from the catastrophic mess that barricaded her, she asked
Eliot to fetch something from the kitchen. "If you don't mind, there is a plastic
bowl, large enough to hold this spinach, in the cabinet next to the fridge.
Careful, oh dear, be careful," she cautioned as he approached. "Just leave it,
thank you, on the coffee table, I can reach."

    She had brought the blade from India, where apparently there was at least
one in every household. "Whenever there is a wedding in the family," she
told Eliot one day, "or a large celebration of any kind, my mother sends out
word in the evening for all the neighborhood women to bring blades just like
this one, and then they sit in an enormous circle on the roof of our building,
laughing and gossiping and slicing fifty kilos of vegetables through the
night." Her profile hovered protectively over her work, a confetti of cucumber,
eggplant, and onion skins heaped around her. "It is impossible to fall asleep
those nights, listening to their chatter." She paused to look at a pine tree
framed by the living room window. "Here, in this place where Mr. Sen has
brought me, I cannot sometimes sleep in so much silence."

---

[2]**serrated:** jagged
[3]**colander:** a metal or plastic bowl with holes in it; used to separate liquid from food

Another day she sat prying the pimpled yellow fat off chicken parts, then dividing them between thigh and leg. As the bones cracked apart over the blade her golden bangles jostled,[4] her forearms glowed, and she exhaled audibly[5] through her nose. At one point she paused, gripping the chicken with both hands, and stared out the window. Fat and sinew clung to her fingers.

"Eliot, if I began to scream right now at the top of my lungs, would someone come?"

"Mrs. Sen, what's wrong?"

"Nothing. I am only asking if someone would come."

Eliot shrugged. "Maybe."

"At home that is all you have to do. Not everybody has a telephone. But just raise your voice a bit, or express grief or joy of any kind, and one whole neighborhood and half of another has come to share the news, to help with arrangements."

By then Eliot understood that when Mrs. Sen said home, she meant India, not the apartment where she sat chopping vegetables. He thought of his own home, just five miles away, and the young married couple who waved from time to time as they jogged at sunset along the shore. On Labor Day they'd had a party. People were piled[6] on the deck, eating, drinking, the sound of their laughter rising above the weary sigh[7] of the waves. Eliot and his mother weren't invited. It was one of the rare days his mother had off, but they didn't go anywhere. She did the laundry, and balanced the checkbook, and, with Eliot's help, vacuumed the inside of the car. Eliot had suggested that they go through the car wash a few miles down the road as they did every now and then, so that they could sit inside, safe and dry, as soap and water and a circle of giant canvas ribbons slapped[8] the windshield, but his mother said she was too tired, and sprayed the car with a hose. When, by evening, the crowd on the neighbors' deck began dancing, she looked up their number in the phone book and asked them to keep it down.

"They might call you," Eliot said eventually to Mrs. Sen. "But they might complain that you were making too much noise."

From where Eliot sat on the sofa he could detect her curious scent of mothballs and cumin, and he could see the perfectly centered part in her

---

[4]**jostled:** pushed against each other
[5]**exhaled audibly:** breathed out noisily
[6]**piled:** crowded
[7]**weary sigh:** heavy, tired sound
[8]**slapped:** hit

braided hair, which was shaded with crushed vermilion[9] and therefore
appeared to be blushing. At first Eliot had wondered if she had cut her
scalp, or if something had bitten here there. But then one day he saw her
95 standing before the bathroom mirror, solemnly applying, with the head of a
thumbtack, a fresh stroke of scarlet powder, which she stored in a small jam
jar. A few grains of the powder fell onto the bridge of her nose as she used the
thumbtack to stamp a dot above her eyebrows. "I must wear the powder every
day," she explained when Eliot asked her what it was for, "for the rest of the
100 days that I am married."

"Like a wedding ring, you mean?"

"Exactly, Eliot, exactly like a wedding ring. Only with no fear of losing it in
the dishwater."

---

[9]**vermilion:** bright red

Vocabulary

A. Vocabulary in Context

Select the letter of the answer that is closest in meaning to the **bold** word or phrase.

1. The beach was **barren**.
   a. dirty
   b. polluted
   c. empty
   d. rainy

2. The seaweed was **strewn** like strips of emerald lasagna.
   a. spread around
   b. lost
   c. collected
   d. growing

3. Eliot placed his sneakers next to a **row of** Mrs. Sen's slippers.
   a. a group of
   b. a line of
   c. a circle of
   d. a mass of

4. Instead of a knife Mrs. Sen used **a blade**.
   a. an old-fashioned fork
   b. the cutting part of a knife
   c. the top part of a hammer
   d. the pointed part of a piece of wood

5. She took whole vegetables between her hands and **hacked** them apart.
   a. cut roughly
   b. cut carefully
   c. cut thinly
   d. pulled quickly

6. She was surrounded by **an array** of colanders.
- a. a variety
- b. a pair
- c. a copy
- d. a crowd

7. She was surrounded by shallow bowls of water in which she **immersed** her chopped ingredients.
- a. put underwater
- b. dried for a long time
- c. stored for a time
- d. salted

8. The sofa was **draped** at all times with a bedcover.
- a. organized
- b. decorated
- c. fresh
- d. covered

9. She was **reluctant** to rise from the mess.
- a. excited
- b. happy
- c. unwilling
- d. bored

10. Eliot could **detect** her curious scent.
- a. imagine
- b. notice
- c. experience
- d. value

Word Partnership	Use **array** with:
adj.	**broad/vast/wide** array, **impressive/dizzying** array
prep.	array **of something**

B. Vocabulary Building

1. Match the verbs with the nouns as they were used in the context of the reading. Look back at the reading to check your answers. Add two more nouns that may be used with each verb.
- a. a potato
- b. your voice
- c. the noise
- d. vegetables
- e. shells

1. __e__ gather   ___shells___ _____ _____

2. _____ chop   _____ _____ _____

3. _____ peel   _____ _____ _____

4. _____ raise   _____ _____ _____

5. _____ keep down   _____ _____ _____

C. Vocabulary in New Context

Make questions about the reading, using verb and noun combinations from Part B. Then, with a partner, take turns asking and answering these questions.

1. Why does Eliot _____ _____ on the beach?

2. How does Mrs. Sen like to _____ _____?

3. How does Mrs. Sen _____ _____?

4. What would happen if Mrs. Sen _____ _____?

5. Why would the neighbors ask her to _____ _____?

Reading Comprehension

A. Understanding the Story

1. Why does Eliot go to Mrs. Sen's house every day?

2. What does Eliot do at Mrs. Sen's house?

3. What differences does Eliot notice between Mrs. Sen's home and his own home? Make a list in the chart below.

Mrs. Sen's home	Eliot's home

B. Interpreting the Story

Answer the following questions. Support your answers with sentences from the story.

1. How does Eliot feel when he is with his mother?

2. What kind of home life does he have?

3. How does Eliot feel when he is at Mrs. Sen's?

4. How old do you think Eliot is?

5. How is the meaning of the word *home* different for Eliot and for Mrs. Sen?

C. Understanding the Characters

Discuss these questions with a classmate. Support your answers with sentences from the story.

1. What values are important to Mrs. Sen?
2. What values are important to Eliot's mother?
3. Make up a conversation between Mrs. Sen and Eliot's mother. What would they agree about? What would they disagree about?

D. Recognizing Style

Discuss the answers to these questions with a classmate.

1. From whose point of view is the story told? Is this different from the author's point of view? How does the narrator's point of view become apparent?
2. Think about how the following images are used in the story. What do they symbolize?
   a. the chopping blade
   b. the car wash
   c. the scarlet powder
3. Find examples of similes and metaphors in the story. How do they help to convey images?

Examples:

Simile: The seaweed was strewn like strips of emerald lasagna.
Metaphor: The weary sigh of the waves.

Discussion Questions

Discuss the answers to these questions with a classmate.

1. Whom do you sympathize more with in the story, Eliot or Mrs. Sen? Why?
2. What do you think will happen at the end of the story?
3. What are some everyday things that are done differently in your culture than in the American culture or another culture that you know?
4. Which culture would you prefer to live in: a culture in which people are close to each other and material things are not important or a culture in which independence, privacy, and money are important? Give reasons.

Critical Thinking Questions

Discuss the answers to these questions with a classmate.

1. This story emphasizes cultural differences. Why did the boy say, "But they might complain that you were making too much noise"? What didn't he understand about Mrs. Sen's culture? How do cultural differences lead to misunderstandings and sometimes conflict? How can we improve cultural understanding?

2. Choose a country with a culture totally different from yours. Now imagine yourself moving to that country. What do you think would be the most difficult thing to adjust to? What do you think would be the most difficult thing for your new countrymen to understand about you? Would you try to assimilate into the new culture? What parts of your culture would you want to hold onto?

3. Does today's world of globalization and mass communication help us understand each other better? Do you think cultures are in danger of losing their identity? Is it important to retain our different cultures? Would people live more peacefully if they were more alike? What advantages are there in retaining our cultural identities? What are the disadvantages?

4. In this "Mrs. Sen's" story, the author creates a vivid picture of the boy's and the woman's lives by using description. What parts of the story are most vivid to you? What words created clear impressions in your mind? Think about a place you have been or a situation you have experienced, and describe it as vividly as you can to your classmates.

Writing

Writing Skills

A. Organizing: *Narrator and Point of View*

Usually, when we ask someone what his or her point of view is, we are asking about the person's opinion. When we are discussing literature, however, *point of view* means the perspective of the person who is telling the story. The story can be presented through the eyes of a character or through the eyes of the author, or the point of view can alternate between characters or between the author and characters. The author can choose from several different options.

First-Person Narrator

The story of "Winterblossom Garden" is told in the first person. This means that we know only what is going on in the mind of the narrator. We know only about events that he sees or experiences. We don't know what his mother thinks, though we can guess by trying to interpret her actions and words. The first-person point of view can be used to increase suspense, because some information can be hidden from readers and then used to surprise them later. It can also create empathy as we try to identify and understand the narrator's feelings. On the other hand, we may come to dislike or distrust the narrator, and in this case we may notice a gap between what the narrator says and what the author wants us to think.

Third-Person Narrator

A story told in the third person refers to all characters as "she," "he," or "they," not as "I." But here there is also a choice for the writer. The author can write as an "omniscient," or all-knowing, narrator who sees everything. In this case, the author is not restricted as to time or location and can see everything that goes on in all the characters' minds. Or the author can write from a limited third-person point of view. In this case, the story is limited to the thoughts of a major character, and nothing is described in the story unless it is seen, felt, or experienced by this character. Look at the excerpt from "Mrs. Sen's." Is it told by an omniscient narrator or by a limited third-person narrator?

B. Exercises

1. Rewrite the following excerpt from the point of view of a third-person narrator. How does the feeling of the story change?

> My mother always manages to find a picture I have not seen before; suddenly I discover I have a relative who is a mortician in Vancouver. I pick up a portrait of Uncle Lao-Hu.

2. Rewrite the following excerpt from the point of view of a first-person narrator. How does the feeling of the story change?

> Eliot didn't mind going to Mrs. Sen's after school. By September the tiny beach house where he and his mother lived year-round was already cold; Eliot and his mother had to bring a portable heater along whenever they moved from one room to another, and to seal the windows with plastic sheets and a hair dryer.

3. Think of an event that happened in your childhood. Write one or two sentences describing what happened in the first person. Then rewrite the sentences in the third person. Read each set of sentences aloud to a partner. How does the feeling of the story change?

Writing Model: Writing about Literature

Read the following essay written by a student.

The Narrator's Point of View in "Winterblossom Garden" and "Mrs. Sen's"

1   "Winterblossom Garden" describes the relationship between an adult son and his mother. It is told in the first person, through the eyes of the son. He and his mother have different views of life, not only because of their age difference but also because she was born in China and he was born and brought up in
5   the United States. "Mrs. Sen's" describes the life of an Indian woman living in the United States who looks after a young boy while his mother is at work. It is told in the third person. The story presents their different understandings of the word *home*. Both stories use the narrator's point of view to present the reader with multiple viewpoints on the meaning of home, family, and culture.
10   Both "Winterblossom Garden" and "Mrs. Sen's" are told through the eyes of one major character. "Winterblossom Garden" is told in the first person,

by the character of the son. He describes himself and his feelings directly: "I have never been sure if my parents really love each other." He describes his mother through her actions and her words: "Soon she stands at the sink, turns on the hot water and washes dishes. My mother learned long ago that silence has a power of its own." By using the first-person point of view, the author helps us to identify with the feelings of the son. We try to understand why the son feels so distant from his mother and why there is a gap between them that makes it difficult to communicate. The author presents the son's point of view in a way that also asks us to challenge and criticize him, and to understand his mother's feelings too.

"Mrs. Sen's" is told in the third person, but the point of view is limited to the thoughts and actions of one main character, the boy Eliot. He is curious about Mrs. Sen's home, and we observe her life through Eliot's eyes as he notices things that seem magical and mysterious to him: "He especially enjoyed watching Mrs. Sen as she chopped things, seated on newspapers on the living room floor. Instead of a knife she used a blade that curved like the prow of a Viking ship, sailing to battle in distant seas." By the end of the story, we find that we are viewing Mrs. Sen's home more positively than Eliot's. Although Eliot does not complain about his home life, as readers we can see that his life is lonely and cold: "By September the tiny beach house where he and his mother lived year-round was already cold. . . . The beach was barren and dull to play on alone; the only neighbors who stayed on past Labor Day, a young married couple, had no children." The author leaves the reader to come to this conclusion about Eliot's loneliness; she does not state it directly. Using the third person to present Eliot's point of view creates a distance between the narrator and the events being described. It allows the reader to view the events from different perspectives: Eliot's, Mrs. Sen's, Eliot's mother's, and the reader's own.

In conclusion, although "Winterblossom Garden" is told in the first person and "Mrs. Sen's" from a limited third-person point of view, both stories present the reader with many different perspectives. As readers we try to understand the main characters' feelings, but at the same time, we also criticize them and reach our own conclusions. In this way, the reader is also encouraged to examine his or her own culture from a new perspective.

Surpuhi
Armenia

Student Essay Follow-Up

1. Underline the thesis statement.
2. What are the similarities in the use of point of view in these two stories? What are the differences?
3. Can you find any additional points of similarity or difference?

Writing Practice

A. Write an Essay about Literature

Write your own interpretation of one of the stories in this chapter. Write an essay on one of the following topics. In your essay, try to include **3** or more vocabulary words from the readings in this chapter.

1. "Winterblossom Garden" illustrates the gap between two generations, but also shows their need to communicate. Discuss.
2. How does the author of "Mrs. Sen's" make the reader examine his or her own culture from a critical viewpoint?
3. In "Winterblossom Garden," we understand more from what the characters do not say than from what the characters do say. Discuss.

B. Pre-Write

Work alone, with a partner, or in a group.

1. Brainstorm the topic. Use one of the techniques on pages 254–256.
2. Select the most interesting points.
3. Work on a thesis statement.

C. Outline

1. Organize your ideas.

   Step 1: Write your thesis statement.

   Step 2: Organize your points in a logical order.

   Step 3: Find sentences in the story to support your points.

2. Make a more detailed outline.

D. Write a Rough Draft

Look at page 257 to find out about writing a rough draft.

E. Revise Your Rough Draft

Use the Revision Checklist on page 258.

F. Edit Your Essay

Use the Editing Checklist on page 259.

G. Write Your Final Copy

When your rough draft has been edited, you can write the final copy of your essay.

Weaving It Together

⏱ Timed Writing

Choose one of the following topics. You have 50 minutes to write an essay about literature.

1. The voice of the narrator in "Mrs. Sen's" is both naïve and wise. Discuss.
2. Compare the character of the son in "Winterblossom Garden" and the character of Eliot in "Mrs. Sen's." How are they similar? How are they different?

Connecting to the Internet

A. Use the Internet to find out about these contemporary writers: Sandra Cisneros, Amy Tan, Alice Walker, and Edwidge Dandicat. What do they have in common? Choose a book by one of these authors that you would like to read. Tell the class the title of the book and why you want to read it.

B. Many thousands of immigrant stories appear in books, magazines, and newspapers every day. Use the Internet to research "immigrant stories." Find a story that you like and summarize it.

C. Use the Internet to research the top issues facing immigrants in the United States or another country of your choice. Write about one of these issues from the point of view (1) of an immigrant, and (2) of a native of the country.

What Do You Think Now?

Refer to page 230 at the beginning of this chapter. Do you know the answers now? Complete the sentence or circle the best answer.

1. "Winterblossom Garden" is/isn't about a Japanese garden.
2. *The point of view* in literature means the _____ of the person telling the story.
3. There is/isn't only one point of view to tell a story.
4. A _____ story can be an autobiography.
5. The feeling of a story changes/doesn't change if it is written in the first person (*I*) or third person (*he/she*).

Resources for Writers

How to Get Ideas, Draft, Revise, and Edit

Getting Ideas

Before starting to write on a specific topic, it is important to develop some ideas. In this section, you will learn a number of strategies for generating ideas. These techniques are useful when you first start thinking about your topic and at other times when you find you have nothing to say about a topic.

Brainstorming

To get ideas and stimulate your thoughts, you can use the strategy of **brainstorming**. You can brainstorm alone or with a group.

These are some guidelines to follow when brainstorming:

- Give yourself or the group a limited amount of time.
- Write down the word or phrase you need to get ideas about.
- Write down all the ideas that come to mind. Do not organize your ideas in any way.
- When your time is up, look over the ideas to see if any can be grouped together.

The following is an example of the ideas that came up in a brainstorming session on the subject of video games for children.

Video Games

addictive	fun
time-consuming	more exciting than TV
bad for eyes	too violent
expensive	take time away from homework

Since there are more negative than positive points written down, the writer might want to write about the negative sides of video games.

Clustering

Clustering is another way of generating ideas. To cluster, you make a visual plan of the connections among your ideas.

Use the following steps for clustering:

1. Write your topic in the center of your paper and circle it.
2. Write an idea related to the topic, circle that idea, and from it draw a line back to the topic. Keep writing down ideas, making circles around them, and connecting them back to the ideas they came from.
3. When you have no more ideas, look at your clusters and decide which ideas seem most important.

The following is an example of the ideas that came up in clustering on the subject of obesity. Using this diagram, the writer could develop an essay on the causes or effects of obesity.

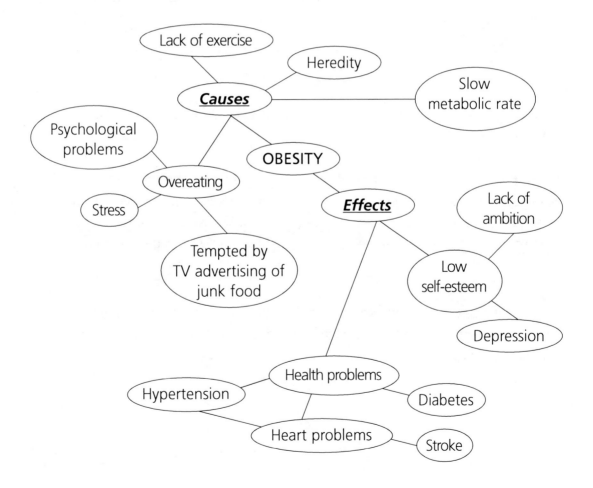

Freewriting

With the **freewriting** technique, you write freely on a topic without stopping. You don't worry about correct grammar or whether what you think is important enough to write down. After you freewrite, you can decide which of your ideas could be useful.

These are some steps to follow when freewriting:

1. Give yourself a time limit.
2. Write the topic at the top of your paper.
3. Write as much as you can about the topic. Don't worry about grammar, spelling, organization, or relevance.
4. Write until your time is up.
5. Read your freewriting and underline the main idea(s).
6. Repeat the process, this time using a main idea as your freewriting topic.

The following is an example of the freewriting technique applied to the subject of a vegetarian diet.

A Vegetarian Diet

I am not a vegetarian, but two of my friends are. They always tell me how cruel it is to kill animals, and I tell them I need meat to get my protein. They tell me you can get protein from sources other than animal products. Animal products contain fat, which can be bad for health, whereas plants are high in fiber and good for health. Even if it were good for me, I just think vegetarian food is boring. But they proved me wrong when I went out to eat with them. The vegetarian dishes were very tasty, and there were so many varieties. There are so many cookbooks now for vegetarians I noticed.

The writer has underlined two ideas that could be explored further. These are "Animal products contain fat, which can be bad for health, whereas plants are high in fiber and good for health," and "The vegetarian dishes were tasty, and there were so many varieties." The writer can take one of these ideas and freewrite about it again.

Drafting

After you have developed some ideas for your essay, it is time to start drafting, or actually writing your essay.

First, you should draft the thesis statement. The thesis statement must tell the reader the main idea you will be discussing and explain your approach to the main idea. A thesis statement should not simply state what you are going to do—for example, "In this essay I will describe my brother." It should present your approach to the main idea, as in "My brother is both an ambitious and a sociable character." The words *ambitious* and *sociable* make clear the focus of your description of your brother. You might write one paragraph on the "ambitious" aspect of your brother, with supporting statements and details, and another paragraph on the "sociable" character of your brother, with supporting statements and details.

Here are some questions to think about as you write your draft:

- What kind of supporting details do I need?
- How many supporting details do I have to give, and how long should the descriptions of them be?
- How do I avoid overlapping supporting details?

As you are writing your first draft, keep these questions in mind. Check and change any sentences that do not support the main idea clearly.

Revising

After the first draft, plan to revise your draft at least once. *Revising* means changing the organization or content of the essay and also editing the sentences.

The questions in the following checklist will help you to see if your essay is focused and well developed. You may wish to ask another person (a classmate) to comment on your essay using the checklist on the following page.

Revision Checklist

Thesis Statement	☐ Does the thesis statement state the writer's main idea adequately?
	☐ Does the thesis statement show the writer's approach or attitude toward the main idea?
Unity	☐ Do the supporting ideas show the writer's attitude toward the main idea?
	☐ Do the supporting details and examples show the writer's attitude toward the main idea?
Development	☐ Is enough evidence provided to support the main idea?
	☐ Are there sufficient supporting details?
	☐ Is the evidence that is provided convincing?
Coherence	☐ Are all the paragraphs logically connected to each other?
	☐ Do the sentences flow logically one after the other?
	☐ Are there sufficient transitions to make the sentences clear?
Purpose	☐ Is the writer's purpose clear?
	☐ Did the writer achieve what he or she wanted to convey to the reader?

Editing

Editing means checking your essay to see if you have expressed your ideas clearly and followed the rules of grammar, spelling, and punctuation.

When editing, focus on one sentence at a time. Make sure your sentences are clear and grammatically correct. Mark them for fragments or run-ons. If you are unsure about a grammatical form, consult a grammar book. When you think you may have misspelled a word, consult a dictionary.

On the following page is a list of editing symbols. The symbols on the left may be used by your instructor or partner to indicate problem areas in your writing.

Editing Checklist

- ☐ Subject and verb in every sentence?
- ☐ Correct tense?
- ☐ Words in correct order?
- ☐ Correct pronoun reference?
- ☐ Subject and verb agreement?
- ☐ Commas in correct place?
- ☐ Wrong words?
- ☐ Missing words?
- ☐ Spelling?

Editing Symbols

Symbol	Explanation
cap	Capital letter
lc	Lowercase— (word or words incorrectly capitalized)
p	Punctuation—incorrect or missing
sp	Spelling mistake
sv	Mistake in agreement of subject and verb
^	Omission (you have left something out)
frag	Sentence fragment (correct by completing sentence)
ro	Run-on sentence (insert period and capital or add comma and conjunction)
vt	Incorrect verb tense
vf	Verb incorrectly formed
modal	Incorrect use or formation of modal
cond	Incorrect use or formation of a conditional sentence
ss	Incorrect sentence structure
wo	Incorrect or awkward word order
conn	Incorrect or missing connector
pass	Incorrect formation or use of passive voice
unclear	Unclear message
art	Incorrect or missing article
num	Problem with the singular or plural of a noun
wc	Wrong word choice, including prepositions
wf	Wrong word form
nonidiom	Nonidiomatic (not expressed this way in English)
coh	Coherence—one idea does not lead to the next
pro re	Pronoun reference unclear or incorrect
pro agree	Pronoun agreement unclear or incorrect
p.o.v.	Shift in point of view
dm	Modifier incorrect or unclear
//st	Sentence structure not parallel
tns	Shift in verb tense
trans	Incorrect transition use or new transition needed
¶	Begin a new paragraph here (indent)

How to Quote

In academic writing, you are expected to support your ideas to make them convincing to the reader. Writing about your own experience alone will not often convince people. If you can refer to a newspaper story, magazine article, or book in which an authority agrees with you, your ideas will have more weight.

The best way to use quoted material is to integrate it into your own writing. You should begin by saying something about the subject in your own words. Then use the quotation to explain the significance of your statement.

Example:

> One aspect of the change in the nature of American society in the 1970s and the 1980s is the change in the pattern of immigration. In his book *The Unfinished Nation*, Brinkley reports, "The nation's immigration quotas expanded significantly in those years, allowing more newcomers to enter the United States legally than at any other point since the beginning of the twentieth century" (1993, p. 898).

The rules for quoting are as follows:

1. Put a comma after the introductory, or *reporting*, phrase. Put quotation marks before and after the words quoted. Capitalize the first word of the quotation if it is the start of a sentence in the original material.

Example:

> He states, "In the 1970s, more than 4 million legal immigrants entered the United States."

2. If the quotation is broken, put quotation marks around both parts and separate the parts with commas. Do not begin the second part with a capital letter unless it is a new sentence.

Example:

> "In the 1970s," he states, "more than 4 million legal immigrants entered the United States."

Omitting Words and Adding Words

It is important to use the exact words of the author you are quoting. If you have to omit part of a quotation to fit the context of your writing, use an ellipsis, which is three spaced periods (. . .).

Example:

> Brinkley states, ". . . the wave of immigration in the twenty years after 1970 was the largest of the twentieth century" (*The Unfinished Nation*, p. 898).

If you need to add words to the original quotation in order to explain it or to make it fit into the structure of your writing, put square brackets [ ] around the words you've added.

Example:

> "Many Asian immigrants [Koreans, Chinese, Japanese, Indian, Filipino, Vietnamese, Thai] were highly educated professionals seeking greater opportunity in the United States," Brinkley stated.

Reporting Words

To introduce a quotation, reporting phrases such as the ones below are used:

As Brinkley said, "_____."

As he stated, "_____."

As he reported, "_____."

As he wrote, "_____."

As he declared, "_____."

As he maintained, "_____."

As he insisted, "_____."

Other reporting phrases without the word *as* can be used in the present or past tense.

Mr. Brinkley said, "_____."

He believes, "_____."

He further stated, "_____."

He continued, "_____."

Example:

Mr. Brinkley further stated, "Already by the end of the 1980s, people of white European background constituted under 80 percent of the population (as opposed to 90 percent a half-century before)."

"It seemed likely that by the middle of the twenty-first century," he continued, "whites of European heritage would constitute less than 50 percent of the population."

Use the phrase *according to* . . . only when you are paraphrasing. Do not use *according to* . . . when citing with quotation marks.

Example:

According to the 1980 Census, 60 percent of Americans identified themselves as having English, German, or Irish ethnic origins.

or

Sixty percent of Americans identified themselves as having English, German, or Irish ethnic origins, according to the 1980 Census.

Remember *always* to document the source of your quotation, even when it is not a direct quotation.

A Note about Plagiarism

Plagiarism is using other people's words or ideas without acknowledging the source of that information. You *must* use quotation marks and cite your source when you use someone's exact words. You *must* cite your source when you paraphrase. It is wrong to use another person's work without giving credit; if you do this in an assignment or on an examination, you may be disqualified from receiving a grade.

How to Paraphrase

Paraphrasing and summarizing are useful alternatives to directly quoting material from books, magazines, and other sources.

When you paraphrase, you put information from another author into different words. In other words, you rephrase it without changing the meaning of the original. When you paraphrase, it is important to use your own words. A paraphrase should usually be the same length as the original passage so that it includes all the information.

Although you are using your own words when you paraphrase, you are expressing another author's ideas. Therefore, you must be sure to give the author credit for them; otherwise, you will be plagiarizing. Begin your paraphrase with a reference to the author and/or title of the work or the source of the article. Use phrases such as:

According to [author's name], . . .
Based on [author's name]'s article in [source], . . .
In [his/her] book [title], [author's name] indicates that . . .

The following is an example of paraphrasing.

Ancient Medicine

Original

Medicinal practices in the ancient world *were as related to* religion and philosophy as they were to science. The Egyptians were *proficient* surgeons who *employed* an *array of medications* and surgical *practices.* Their *extensive expertise involving* the human anatomy was *derived mainly from* their *practice of embalming. The ideology behind this* was that the *deceased* person's spirit, or Ka, would *perish* if the body *decomposed. To furnish an eternal abode* for the spirit, the body was *meticulously preserved.* In *another part of the ancient world,* Chinese medicine *was also linked to*

---

ideology, in particular the belief that people are *closely linked to* a universe *dominated* by two *opposing* types of forces known as *yin* and *yang*, the negative and the positive. Physicians *were part philosophers who believed* that the harmony of the universe and the health of people depended on keeping a balance between the two forces. (*Discovery*, Everett, Reid, and Fara)

Paraphrase

In their book *Discovery*, Everett, Reid, and Fara indicate that the practice of healing in the ancient world had as much to do with religion and philosophy as it did with science. Extremely skillful surgeons, the Egyptians used a variety of drugs and surgical techniques. Their broad knowledge of the human anatomy was primarily due to their preservation of the dead. Their belief was that the dead person's spirit, or Ka, would die if the body rotted away. To provide a lasting home for the spirit, the body was mummified as carefully as possible. In the ancient Far East, Chinese medicine also involved philosophical beliefs, especially the idea that people are part of a universe controlled by two conflicting forces known as *yin* and *yang*, the negative and the positive. Physicians endorsed the philosophical belief that the harmony of the universe and the health of people depended on keeping a balance between the two forces.

These are the substitutions for the italicized words in the original.

Original	Paraphrase
Medicinal practices	the practice of healing
were as related to	had as much to do with
proficient	extremely skillful
employed	used
array of medications	variety of drugs
practices	techniques
extensive expertise involving	broad knowledge of
derived mainly from	was primarily due to
practice of embalming	preservation of the dead
The ideology behind this	Their belief was

(continued)

Original	Paraphrase
deceased	dead
perish	die
decomposed	rotted away
To furnish an eternal abode	To provide a lasting home
meticulously preserved	mummified as carefully as possible
another part of the ancient world	ancient Far East
was also linked to ideology	also involved philosophical beliefs
in particular the belief	especially the idea
closely linked to	depended on
dominated	controlled
opposing	conflicting
were part philosophers who believed	endorsed the philosophical belief

Some words in the original text cannot be changed because there are no synonyms for them, such as the names of people, countries, religions, and scientific terms. In this passage, for example, there are no synonyms for *Egyptians, science, Ka, Chinese, yin*, and *yang*. Not every word has to be changed in a paraphrase; a few of the original words may be kept to maintain the accuracy of a piece. In this passage, for example, important words like *ancient, religion, science, philosophy, anatomy, spirit, negative, positive, harmony*, and *universe* have not been changed.

The following are useful steps to follow when paraphrasing:

Paraphrasing Checklist

- ☐ Read the section of the book or article over several times until you fully understand it.
- ☐ Underline any words you do not understand. Look them up in a dictionary or use a thesaurus to find a good synonym.
- ☐ Begin your paraphrase with a reference to the author and/or title of the book or article.
- ☐ Rewrite each sentence, simplifying the structure and using synonyms. Rewrite each sentence one after the other.

☐ Review your paraphrase. Make sure it sounds natural and like your own writing. Check to see that you have included all the information in the original, and that you have not changed the meaning in any way.

Exercise

Working with a partner, in a group, or on your own, paraphrase the following selections. Use a dictionary or thesaurus to find synonyms. Follow the steps listed above.

1. Although many women throughout history have been involved in the development of science, their work has gained little recognition. For a number of reasons their achievements have been ignored and their names left out of books. (Everett, Reid, and Fara, *Discovery*, p. 92)

2. Observe a group of listeners the next time a good storyteller tells an obscene joke. Skilled joke tellers elaborate on details. They allow the tension to build gradually as they set up the punch line. Listeners smile or blush slightly as the joke progresses. According to Freud, this long building creates greater tension and thus a louder and longer laugh when the punch line finally allows a tension release. (Burger, *Personality*, p. 99)

3. Three decades of research has demonstrated that people exposed to aggressive models sometimes imitate the aggressive behavior. This finding holds true for children as well as adults. But clearly, simple exposure to an aggressive model is not enough to turn us into violent people. Anyone who has watched television or attended a few movies recently undoubtedly has seen some murders, beatings, shootings, and the like. Yet rarely do we leave the theatre in search of victims. (Burger, *Personality*, p. 445)

How to Summarize

A summary is very similar to a paraphrase, only shorter. When you summarize, you put published information in your own words and include all the important information, without changing its meaning, just as you do when you paraphrase. However, when you summarize, you reduce the amount of information. The length of summaries varies. For example, the summary of a book may be several pages long, while the summary of an article may be one paragraph.

In a summary, only the main ideas and key points are stated, and repetitions of the same idea are left out. Since you include only the main ideas in a summary, it is helpful to make a brief outline before you begin to summarize.

The following is an example of a paraphrase, outline, and summary.

Personality Types

Original

What kind of people are likely candidates for heart attacks and what kind are not? Typical Type A people are the most susceptible to heart problems, because they are strongly motivated to overcome obstacles and are driven to achieve and to meet goals. They are attracted to competition, enjoy power and recognition, and are easily aroused to anger and action. They dislike wasting time and do things in a vigorous and efficient manner. On the other hand, Type B people are relaxed and unhurried. They may work hard on occasion, but rarely in the driven, compulsive manner of Type A people. These people are less likely than Type A's to seek the stress of competition or to be aroused to anger or action. Naturally not all people classified as Type A or Type B fit these profiles exactly, and there are times when Type A people behave in a Type B manner and vice versa. But, as with other traits, researchers can identify the extent to which each of us behaves, on the average, and assign us a personality type on the basis of which some startling predictions can be made. (*Personality*, Burger)

Paraphrase

Which personalities are prone to heart attacks and which are not? According to Burger in his book *Personality*, classic Type A people are most at risk for coronary problems because of their intense desire to conquer barriers and their drive to realize their goals. They like competition, relish power and recognition, have quick tempers, and are readily provoked to action. Time is of the essence, so they do things energetically and efficiently. On the other hand, Type B people are calm and unhurried. Sometimes they may work hard, but they hardly ever do so in the compelling, compulsive way of Type A people. Type B's are less likely than Type A's to be competitive or to be incited to anger or action. Of course, not all people identified as Type A or Type B conform to these profiles exactly. Occasionally, Type A people exhibit Type B characteristics, and vice versa. But, as with other traits, researchers can determine the measure of our average behavior and attribute a personality type to us—which can reveal some very surprising things about us.

Outline

A. Type A people
   1. At risk for heart attacks
   2. Driven, competitive, quick-tempered, time-conscious, energetic, and efficient

B. Type B people
   1. Calm and unhurried
   2. Less competitive and slower to react

C. On the basis of average behavior, people can be categorized according to well-defined personality types.

Summary

According to Burger in his book *Personality*, people can be categorized into well-defined personality types on the basis of their average behavior. Type A people tend to be more at risk for heart attacks because they are driven, competitive, quick-tempered, time-conscious, energetic, and efficient. Type B people, on the other hand, are calm, unhurried, less competitive, and less reactive than their Type A counterparts.

You can see from the outline that the main idea (item C) is stated in the last sentence of the passage. In your summary, however, you write the main idea first and then add one sentence for each of the two supporting ideas (items A and B).

Summary Checklist

☐ Begin with a reference to the author and/or title of the book or article. Include the source of the article.
☐ Identify and write the main ideas and key points.
☐ Do not include details or repeat ideas.

Exercise

Summarize the following passages in a few sentences. Check your work against the summary checklist.

1. Music video is a relatively new entry into the world of television, having become common only in the 1980s. Music video is difficult to categorize and to illustrate with one example, because it includes so many different types of expression. The definitive characteristic is in its name: There is music and there is video imagery. Some music videos dramatize the words of a song or even create brief visual dramas that are only vaguely related to the music. Some offer a message or statement. Some are relatively straightforward recordings of the performers at work. Obviously, defining the art of music video is not an easy task. (*Living with Art*, Rita Gilbert)

2. Charles Darwin, an English naturalist and explorer, began a five-year expedition in December 1831 on a ship called the *Beagle*. The expedition reached Bahia in Brazil in the spring of 1832. Darwin was amazed by the number and dazzling colors of the flowers and birds he saw. The *Beagle* then sailed south along the coast of Patagonia where the crew discovered the fossil remains of several extinct animals. In September 1835, the expedition reached the remote Galapagos Islands. There Darwin saw birds, animals, and plants that are found nowhere else on earth because they had developed in isolation from their relatives in America. They were to play an important part in Darwin's theories on how animals and humans evolved. (*Discovery*, Everett, Reid, and Fara)

3. Beginning in the Middle East at least 10,000 years ago, some peoples began to purposely sow the seeds of their food plants. It was a practice that allowed them to produce adequate amounts of food in the areas near their settlements rather than pursuing game and living as nomads. At the same time, they gradually tamed and domesticated wild animals for their food, hides and labor. An agricultural lifestyle led to the first towns and cities, the development of tools, baskets and pots, which led to the development of commerce and new crafts and skills. Agriculture played a significant role in developing the control over our existence that distinguishes humans from other species. (*Biology!* Postlethwait, Hopson, and Veres)

Photo Credits

This page constitutes an extension of the copyright page. We have made every effort to trace the ownership of all copyrighted material and to secure permission from copyright holders. In the event of any question arising as to the use of any material, we will be pleased to make the necessary corrections in future printings. Thanks are due to the following authors, publishers, and agents for permission to use the material indicated.

Chapter 1. 1: Self Portrait with Velvet Dress, 1926 (oil on canvas), Kahlo, Frida (1910–54) / Private Collection / Photo: Jorge Contreras Chacel / The Bridgeman Art Library International **2:** The Philadelphia Museum of Art / Art Resource, NY **3:** top, The Waterlily Pond with the Japanese Bridge, 1899, Monet, Claude (1840–1926) / Private Collection / Peter Willi / The Bridgeman Art Library International; center, Wheatfield with Cypresses, 1889 (oil on canvas), Gogh, Vincent van (1853–90) / National Gallery, London, UK / The Bridgeman Art Library International; bottom, The Persistence of Memory, 1931 (oil on canvas), Dali, Salvador (1904-89) / Museum of Modern Art, New York, USA / © DACS / The Bridgeman Art Library International **4:** © SuperStock / SuperStock; bottom, © Harald Sund / Getty Images **14:** © PNC / Getty Images

Chapter 2. 33: © The Art Archive/Corbis **45:** top right, © africa924 / Shutterstock; bottom left, © LoopAll / Shutterstock **46:** top, © Victor de Schwanberg / Alamy; center, © Shawn Talbot / Shutterstock; bottom, © Mar Photographics / Alamy **47:** © Yuri Arcurs / Shutterstock

Chapter 3. 62: © Frédéric Soltan/Sygma/Corbis **72:** © Marty Snyderman/Corbis

Chapter 4. 90: top left, © Visions of America, LLC / Alamy; bottom right, © cultura/Corbis **101:** © AP Images/ Rick Rycroft

Chapter 5. 116: left, © chilkat / Alamy; right, © Angela Hampton Picture Library / Alamy

Chapter 6. 145: © Klaus Tiedge/Corbis **155:** © Blend Images RF/ Photolibrary

Chapter 7. 174: © 4736202690 / Shutterstock **175:** top, © studiomode / Alamy; middle top, © Cephas Picture Library / Alamy; middle bottom, © Dana Hoff / Getty Images; bottom, © Eye- Stock / Alamy **185:** © Kevin Fitzmaurice-Brown / Alamy

Chapter 8. 205: © Olivier DIGOIT / Alamy **206:** top left, © David Noton Photography / Alamy; top right, © AP Images / U.S. Navy, Brien Aho, HO; bottom left, © Don Farrall / Getty Images; bottom right, © Wolfkamp / Shutterstock **213:** © Wave Royalty Free / Alamy

Chapter 9. 230: © John Nordell/ Photolibrary **232:** © JUPITERIMAGES/ GOODSHOOT / Alamy **239:** © Bonnie Kamin

Skills Index

Charts and Tables, 244

Grammar and Usage
Comparison and contrast indicators, 163–169
Compound adjectives, 151, 189, 190
Prepositions of time, 54–56
Quotations, 261–263

Listening/Speaking
Ask and answer, 10, 76, 97, 105, 131, 181, 211, 216, 236, 244
Critical thinking questions, 13, 20, 44, 51, 71, 79, 100, 107, 125, 134, 162, 184, 192, 212, 218, 238, 246
Discussion questions, 12, 20, 43, 51, 71, 79, 91, 100, 106–107, 125, 134, 162, 183, 192, 212, 218, 237, 245
Group activities, 58, 86, 112, 141, 170, 201, 227, 250
Partner activities, 10, 58, 76, 86, 97, 105, 112, 131, 141, 170, 181, 201, 211, 216, 227, 236, 244, 250

Reading
Comprehension, 10–12, 18–20, 41–43, 49–51, 69–71, 76–78, 98–99, 105–106, 123–124, 131–133, 152–154, 159–161, 181–183, 190–192
Details, 10, 19, 42, 50, 70, 77–78, 98–99, 105, 123–124, 131–132, 152–153, 160–161, 182, 191
Main ideas, 10, 18, 41, 49, 69, 76, 98, 105, 123, 131, 152, 159, 181, 190
Making inferences and drawing conclusions, 12, 19–20, 42, 50–51, 70–71, 78, 99, 106, 124, 133, 153–154, 161, 182–183, 191–192
Narrator and point of view, 247–250

Pre-reading activities, 2–4, 34, 63, 91–92, 117, 146, 175
Spelling, 34–43

Technology—Internet, 32, 61, 89, 115, 144, 173, 204

Test-taking skills
Circling choices, 1, 10, 12, 32, 33, 41, 42, 61, 62, 63, 69, 70, 75, 89, 90, 106, 115, 116, 123, 124, 131, 133, 144, 145, 152, 153, 166, 173, 174, 181, 182, 190, 204, 205, 217, 229, 230, 252
Filling in blanks, 18, 19, 49, 50, 55–56, 76–78, 98, 99, 131, 138, 146, 158, 161
Identifying, 137, 138, 142, 197
Matching, 2–4, 9–10, 34, 40, 55–56, 68, 76–78, 91–92, 97, 158, 175, 180–181, 189–190, 216, 243
Multiple-choice questions, 8–9, 10–11, 38–43, 47–48, 67–71, 75–76, 82–84, 96–97
Rewriting definitions, 82
Sentence completion, 10, 40–42, 48–51, 61, 68, 70, 77–78, 89, 98–99, 106, 109–110, 115, 122, 130–132, 144, 151, 152–153, 159, 160–161, 173, 190, 204, 229, 236, 252
True-or-false, 63, 69
Underlining choices, 55, 58, 111, 141, 169, 198, 201, 226, 250
Yes or no questions, 1, 33, 62, 90, 116, 145, 174, 205, 230

Topics
Artists, 1–32
    Frank Gehry, 14–21
    Frida Kahlo, 1–13
Gender, 145–172
    Culture and the sexes, 155–172
    Differences between men and women, 145–154

Vocabulary

Writing